I0605584

EVERY DAY IS SUNDAY

How Jerry Jones, Robert Kraft, and Roger Goodell Turned the NFL into a Cultural & Economic Juggernaut

KEN BELSON

NEW YORK BOSTON

Grand Central Publishing
Hachette Book Group
1290 Avenue of the Americas, New York, NY 10104
grandcentralpublishing.com
@grandcentralpub

First Edition: October 2025

Library of Congress Cataloging-in-Publication Data

Names: Belson, Ken author
Title: Every day is Sunday : how Jerry Jones, Robert Kraft, and Roger Goodell turned the NFL into a cultural & economic juggernaut / Ken Belson.
Description: First edition. | New York, NY : Grand Central Publishing/ Hachette Book Group, 2025. | Includes bibliographical references and index.
Identifiers: LCCN 2025017583 | ISBN 9781538772553 hardcover | ISBN 9781538772577 ebook
Subjects: LCSH: National Football League—History | Jones, Jerry, 1942– | Kraft, Robert Kenneth | Goodell, Roger, 1959– | Football—Economic aspects—United States | Football—Social aspects—United States
Classification: LCC GV955.5.N35 B45 2025
LC record available at https://lccn.loc.gov/2025017583

ISBNs: 978-1-538-77255-3 (hardcover), 978-1-538-77257-7 (ebook)

Printed in the United States of America

LSC-C

Printing 1, 2025

For Harumi

CONTENTS

EVERY DAY IS SUNDAY

INTRODUCTION

THE BEST ACROBATS

"The NFL under Pete Rozelle was Madison Avenue. The NFL under Paul Tagliabue was Wall Street. The NFL under Roger Goodell is Broadway."

—Bob LaMonte, sports agent

In August 2024, the thirty-two NFL owners convened for a special one-day meeting at the Omni Viking Lakes Hotel in Eagan, Minnesota, next door to the Vikings training facility. The matter at hand was a plan to tap a new gusher of money that would make these very wealthy and mostly elderly owners even wealthier. Before the meeting began, the league's two most powerful owners stopped in the lobby to share fist pumps. Dallas Cowboys owner Jerry Jones and his oldest son, Stephen, greeted New England Patriots owner Robert Kraft and his oldest son, Jonathan. "Boy, you're looking trim," the elder Jones, graying and pale, said to the elder Kraft, suntanned and in sneakers. The two octogenarians beamed like school chums meeting after summer break. Kansas City Chiefs owner Clark Hunt, by comparison a youthful fifty-nine, and Pittsburgh Steelers owner Art Rooney, seventy-two, passed by. Commissioner Roger Goodell, the trim, barrel-chested confidant, and leader to them all, chatted with the group. About the only people not smiling were the players who had just been cut by the Vikings and were checking out of the hotel, their fates unknown.

A few hours later, Jones, Kraft, and the other owners voted 31–1 to allow teams to sell up to 10 percent of their multibillion-dollar franchises to private equity groups that include Carlyle and Sixth Street Partners. (Cincinnati Bengals owner Mike Brown, a staunch traditionalist, was the lone dissenter.) As the meeting broke and the owners headed for their limousines to take them to their private jets, Jones told reporters: "This is good for anybody that's in love with the N.F.L., any part of it—the game part, on the field, off the field. This is a good thing."[1]

Most of all, it was also a good thing for Jones and his fellow owners. The decision, which came after five years of study and debate, included rules preventing private equity groups from having any say in the running of the teams they invested in. They had to hold their stakes for at least six years. And the owners didn't have to share the proceeds with the players who helped create the value of the teams. The owners would have their cake *and* eat it, getting piles of cash without ceding control. Within a few months, the Buffalo Bills, the Miami Dolphins, and other teams sold pieces of their teams for hundreds of millions of dollars. Asked what he planned to do with the money from the sale of stakes in his $7 billion team, Las Vegas Raiders owner Mark Davis joked: "I'm going to In N Out Burger."[2]

The NFL had won again. Just a decade before, the league was under mortal threat. Thousands of retired players sued the league, claiming they were deliberately misled about the dangers of concussions. Concerned about the brutality of football, parents were steering their kids toward safer sports. Women fans were turned off by reports of players beating their girlfriends and wives. Players who knelt during the national anthem to protest social inequality and police brutality ensnared the league in a bitter debate about free speech and patriotism. The league lost fans along the way, but it largely weathered these crises. Rather than risk seeing players with dementia called as witnesses, the league agreed to a settlement that has paid out more than $1.5 billion, with each player getting as much as $5 million.[3] But after insurance claims and split thirty-two ways, the teams would pay just a few million dollars each a year on average. At the same time, the league created marketing campaigns and donated millions of dollars to nonprofit groups and research institutions to change the narrative and refocus the public's attention on the games, with their irresistible blend of American pageantry, violence, and high-wire outcomes.

With more than $23 billion in revenue in 2024, the NFL is the biggest sports league in the world. It's grown as large as Fortune 500 companies like Colgate-Palmolive and Goodyear Tires. The NFL drew the largest audiences on television, sold the most valuable media rights and sponsorships, and played in the most lavish stadiums. The Super Bowl was a de facto national holiday; wedding planners recommend picking any other Sunday to tie the knot.[4] As networks struggled to attract viewers, NFL games made up ninety-three of the one hundred most watched programs in 2023; its deals with HBO, Netflix, and other media outlets created nongame programming such as *Hard Knocks* that kept the league in the news throughout the year. New revenue came in from overseas and sports gaming. Thirteen of the world's twenty most valuable sports franchises in 2024 were NFL teams.[5] The NFL wasn't just a sports league, it was an immensely profitable American religion, complete with acolytes, pomp, and tax breaks.

None of this was preordained. The NFL almost folded during World War II when owners had to sell players from their depleted rosters to pay their bills.[6] The pro game lagged behind baseball, boxing, and college football until the 1960s, when Commissioner Pete Rozelle harnessed the power of television and the country's growing economy to catapult the league up the sports food chain. Younger fans gravitated to the NFL's flashier, more brazen game just as Wall Street's winner-take-all ethos bled into American society. George Will seemed quaintly out of touch when he complained that "football combines two of the worst things in American life: It is violence punctuated by committee meetings." Many Americans, it seemed, were hooked on both.

The league endured player strikes, legal challenges, and drug scandals in the 1980s. Starting in 1989, Rozelle's successor, Paul Tagliabue, worked with the players union chief, Gene Upshaw, and fair-minded owners like Dan Rooney of the Steelers to craft a new revenue sharing agreement with a salary cap and free agency that provided the economic foundation the NFL still stands on.

"In the span of two generations in postwar America, pro football became a truer and more vivid reflection of the American preoccupations with power and passion, technology and teamwork, than any other sporting institution in the country," Michael MacCambridge wrote in *America's Game: The Epic Story of How Pro Football Captured a Nation*.

Jones and Kraft entered the league at this critical juncture. Self-made businessmen who went deeply into debt to buy money-losing teams, they were hungry for success on the field and desperate for money off it. "He was the first and we were the next to pay up big,"

Kraft said, referring to Jones. "We had to make it work. We had to do things to generate revenue from something that only held events ten days a year." Over the following three decades, they built their teams into two of the world's most valuable franchises and had a hand in nearly every major financial decision the league made. After Tagliabue stepped down in 2006, they backed his long-time protégé, Goodell, who took a maximalist approach to growing the NFL. During Tagliabue's seventeen years as commissioner, the league doubled in size to $8 billion. Goodell, channeling Jones, Kraft, and other owners, set a target in 2010 of *tripling* revenue in the following seventeen years—a goal the league is on track to exceed.

Their empire building did not happen overnight or by accident. Given its prominence, the NFL is often viewed as progressive. In fact, the league moves deliberately, waiting to see what other leagues do first, say, with international expansion or putting a team in Las Vegas, before adapting the best elements to suit its needs. Goodell and the owners use demand for NFL games to cut record-setting deals with networks, sponsors, and other businesses that have turned the league into a 365-day-a-year enterprise that now bleeds into Black Friday, Christmas, and other formerly sacrosanct days. The Draft, once a sleepy event for football nerds, draws hundreds of thousands of fans. The NFL unveils its season schedule on prime-time television. "Because now there's just, well, there *is* no off-season, there's just a time you don't play the games,"[7] former coach Dick Vermeil once said.

To Goodell, the NFL isn't just a sports league, it's a cultural institution that gobbles mindshare and captures the national zeitgeist. The owners are considered celebrities—and mocked—including Jones and Kraft, who are shown in their luxury boxes during games and starred in ten-part documentaries about their clubs. Roger Goodell is lampooned mercilessly on TikTok, *South Park*, and Barstool.[8] He and the owners like to say that football mirrors American life. If that is true, then the reflection includes not just teamwork, perseverance, and spectacle but also some measures of greed, corporate welfare, violence, misogyny, self-promotion, and bland officiousness.

For more than a dozen years, I have documented the business of the NFL as a reporter for *The New York Times*. I have interviewed hundreds of owners, league executives, and team officials; union bosses and players; network executives and sponsors; coaches and fans. Jones took me in his helicopter and Kraft invited me to his apartment to break bread. I watched Goodell tell a convention of neurosurgeons about the league's efforts to make football safer. I saw Seattle Seahawks coach Pete Carroll mobbed by television cameras moments after his team blew Super Bowl XLIX, his grandson crying at his knee. One fan told me he was so angry that the Chargers left San Diego that he drove to Los Angeles to tailgate with friends but refused to buy a ticket because he didn't want to give Chargers owner Dean Spanos his money.

I have also seen the carnage football produces in abundance. NFL players compete in an extraordinarily dangerous game for our collective entertainment. Fans witness horrific injuries: Tua Tagovailoa getting knocked unconscious, Damar Hamlin's heart stopping. Every game, players are part of high-speed collisions, akin to car crashes, that fans take for granted. Former referee Ed Hochuli saw this up close: "There wasn't a single game right up to the very last one that there weren't a half a dozen times in that game [where] I said, 'Oh my god, how's that guy gonna get up off the ground? He's gotta be dead.' And they hop up and they go back to the huddle."[9]

Players have access to doctors who patch them up for the next game, sometimes delivering high doses of Toradol, a pain reliever provided before games as a prophylactic. But after they leave the game, they lose a lot of that support. The fallout from many of their injuries, including concussions, manifests itself years after they stop playing. The players' families become caregivers, sometimes with help from the league's benefit plans but often in silence. Super Bowl rings provide no immunity. At least seven players from the 2001 New England Patriots died before they passed fifty years old.[10] Liz Nicholson told me her husband, former offensive lineman Gerry Sullivan, had advanced dementia and was so paranoid that he kept a loaded pistol in the house. When she tried to take away his bullets, he became more paranoid. He shot a hole in their hardwood floor and threatened to kill them both. The next day, he remembered none of it. She coped by crushing his Valium tablets and mixing them into his red wine to knock him out at night.

Fans tiptoe past the wreckage, if they notice at all. The games are too much of a narcotic. The NFL didn't invent the circus; they just have the best acrobats. A media ecosystem including NFL Network and NFL Films fuels interest in the games, players, and league. Networks, radio stations, and websites create outrage over issues with the half-life of a punt return. Take Mina Kimes, an ESPN reporter. The website Awful Announcing congratulated her for calling Aaron Rodgers a hypocrite after he complained to Pat McAfee, a former player who has his own show on ESPN, about television analysts who make "unfounded or asinine" comments.[11] "He's espousing that opinion on a personality-driven program that employs him as a personality during the NFL season," Kimes said on *First Take*, a personality-driven ESPN talk show hosted by Stephen A. Smith.[12] Around and around it goes.

The NFL was a rare institution that emerged from the Covid-19 pandemic stronger. Stuck at home and starved for entertainment, fans tuned into games, many of them played in empty stadiums. The owners lost about $4 billion that season but clawed it back in successive years. While many businesses hunkered down, Kraft, Goodell, and others at the league negotiated ten-year media rights deals worth twice as much as the previous ones. Once the pandemic subsided, Goodell began talking about adding an eighteenth regular-season game and playing sixteen games overseas each year, player safety be damned.

"It just shows that it's all about money and this is a way that they can, you know, make more money and figure this thing out because it's not fair for the players," retired Steelers quarterback Ben Roethlisberger said about his old team, which played three games in eleven days in 2024.[13]

This book is not about those games, but the owners and executives—Jones, Kraft, and Goodell chief among them—who package and sell the games as America's last true mass entertainment. It is also about Goodell's predecessor, Paul Tagliabue, and the union boss, Gene Upshaw, and others who created the revenue sharing model that led to the league's meteoric growth. This book will illustrate how they extracted billions of dollars in stadium subsidies from local governments—and abandoned cities that refused to bend—and convinced networks, sponsors, and gaming companies to pay billions more for rights fees while producing games that kept fans hooked. This is the story of how this unlikely trio—a hard-drinking wildcatter from Arkansas, an opportunistic striver from Boston, and the alpha dog son of a senator—helped turn the NFL into an undeniable juggernaut.

1.

"DO YOU WANT A YARMULKE OR A HELMET?"

Paul Tagliabue was as sharp a lawyer as there was, but his memory was foggy the day after he celebrated the end of five years of NFL labor strife. Tagliabue, Steelers owner Dan Rooney, NFL Players Association chief Gene Upshaw, and his top lawyer, Jim Quinn, worked feverishly in December 1992 to complete a groundbreaking labor deal that would alter the trajectory of the NFL.

It was getting late that night, so the men walked a few blocks from the league headquarters to the Hilton Hotel to hash out loose ends over dinner. At the end of the meal, they felt like they had everything resolved. They had one more drink to toast what they felt was the start of labor peace. After four bottles of wine, they called it a night.

The next day, they reconvened to put the last details on paper. They joked that they couldn't recall everything they had agreed to because of all the wine the night before. But after shaking off the rust, they remembered: For the first time, players would get free agency after five years in the league. In return, a salary cap would be installed to prevent the kind of runaway spending that plagued Major League Baseball, where clubs like the Yankees and Dodgers used their financial muscle to sign the biggest stars. Most important, Tagliabue and Upshaw agreed to divide the league's revenue roughly in half between the owners and players, a major shift in how the NFL had operated since its inception seventy years before.

This new labor deal didn't just end years of bickering, court battles, and work stoppages; it made the NFL and players partners, laying the foundation for the league's startling success over the following three decades.

"What we had produced was complicated and imperfect, but also innovative and built to last," Tagliabue wrote in his memoir.[1] "It did more than ensure labor peace for seven years. It created a partnership with the NFL Players Association that produced other improvements, and not just on economic issues."

Fans take concepts like free agency and salary caps for granted. But the NFL adopted them only after great resistance from owners like Mike Brown in Cincinnati and Hugh Culverhouse of the Tampa Bay Buccaneers, who felt they had more to lose than gain.

Tagliabue had worked as outside counsel for the NFL for two decades before becoming commissioner in 1989, and much of that time included tension between the players and owners. Since 1987, when the players went on strike for twenty-four days and the owners hired scab players, the two sides operated without a collective bargaining agreement (CBA). The lack of a labor deal meant the constant threat of disruption, which was bad for business. The players union sued the league for violating antitrust laws, but the case was dismissed in 1989. Then the union took the extraordinary step of disbanding. Eight players, led by Jets running back Freeman McNeil, sued the NFL, this time as individuals. The case took more than two years—fast for an antitrust suit—and included depositions of owners, who were reluctant to open their books.

"They fought tooth and nail, but Judge Doty ordered them to produce" their financials, said Jeffrey Kessler, outside counsel for the players, referring to the judge presiding over the case.

On September 11, 1992, a jury in Minneapolis sided with McNeil and the other players, finding that the league's compensation rules were "more restrictive than reasonably necessary to achieve the objective of establishing or maintaining competitive balance in the NFL, and that the rules caused economic harm to the players."

The players became unrestricted free agents. Within a week, Kessler filed a new claim on behalf of ten other players who were not under contract. They, too, were declared free agents and were quickly signed by teams. Another 250 players who had expiring contracts then filed a third case, with star defensive end Reggie White as the lead plaintiff. Lawyers for the players estimated that damages, when trebled in antitrust cases, would top $1 billion. Tagliabue pushed to settle the White case, and on a December night in 1992, he and Upshaw shook hands on a deal that would revolutionize the league. No wonder the wine flowed.

The celebration was brief. Raiders owner Al Davis, who took extreme positions on many issues, tried to derail the agreement, fixating on minor features of the deal and one very big one: He wanted players to get free agency after six seasons, not five. Rooney and New York Giants owner Wellington Mara tried to convince

Davis to back down. But they couldn't clinch a deal before heading back to Minnesota in early January to meet Judge David S. Doty. A cigar-smoking former Marine, he did what many judges did: He threatened to impose a deal that neither side would like. For emphasis, he waved a thick manila envelope, which presumably included his ruling.

"He had the decision already written, and he showed it to us on his desk," said Kessler. "He wouldn't tell us what it said. Doty made it very clear—it was on a Friday—that 'if I have to issue this on Monday, let me just say, you're not going to be happy.'"

After meeting for forty-five minutes with Upshaw and his team, Doty went to Tagliabue, Rooney, and the other owners and told them he would grant players free agency after three years, not five years. The owners were stunned. But unsure whether Doty was bluffing—they hadn't seen the contents of his envelope—they agreed to take the deal to all the owners.

Tagliabue, Rooney, Mara, and the other owners, as well as Quinn representing the players, flew to Dallas. There, they presented the deal to the full ownership: The league would pay $200 million in damages to settle the White case and cover the players' legal expenses. White and hundreds of players with at least five years in the league would become unrestricted free agents. Each team, however, could assign a "franchise tag" to one player to prevent him from leaving. The college draft would be trimmed to seven rounds from twelve, and salaries for rookies would remain capped at roughly $2 million.

The owners agreed to the deal, and on January 6, 1993, the two sides announced a seven-year labor agreement,[2] ending more than five years of acrimony. Upshaw was ecstatic. "This puts us right there with baseball and basketball," he told *The New York Times*. "The landscape of the N.F.L. will never be the same. For the first time, we're the partners of the owners."

Tagliabue was privately relieved but publicly channeled some of the displeasure of owners like Jack Kent Cooke in Washington and Eddie DeBartolo in San Francisco, who built dynasties during the pre–free agency era and reluctantly gave in only after the string of losses in court.

"We hope it won't change football," Tagliabue said. "The teams wanted to strike a balance, meeting players' desires as well as team unity. There will be some surprises, some stumbles."

Davis, though, knew he and the other owners would find this new world disorienting. For years, they had leverage in negotiations because without free agency, players had few alternatives for employment outside of the Canadian Football League. Most players' careers lasted only a few years, and they had little appetite to go on strike because they would miss paychecks.

Now the best players would have the owners bidding for their services, and frugal owners would have to compete against the likes of Cowboys owner Jerry Jones, who made a fortune gambling on oil and gas wells. Chaos would surely follow.

"It'll be like the Russians learning the free market," Davis said of how the owners would respond.

After the announcement, the league and players rushed to get everything in place for the coming season.

"We were too busy to celebrate," said Doug Allen, Upshaw's longtime point man. "We created a monster and then we had to figure out how we could make it work."

The first task for Upshaw, Allen, and the players was to recertify as a union so they could sign the new collective bargaining agreement, which would provide the NFL with an antitrust exemption to insulate it from more lawsuits. The union also needed to resume functions like distributing benefits and handling grievances. During the lawsuits, Upshaw and Allen had been careful not to act like a union lest the owners argue in court that the decertification was a legal fiction. No dues were collected. Upshaw paid the players' legal bills with money from licensing agreements that Allen and his wife struck with Topps, Electronic Arts, and others. With the court battles over, "we had to ramp all that back up again," Allen said.

Though the players agreed to the deal, many of them were not fans of the salary cap, which they said would give owners a tool to lowball rank-and-file players. They wanted to earn as much money as they could as quickly as they could. Now the owners would have a set amount of money to spend, and the lion's share would likely go to a handful of stars.

"The dynamic among the players has proven, if you go wild on the upside, what happened to the lower-priced players?" said Steve Gutman, the longtime president of the New York Jets who, along with general managers Bill Polian, Jim Irsay, and George Young, created a hard salary cap without loopholes owners could exploit. "We tried to develop concepts where parity and equity and fairness would allow the league to function," he added.

A hard cap sounded nice in principle, but the owners wanted the flexibility to break it when it suited them. The owners were businessmen who were not used to being told how to spend their money. Gutman and Polian reminded them the hard cap was designed to protect them from their worst impulses.

"We came up with a hard cap, but every owner, every general manager in the league was looking for every exception that they could possibly have," Gutman said. He explained the merits of the plan in a way he thought they could grasp.

"I'm sure you guys will understand," Gutman told them at one meeting, "but do you want a soft cap or a hard cap, do you want a yarmulke or a helmet?"

The owners chose a helmet. Even then, some small-market owners who had less revenue than the Cowboys, Giants, and San Francisco 49ers spent well below the maximum on salaries. Years later, a salary floor would be added.

The first big-name free agent of the era was White, the star defensive end who had spent his first eight years with the Philadelphia Eagles. He was heavily courted, including by the Jets, who invited him to New York to meet owner Leon Hess. Hess owned a chain of eponymously named gas stations that each Christmas sold toy gas trucks.[3] He took out a prototype of that year's truck and told White he wanted to make sure his trucks never broke so no child would be disappointed. He put the truck on the floor and asked the three-hundred-pound lineman to stand on it. Dumbfounded, White complied. The truck survived. Hess called his secretary and told her the truck was solid enough to put into production.

"It was his way of breaking the ice," Gutman said.

Hess's charm didn't work. White signed with the Green Bay Packers and helped them win a Super Bowl a few years later. The Jets wouldn't make the playoffs for another six years.

The NFL's unparalleled stature makes it easy to forget the significance of the 1993 labor deal. The league and the union have butted heads over many issues, including Roger Goodell's aggressive policing of the players' conduct. But except in 2011, when the owners locked out the players during the offseason to reclaim a chunk of shared revenue, the NFL has had no work stoppages. This has given television networks and sponsors comfort and emboldened owners to pour hundreds of millions of dollars into new stadiums. It also boosted team valuations into the billions of dollars.

Shad Khan learned this firsthand. He used the money he made in the car bumper business to buy the Jacksonville Jaguars in 2011 for $770 million.[4] He recalled meeting Jones and Washington Redskins owner Dan Snyder in 2007. Jones and Snyder were enamored with Khan's new yacht, *Kismet*, which was moored in the South of France near their vessels. They invited themselves on board, their entourages in tow. As they partied for several days, Khan milked them for information about owning a team. Nearly two decades later, one thing Jones said stuck in Khan's mind.

"He said the teams are going to be worth a billion dollars," Khan said with a chuckle. "I was like, okay, Jerry, you can stop exaggerating now."

As it turned out, Jones was conservative. By 2024, the Cowboys were worth more than $10 billion—the world's most valuable sports franchise, according to *Forbes*. The Jaguars, who play in one of the smallest NFL markets, were worth $4.6 billion.[5]

As the owners raked in more money, so did the players. Under the CBA, team payrolls are based on the players' share of the league's revenue minus what the players spend on their retirement and medical benefits. In 1994, the first year of the new system, teams had up to $34.6 million to spend on player salaries.[6] By 2001, that amount had doubled as the league signed more lucrative media and sponsorship deals. By 2014, the number had doubled again to $133 million. By 2025, teams had $279.2 million to spend on player salaries, about eight times more than three decades before and far outpacing inflation over that time.

The salary cap and free agency forced teams to not only scout college players but figure out how to spend money efficiently. That meant an owner like Davis, a former coach with an eye for talent, would lose his best players to free agency. Gone were the days when the Dolphins and Steelers built dynasties with stars who had no option of leaving. The Cowboys, who won three Super Bowls in four years in the early 1990s, were the last of the pre–salary cap dynasties. Since then, only the Denver Broncos, Patriots, and Chiefs have won back-to-back titles; the Cowboys haven't been back to the NFC Championship Game.

"As it turned out, free agency has had as much to do with the success of the league as it has the enriching of the players because it made the building of a winning team much more interesting to the fans, and sometimes teams could be turned around in a much faster period of time," Allen said. "That worked to the benefit of the league and the value of the league and the networks."

When Tagliabue ran to replace Rozelle, he foresaw how labor peace would lead to the riches that followed. As outside counsel to the NFL, he and Rozelle dined often at 21, the restaurant on Fifty-Second Street, where Rozelle drank rusty nails and Tagliabue sipped Campari with a twist. He learned that having the owners run labor negotiations was not working because they could not see the bigger picture: Stiff-arming the players was leading to strikes and the threat of strikes, and that was bad for business.

By the 1980s, Rozelle had little role in labor negotiations and was consumed with fending off lawsuits by Donald Trump, the United States Football League, and others. The league's Management Council, which had separate offices and legal counsel, and which leaned hard right when it came to paying players, ran negotiations. Culverhouse and other owners resisted free agency, and they weren't fond of Tagliabue, whom they viewed as conciliatory. In the late 1980s, Culverhouse fired Tagliabue—calling him a "traitor in our midst"—for not doing the owners' bidding. Rozelle told Tagliabue that he worked for the league, not the Management Council, and hired him back the next day.

The owners' condescending attitude toward the union prompted the players to walk out in Week Three of the 1987 season. Rooney, one of the few owners with any credibility with the players, almost had a deal with Upshaw that would have avoided the use of replacement players the following week.[7] Meeting near Dulles Airport, the two men agreed on a new free agency system. But Rooney couldn't win over Culverhouse and other hardliners. At a meeting with the union, Cowboys president Tex Schramm made what turned into a rallying cry for the players: "You guys are the cattle and we're the ranchers," he said to Upshaw, Allen, and the other union officials. "And ranchers always get more cattle."

The owners hired scabs for a couple of games before the players returned and filed an antitrust suit. By 1989, most owners recognized the toll that the fight was taking on business. The networks, fearing that games would be canceled, were reluctant to pay more for media rights. In his pitch to become commissioner, Tagliabue said that he would take the top job only if he could lead labor negotiations.

Tagliabue lacked the football credentials of the other candidates: Jim Finks, a former player, coach, and team executive; and Jack Kemp, a former quarterback who had a second career in politics. But on October 26, Tagliabue was chosen on the twelfth ballot. One of the first things he did was seize power from the Management Council and start rebuilding relations with Upshaw and a skeptical union.

"At first, we were really worried about him because we were fighting tooth and nail in court, and he was one of the lead guys in the whole litigation fight," Allen, Upshaw's deputy, said. "We were very wary of him as commissioner."

Tagliabue, Allen said, "wasn't going to give up much until he had to, until we had the leverage that required him to. And that required us to win the lawsuit, which we ultimately did. Once that happened, almost immediately, his attitude was, 'Okay, we lost, now we've got to figure out how to make this relationship work.' Gene had the same attitude."

Jones and other hardline owners criticized Tagliabue for being chummy with Upshaw. Tagliabue and Upshaw had a good working relationship, speaking frequently and even dining at each other's homes. But they weren't buddies. "They just had enormous respect for the role each was playing in their own organization, and the role they were playing across the table," Allen said. "They didn't waste a lot of time on histrionics."

The new, more equitable labor agreement was a turning point. But Tagliabue modernized the league's business operations in other ways. The NFL that Tagliabue took over was, by today's standards, remarkably small. Rozelle knew everyone in the league office—less than one hundred people in all—and wrote them personal Christmas cards. If you bumped into him, he would recall a wedding or a birthday. Nancy Behar, who worked in the broadcast department for more than forty years, typed television contracts that back then were just four or five pages long.

But the business of pro sports exploded in the 1990s. Nike and other sponsors threw so much money around that some players earned more off the field than on it. Fox blew up the cozy broadcast model by wildly outspending CBS for the NFC television package. Cable and satellite services provided more ways to distribute NFL games, creating new sources of revenue.

For years, the league office ran everything related to the games, the stadiums, events like the Super Bowl, and network contracts. NFL Properties cut licensing and sponsorship deals. After several

Properties employees were arrested for theft and fraud, Tagliabue oversaw the subsidiary.

He also hired Neil Austrian as the league's president in 1991. Austrian was a business savant who had worked at IBM, in advertising, private equity, and media. When he ran Showtime's Movie Channel, he pitched Rozelle on a subscription satellite service that would show all out-of-market games to fans around the country. Rozelle was intrigued, but CBS chairman Larry Tisch feared the service would lead to a pay-per-view model. The concept went no further.

When Austrian joined the NFL, he had the leverage to get the networks to agree. In 1994, the satellite provider DirecTV bought the rights to sell NFL Sunday Ticket and paid hundreds of millions of dollars to the league for years to come. Sunday Ticket also solved one of Tagliabue's headaches. Every year, the league would sue bars and restaurants that used satellite dishes to poach the broadcast signals of games that were blacked out locally, an expensive process and a terrible look. Now the establishments could pay for Sunday Ticket, turning a cost into a source of revenue for the NFL.

"It was the big bad NFL coming into Cleveland and suing this little working-class tavern," said Frank Hawkins, a lawyer Tagliabue recruited who worked at the league until 2008. "I always said, instead of being defensive, make an offensive solution to your problem."

Austrian updated the league's operations, giving everyone personal computers. Budget presentations, which had been essentially two slides, needed to break down every department's functions. "I think the owners appreciated the fact that we put together a very detailed budget," Austrian said.

The old guard in the league office—men who felt the NFL's primary mission was to promote football—pushed back against the executives Austrian hired to supercharge the NFL's businesses. Howard Handler, the senior vice president of strategic marketing and fan development in the 1990s, saw it as "a church versus state kind of thing." He recalled being cut off in one meeting when he began to talk about the league's brand. "We don't use that word here, we are a league," he was told.

Handler and other business executives shook off the starchy traditionalists and found new gushers of money by launching websites, opening NFL Shop, which had been a sleepy catalog business, and promoting NFL merchandise on shopping channels.

"The mid-1990s were the inflection point where we started to think about the league as this vibrant sports media enterprise," Handler said. "It was just a question of how we could bring this to life."

Some owners bristled at Austrian's approach for other reasons. Since the NFL's founding, the owners had their fingerprints on nearly every critical decision. Austrian added layers of executives that created barriers in the league office. Jones, for instance, took exception to Sara Levinson, an executive hired from MTV to promote the league with younger fans. Jones felt that her approach devalued the league's brand. He and other owners hounded her out of the job.

"She never acknowledged that she worked for the owners," Hawkins said. "She'd say she worked for Neil," and that irked owners who felt that league executives answered to them.

The corporatization of the league office came to a head in 1999. Austrian wanted to create a long-term plan to incentivize executives, including Tagliabue. Owners on the finance committee approved the plan. But the details came out during a lawsuit that Al Davis had brought against the league, and he, Jones, and Miami Dolphins owner Wayne Huizenga felt Tagliabue and Austrian were trying to turn the league into a media company. Austrian quit, allowing Tagliabue to save his job. But the message had been sent: The owners were in charge, not league executives.

Still, the game was as healthy as ever. A Harris poll in 1992 showed that despite years of dysfunction, football remained the country's most popular sport. The next year, the Cowboys beat the Bills, 52–17, in Super Bowl XXVII, their first title since 1978. The NBC broadcast was seen by 133.4 million, the most watched program in television history.

Tagliabue established an expansion committee in 1991, and in the fall of 1993, the owners awarded the league's twenty-ninth and thirtieth franchises to the Carolina Panthers and the Jaguars, which each paid a $140 million fee. That gave the league two more teams in growing Sun Belt markets, which drove up the value of the NFL's television rights. The owners also approved a plan to relaunch a European football league.

No one was more optimistic than Jones. He was the league's most ambitious—and reckless—owner and its biggest cheerleader. His bet on the Cowboys wasn't just a bet on the team, it was a bet on a league he believed was the future of American sports and entertainment. He would in the coming years work harder than anyone else to modernize the NFL.

"It's not business," Jones told me years later while sitting in his office near the three Vince Lombardi Trophies his teams won in the 1990s. "In Mudville, it's important for the joy to include making it work. That's kind of the art of the deal. That's the ten-pound bass being reeled in on the one-pound test line. That's the art of the deal because sports is challenging."

2.

"RUPERT, YOU DON'T HAVE TO DO THIS!"

The lights were burning late at the NFL's Park Avenue headquarters on a Thursday night in December 1993. While workers in New York were at Christmas parties or away for the holidays, the league's top leaders—including Paul Tagliabue and his head of media, Val Pinchbeck—were negotiating the rights to broadcast NFL games with one of the country's largest television networks, and the stakes had never been higher.

Earlier that year, the league and the players union signed a new collective bargaining agreement that ushered in labor peace, which Tagliabue and the owners would use to wring more out of their broadcast partners.

Some networks, though, were pleading poverty. CBS claimed it lost tens of millions of dollars on its NFL rights deal during the recession of 1990–1991, and Larry Tisch, the chairman of the network, wanted to pay *less*, not *more*, in the next agreement. Cleveland Browns owner Art Modell, who ran the broadcast committee for years, was cozy with the networks and was inclined to give them the discounts they wanted.

But this was the new NFL, one increasingly dominated by younger, hungrier owners like Jones and Pat Bowlen of the Broncos, entrepreneurs who went into debt to buy their teams and wanted to recoup their investments as fast as possible. Modell's health was poor, and he quit the committee, leaving Jones and Bowlen. Jones wanted to add a fourth bidder for the league's three main television packages, and Rupert Murdoch from Fox was that bidder. The bare-knuckled Australian had inquired about the rights to *Monday Night Football* years before but was rebuffed. Now he was back and wouldn't take no for an answer.

Frank Hawkins, who had been handling many of the league's complex transactions, was in the office that night, ready to draw up any critical paperwork. Hawkins had stepped out for a cup of coffee, and when he returned, he passed Tagliabue's office. Standing near the door was Chase Carey, one of Murdoch's lieutenants, talking on the phone to his boss.

Fox, which was launched in 1986, was best known for its comedy shows like *In Living Color* and *The Simpsons*. It had no sports or news divisions. In many markets, its channels were hard to find or it had no presence at all.

But Murdoch had learned in Britain, where his Sky Sports subscription service showed Premier League soccer matches, that must-see sports attracted viewers and advertisers. In the United States, he hoped that showing NFL games would convince affiliates to carry Fox. Murdoch told Jones that he wasn't interested in being a stalking horse, he wanted to be taken seriously. "Mr. Murdoch, I wasn't part of that negotiation," Jones said to Murdoch. "But I am [in] this one."

As Hawkins passed Tagliabue's office, Carey said, "Rupert, you don't have to do this." Hawkins wasn't entirely clear what "this" meant. But he soon found out. Carey returned to the commissioner's office, where Tagliabue, Jones, and the others were waiting. Fox had already bid a record $340 million for the rights to show NFC games, which included the Cowboys, 49ers, and Giants. That was well beyond the $250 million that Tisch said CBS was considering. CBS executives weren't aware Murdoch was so hungry.

"We did not get the feeling that he would be chasing our package," said Neal Pilson, the head of CBS Sports then. "We thought, given the fact that he had no sports division, that the Monday night package made more sense for Fox. We certainly talked about it. But there was frankly no sense of urgency. We felt the problem was NBC, which wanted to upgrade from the AFC to the NFC."

But Pilson knew that $250 million wasn't going to get a deal done. The Sunday before bids were due, Pilson invited Tagliabue onto CBS's pregame show, *The NFL Today*. Off camera, he asked what it would take to get a new deal. Tagliabue said a number that started with a three.

By the end of the week, Fox was already well above that, and when Carey returned to Tagliabue's office that night, Fox went even further, bidding a staggering $395 million a year for four years, which would be the first ten-figure media deal in league history. Jones was unable to contain his glee. "Underneath the table we were kickin' the living shit out of each other," he said later.

Carey later explained Rupert's logic:[1] "You had to have a number that—I don't have a better word for it—made them choke."

The NFL wanted to give CBS a chance to respond, so Austrian, Tagliabue's deputy, called Hawkins into his office and told him to type a memo with Fox's bid. Hawkins remembered Austrian cackling and saying, "An average of $395 million per year for a four-year total of $1.58 BILL-ion dollars," with an emphasis on the first syllable of "billion," like Dr. Evil.

That was when Hawkins realized that Carey was trying to tell Murdoch on the phone that Fox's initial bid was probably enough. But Murdoch wanted to blow CBS away and show the NFL he was serious.

"It was like, 'Fuck 'em,'" Hawkins said of Murdoch's strategy.

Pinchbeck called Peter Lund, the head of the CBS Network, at a Christmas party at CBS president Howard Stringer's home in Manhattan. About a dozen top executives crammed into Stringer's bedroom to persuade Tisch to raise his bid. He agreed that CBS would offer $295 million, but it was too little, too late.[2]

Lund left the room to speak to Pinchbeck, and when he returned, his face was ashen. "He looked like somebody died," Pilson remembered. "He said, 'Guys, there's a new number. Fox has offered 400. We need to step up.'"

Tisch said to forget it.

The next day, Lund told Tagliabue that CBS wanted to bid for the AFC package, which was less expensive because of the mix of teams and markets. To his surprise, Tagliabue said that the league had already shaken hands with NBC on a deal that turned out to be worth $217 million a year.

Never shy about pressing for more money, Jones urged Tagliabue to reopen the bidding for the AFC package. Tagliabue was reluctant because he did not want to renege on a deal. To be sure, he called Jets owner Leon Hess, who was also a board member at ABC Capital Cities. Hess asked Tagliabue if he had given NBC his word. Yes, the commissioner said. Then that's it, Hess replied. Your word is your bond.

"There were owners led by Jerry who wanted to start a second bidding war," said Hawkins. "But Paul and Neil were very clear about honoring the deal with your buyers."

The enormity of the NFL's gamble on Fox was clear for both sides. Fox had no sports division, cameramen, producers, or announcers. All the league had was a glimpse of what Fox said it might do. That came via David Hill, who produced soccer games for Murdoch's Sky Sports in London. In mid-December 1993, before the bidding ended, he had wowed the owners at a meeting near the Dallas–Fort Worth Airport.[3]

At Murdoch's request, Hill, a fellow Australian, put together a "sizzle reel" to show the NFL brass what he thought a football game should look like, with three cameras following the action from different angles and closeups of the players. There would be more music and graphics. The pregame show would be livelier, with more of a frat boy vibe than the sober feel of a newsroom.

"We were charging for subscribers to watch the English Premier League, so I had to make the coverage look so much better than it ever looked before, which was relatively easy to do because English broadcasting then was very lazy and the coverage was virtually a wide shot pan and the only time you ever saw the players was when the ball went out of play," Hill said.

After Hill played his tape for Jones, Bowlen, Tagliabue, Austrian, and Pinchbeck, someone on the NFL side who had seen one of Hill's broadcasts on a trip to London said: "Well, if he can make English football interesting, imagine what he can do with the NFL." It was a sign the owners believed Fox might have the chops to broadcast NFL games.

Hill flew back to London assuming Fox had no shot to land an NFL deal because CBS was the longtime incumbent. Besides, Hill had his hands full at Sky Sports.

"It's like anything in the world of television, you pitch a lot and occasionally everything works out, and I thought this was just another pitch," Hill said. "I was having enough problems getting Sky Sports up and running and didn't give a rat's ass what was happening out here."

Then at Christmas, "Rupert rang to say, 'The Eagle has landed,'" Hill said. "I said, 'What does that mean?' and he said, 'We've got the NFL.'"

Murdoch didn't tell Hill one key fact, which he learned the next Monday when he got a call from George Krieger, a Fox executive. He asked Hill if he had seen *The Wall Street Journal*, which Hill had not. Krieger faxed him the article. The first paragraph of the story said that Fox had won the NFC broadcast rights. The second paragraph said that Hill would be president of Fox Sports.

"So, I rang Rupert, who was in LA, and said, 'Is there something you want to tell me?'" Hill recalled. "Murdoch said, 'Can you get here as soon as possible? There's so much to be done.'" The job of building a sports division from scratch in eight months was so daunting, and the money riding on it so immense, that Hill assumed he would be sacked after the first week of the new season. He was so sure of it he kept his apartment in London.

When a colleague in London asked Hill when he'd be back, he said: "When they fire me on September seventh," after the first week of the season.

The NFL might have been sold on Hill's vision and Murdoch's $1.58 billion bid,[4] but they were uncertain whether Fox would be ready in time for the 1994 season, or even be able to pay its bills. Some owners, Jones said, suggested that the league take out a line of credit in case Fox faltered. But ultimately, they put their faith in Murdoch to deliver what he promised.

With the NFL rights, Murdoch got to work expanding his network by getting off hard-to-find channels in major markets that were less valuable to advertisers. Murdoch needed affiliates willing to ditch CBS or other networks.

"The biggest leap of faith for us was that they would go after those affiliates and get them," Tagliabue said. "But Rupert said, 'I'll pay what it takes to get it.'"

In May 1994, Fox invested $500 million in New World Communications, which controlled a string of stations. As part of the deal, New World agreed to switch up to a dozen of its local stations to Fox from CBS, ABC, and NBC. That put Fox—and its NFL games—on channels higher on the dial in Atlanta, Dallas, Detroit, Tampa, and other cities with NFC teams.

"This agreement will forever change the competitive landscape of network television," Murdoch said in a statement.

Fox needed a sports division to produce those games. Hill had a choice of moving to New York or Los Angeles but chose the latter because he felt the network studios in New York were more focused on news and serious programming.

"I've always seen sport as pure entertainment," Hill said. "In New York, people are doing news and *60 Minutes* and all that shit. In LA, I got an opportunity to work with people that are making shows that the world watches and make people laugh. So I can get cameramen and editors and audio guys and the people that actually, you know, create the magic."

Hill started building a team, and the most obvious source of talent was at CBS, which would be out of the football business after the NFL playoffs ended. Hill sought out Ed Goren, the lead producer of NFL games at CBS. Goren was not surprised. Even before Fox won the NFC rights, Goren went to his agent and told him, "If this Rupert Murdoch rumor is true and he's the wild man he certainly is, the deal is going to Fox," Goren later said. "What people didn't realize is, Rupert wouldn't take the second best. If he was going to overpay, he might as well overpay for the best," and the best was CBS's NFC package.

After Murdoch won the NFC rights, Goren knew football would no longer be in his portfolio at CBS. He asked Lou D'Ermilio, a CBS Sports spokesman, to send a fax for him. D'Ermilio saw it was Goren's résumé. Goren told him to keep it quiet because he still had to work the Winter Olympic Games in Lillehammer, Norway, a few weeks later. Goren then flew to California to meet Hill.

Goren quickly realized that building a sports division from scratch was the chance of a lifetime. He and his wife were set to fly to Los Angeles from their home in Connecticut when the Northridge earthquake hit Southern California on January 17, 1994. Despite the ominous start, Goren was itching to get going. He never made it to Norway.

"It was great because first off, we had nobody," he said. "It was David who comes in from London and I come in from CBS and that was it."

Hill, Goren, and their small team moved into the offices of KTTV, a channel Fox owned. The lot on Sunset Boulevard included the set where *All in the Family* had been filmed. Hill's office had been used by Norman Lear, the show's creator.

"I arrived at Fox in January 1994, and was given an IBM Selectric typewriter, a yellow legal pad, and two HB pencils," Hill said. "There was nothing. I had six months to put together eight production teams, a logo, a studio, engineering infrastructure, a publicity machine, a sales department. I hired Ed because he was at CBS in production management, and he knew everyone. He had the best Rolodex in town, and he was universally liked."

Everything was up for grabs, from the graphics to the theme song to the announcers and pre- and postgame shows. Days were long and often stretched into late-night sessions at nearby restaurants where ideas were scribbled on napkins and, hopefully, deciphered the next morning.

"The launch," D'Ermilio, whom Goren brought over from CBS, said, "was powered by red wine and Marlboro Lights."

Hill knew that fans wanted to see and hear the players, so he added more cameras and parabolic microphones on the field. At CBS, some games had only four cameras and two tape machines for editing replays. Hill and Goren decided to go with six or seven cameras for lesser games and ten or more cameras for bigger games.

They developed new graphics. At CBS, the producers would show scores from other games during breaks in the action, not while the game was going on because it was considered distracting and could give viewers a reason to change channels.

Hill and Goren put a box at the top of the screen with scores from other games so fans could keep track in real time. Hill had created a similar box for soccer games. Dubbed "the Fox Box," it was initially panned by industry insiders, including Dick Ebersol at NBC. Ultimately it became the standard. Goren's only regret was not patenting it.

"David, when all is said and done, was a producer, and I was a producer," Goren said. "At a lot of the networks, it was ad guys, business guys" who controlled things. But "we spoke the same language. We were going to be different."

Murdoch left most of the details to Hill, Goren, and others, but he did weigh in at times, like when Fox wanted to sign John Madden, the king of football analysts. Madden's everyman persona made him the top color man in sports. He pioneered the use of the Telestrator to diagram plays, and his syncopated delivery and slovenly dress complemented Pat Summerall, his straight man partner at CBS.

Murdoch didn't know much about football, but he knew Madden. Richie Zyontz, an NFL producer who joined Fox in 1994 after sixteen years at CBS, recalled a comment Murdoch made about the former Oakland Raiders coach: "If I have to introduce someone new to our country to one person who is uniquely American, it would be John Madden," Murdoch said.

Madden was going to be out of a job, and Bob Iger at ABC tried to lure him to *Monday Night Football*. Madden's agent, Barry Frank, was in talks on a deal worth $10 million over four years. Murdoch got wind of it and called Frank and Sandy Montag, who also represented Madden. Murdoch wanted to know "Madden's number." When he was told, Murdoch said he'd call back in five minutes. Murdoch's CFO called back and asked for the address to send the contract, worth about $30 million over four years. Madden told Frank to tell ABC the deal was off, something Iger never forgot.

"I know, but this isn't my money, and it's not your money," Frank told Iger.[5] "It's John Madden's money."

Madden wasn't just in it for the money. He liked Murdoch's style. Madden visited Murdoch's ranch in Carmel, California, and when the Fox chief was grilling at the barbeque, a sausage fell on the ground. Madden was impressed that Murdoch picked it up, dusted it off, and threw it back on the grill.

After years of heavy drinking, Summerall was sober.[6] But he worried that Fox would pick someone else to work with Madden. Fox, though, knew the pair were inseparable in viewers' minds, and it signed Summerall, too.

"That was a no-brainer in a lot of ways," Goren said. "Pat and John, you can't go wrong."

Madden and his longtime sidekick traded the most established network in sports for a newcomer. At a meeting to discuss the vision for the new division, Madden asked David Hill why it was called Fox Sports when it had only one league to cover. "Why not call it Fox Sport since we only have one sport?" he asked.

Goren hired Dick Stockton and Matt "Mini Madden" Millen from CBS to be the B-team. Goren then looked for young play-by-play announcers who could grow with the network. Fox signed Marv Albert's son, Kenny; and Thom Brennaman, whose father, Marty, called Cincinnati Reds games. Kevin Harlan, whose father was president of the Packers, joined, too.

Goren found another announcer at the Super Bowl in Atlanta, where he accompanied Murdoch. One night, Goren and his wife bumped into Jack Buck, who had worked at CBS for many years, and his wife, Carol. Buck rarely pushed his son to television executives, but Carol wasn't shy. After some pleasantries, she told Goren, "I have a son who's a sportscaster" and then reached into her bag, took out a VHS tape, and gave it to him.

"He's done a little bit of this, a little bit of that, you think you might watch it?" she asked.

Patty Goren jumped in. "If he expects any action tonight, Carol, he's going to look at the tape first."

Buck had called only baseball and basketball at that point, but Goren signed him anyway. He later joked that Buck joined the "lucky sperm club" with Albert, Brennaman, and Harlan.

Hill and Goren had ideas for the pregame show, which would set the tone for the broadcast. Hill had seen Terry Bradshaw on CBS's *NFL Today* show and thought he was perfect. Bradshaw agreed to move to Fox before Goren arrived. In Atlanta, Goren met Howie Long, who had just retired after a thirteen-year Hall of Fame career with the Raiders. He had the looks and personality for television and had been a defensive end who could complement Bradshaw, a former quarterback.

But at his audition, Long came across as wooden and overprepared. Goren went to the set and asked Long how many notes Bradshaw had. "None," he replied. Goren said, "Right, come back tomorrow and audition again without notes." Long nailed the second audition.

After the Cowboys won their second consecutive Super Bowl, Goren and Hill were watching ESPN as the announcers discussed the messy divorce between Jerry Jones and his coach, Jimmy Johnson. After the report ended, Goren turned to Hill and said, "I'll see you in a couple days." Hill replied: "Dallas?"

"He knew, he just read it," Goren said, explaining how he and Hill thought alike.

Goren knew Johnson when he coached at the University of Miami. Most coaches pulled their punches on television because they didn't want to offend potential employers. Johnson wasn't afraid to throw darts. Goren called Johnson from the plane and told him that he wanted to talk about working for Fox.

"Ed, I just got my butt kicked—not today," Johnson said.

Goren said he was on the plane and would be in Dallas soon. Johnson relented but told Goren to meet him at an airport hotel to avoid reporters.

A month or so later, Rich Dalrymple, the Cowboys spokesman, called Goren to say that Fox's offer was too low. Goren said he'd take care of it. Then Dalrymple told Goren that Johnson hated to fly and didn't want to commute from his home in the Florida Keys to Los Angeles every week during the season.

That spring, Johnson called Goren before he flew to New York. ESPN, it turned out, was also courting Johnson. Goren demanded to know ESPN's offer so he could match it.

"This isn't a negotiation," Goren told Johnson. "Right now, Rupert's got my balls in one hand, and he can find the other one to squeeze."

Johnson added that ESPN would let him appear on their show from his home.

"I said, well, they lied," Goren said. "What kind of fucking charisma will you and your lazy fucking white ass have in Islamorada?"

As a compromise, Goren told Johnson that he could pick two Sundays each season so "you can be on the show sitting on your lazy white ass by your pool."

Goren wanted Johnson's deal sewn up, so he called Lucie Salhany, the chairwoman at Fox.

"When will it end? First you want Madden and Summerall, then you want Bradshaw. Now you want Jimmy Johnson," Salhany said before hanging up.

Goren persuaded the head of advertising sales at Fox to tell Salhany the extra money was worth it. She relented.

Goren received a call from Madden after the 1994 schedule was released. The gold star game was a rematch of the previous year's NFC Championship Game between the Cowboys and 49ers. Madden wanted to make sure Fox secured that game. Goren told Madden he was working on it.

A week later, Madden called back. "Did you get the game yet?" Goren said he was lobbying Pinchbeck, who created the season schedule. Madden called back a third time. "Al Michaels says that the game will be on ABC," on a Monday night, Madden said.

Panic ensued. Fox didn't pay $395 million a year to not carry the marquee matchup. Goren told Hill that Murdoch had to intervene. Murdoch called Tagliabue and said Fox paid dearly for the NFC package and deserved the biggest NFC games.

"They want me to tell you that we need these matches for this to work," Murdoch told Tagliabue, who remembered how Murdoch called them "matches," not "games."

Tagliabue asked him which games he wanted. There was a pause. Then Murdoch said: "God damn it, I can't find the card they gave me with the matches on them."

Murdoch put Tagliabue on hold and called Hill and said, "What bloody games do you and Ed want?"

Murdoch returned and told Tagliabue the list of games, starting with Dallas–San Francisco. Tagliabue said he thought he could get it done. Murdoch thanked him and then added, "I apologize for not knowing anything about any of these matches."

One of Hill's more serendipitous creations was Fox's theme song. To that point, *Monday Night Football* had the most memorable intro song in sports, with blaring trumpets and pounding tympanies that was a prime-time clarion call.

Hill described a successful theme song this way: "If you hear it playing, it makes you want to come to the set, and if you're sitting in front of it and you hear it, it gets your endorphins going when you hear it."

Hill's inspiration came in March 1994 when he was waiting to board the new Batman ride at Six Flags Magic Mountain with his son, Jules. The Gothic orchestral Batman theme song wormed its way into Hill's head.[7] Impressed with the tune, he called George Greenberg, who had left ABC Sports to become the creative director at Fox Sports. Hill told him about the music he heard and told him to come up with a song that conveyed "Batman's got a football team."

Hill told Greenberg to call Scott Schreer, a composer who wrote commercial jingles in New York. Greenberg told him that Hill wanted something along the lines of "Batman on steroids."

Days later, Hill picked up Greenberg at his hotel in Los Angeles and Greenberg popped a CD in with Schreer's three versions. They were big and brassy, with dozens of horn players. There was no ambiguity. It smacked listeners in the face. Hill loved it.

"We made sure we embedded that so when you heard it over and over again it was subliminally and overtly embedded in your brain," Schreer said.[8]

Hill asked to combine the introduction and middle 32 in the first version with the thematic melody in the second version. The reason the song "works in such a minor key is that it has that combative warrior vibe to it," Schreer said. "It's both conscious and subliminal to the listener. It's how we're coded. It's an association thing."

Like its in-your-face announcers and theme song, Fox Sports was not shy about trumpeting its own arrival. Hill told Tracy Dolgin in the marketing department to come up with a slogan for the show. An ad agency created about fifty examples. Hill chose the second-to-last one: "Same Game, New Attitude." There would be less focus on the intricacies of the game, and more graphics and banter in the studio instead of the stuffiness at other networks. A lot was riding on Fox pulling off the broadcast without a hitch, and Hill knew it.

"I had five months to create a full-blown sports division from nothing," Hill said. "I had no time to ponder committees. I had to trust my gut, make the call, and move on."

Viewers quickly noticed the difference in Fox's first preseason game in August 1994. Some fans didn't like the Fox Box with the scores of other games. Goren found a voice message on his phone from a viewer who said Fox had ruined his viewing experience. Hill received five death threats from people who accused him of being a foreigner out to ruin America's game, and that if Fox didn't remove the box, he and his family would be killed. Hill met with the FBI and police, but the threats stopped. The window of Goren's office was shot out, but the police said it might have been related to gang violence, not Fox's new graphics. Still, it was unnerving.

Football fans got their real introduction to Fox Sports on the opening weekend of the season. The broadcast began with Bradshaw dressed as a cowboy standing next to a horse.[9] "Now, it's a new day for the fan, a new day for Fox, it's a new day for this old country boy," he said, his image tinted in sepia. Bradshaw then mounted the horse. "Well, new frontier. They ain't gonna change the game. Sure ain't gonna change me, not even in Hollywood."

Then Bradshaw trotted off as the camera panned to the white Hollywood sign in the hills above the city. The camera followed Bradshaw riding down Sunset Boulevard, past Grauman's Chinese Theatre, and onto the Fox lot, where he parked his horse next to Arnold Schwarzenegger's Rolls-Royce.

After Bradshaw walked into the studio, Fox's NFL graphics rolled and the theme song began. "This is it," a narrator intoned. "Today, the curtain opens on a new era. Football at its best. Coverage at its finest. The NFL on Fox."

Confidence and swagger—or hubris, to critics—would define Fox Sports.

"Schwarzenegger, this celebrity or that celebrity," Goren said. "That's all you needed to know as to what we were going to be about."

More than three decades later, the impact of Murdoch's entry into the NFL continued to ripple through the sports world. By wildly overpaying, Murdoch drove up the value of the NFL's media contracts by 22 percent. He also changed the paradigm for sports media rights. For the networks, broadcasting the NFL had gone from being a cash cow to a break-even proposition to a loss leader. Other sports leagues took note.

"Everyone was looking at the NFL deals and saying, 'We're being underpaid for our rights fees,'" Goren said. "Everyone went into negotiations with that in mind. The valuations of those teams went up dramatically. How do we get to a quarterback making $35 million a year or a right fielder making $50 million a year? It was all coming from TV money. If there was no Rupert Murdoch, who knows what the numbers actually would have been."

Despite the rising prices, the networks knew they needed marquee sports rights. They saw how CBS shows like *60 Minutes* suffered without NFL games to promote them.

"It was a disaster," Neal Pilson said. "A significant number of CBS affiliates switched to Fox. That hurt because we went from the number one or two station in a market to the number four station. That hurt ratings as much as the loss of the promotion power. We lost the male audience because we had nothing effective to promote to get men to watch."

Pilson added: "I never liked Rupert's politics, but he is a pretty smart dude."

Some NFL executives regretted that CBS was pushed out. But the avalanche of media money arrived as the owners entered a new revenue sharing agreement. The windfall from Fox would raise player salaries and help pay for stadiums, training facilities, and team planes. It would make the owners far wealthier, too. In 1998, CBS bid $500 million a year for the rights to AFC games, twice what it had offered four years earlier for the more valuable NFC package.

"Once again, thank you, Rupert," said Robert Kraft, who helped negotiate that deal. "He was really a pioneer. No one wanted to do battle with Rupert. He was really the catalyst."

Within a few years, the NFL's media money grew so large it ensured that every team broke even. The owners could not believe their luck, no one more than Jones. He had courted Murdoch, elbowed his way onto the broadcast committee, which he helped reshape, and was in Tagliabue's office that December night when Murdoch's deputy pushed all of Fox's chips across the table.

The Fox deal "was a watershed moment for the NFL, period," he said. "We went from one thing to something else when Fox came in."

3.

"I LIKE TO SMEAR THAT COWBOYS PEANUT BUTTER ON EVERYTHING."

NFL owners generally fall into three groups. The first comprises multigenerational owners like Art Rooney of the Steelers and John Mara of the Giants, men who inherited their clubs and have most of their wealth wrapped up in their teams. Atlanta Falcons owner Arthur Blank, who cofounded Home Depot, is typical of the second group of men who bought their teams with money they made elsewhere. A third group, which includes Stan Kroenke of the Los Angeles Rams, are even wealthier and as reclusive as Howard Hughes.

Then there's Cowboys owner Jerry Jones. He turned a bankrupt team into the world's most valuable sports franchise. He made his wealth in oil and gas, real estate, and other industries, so he fits in the second group. But he is also the only owner who is team president *and* general manager, running the Cowboys' business *and* football operations. Jones is the only owner who makes weekly radio appearances and speaks to the media after every game. He is the only owner to host Elizabeth Taylor, Nelson Mandela, and Rush Limbaugh at games. He gave Supreme Court Justice Clarence Thomas a Super Bowl ring and invited him on his private jet.[1]

Jones generates reams of news stories about his scandals, from infidelity to failed business ventures, yet he never misses a chance to promote himself and his team (it's often unclear which takes priority), including flying on private jets with the Cowboys' blue star on the tail. He is the NFL equivalent of the late George Steinbrenner, the ever-present and controversial owner of the New York Yankees.

So, it is unsurprising that the last stop on the "Owners Experience Tour" at Jones's AT&T Stadium is a hologram of Jones himself. Guests who pay $65 can visit "exclusive areas" of the stadium affectionately known as Jerry World, including the private box where Jones sits during games. They pass black-and-white photos of Cowboys greats from before Jones bought the team in 1989, and color photos taken afterward, as if the world was drab before Jones arrived. One hallway included portraits of Jones and his wife from his induction into the Pro Football Hall of Fame in 2017. A few feet away is a small theater where an emcee greeted the dozen fans who took the VIP tour with me.

"If you've ever wondered what it would be like to have dinner with Mr. Jones, or 'If I was a member of the media, what would I ask Mr. Jones about?'," the twentyish man in chinos and a golf shirt said, "well, today you get the opportunity to do that!"

Jones's image popped up on a wall-sized screen. Virtual Jerry sat on the edge of a chair in a blue suit, black boots, and a diamond lapel pin in the shape of a star. Artificial intelligence engines found words in Jerry's vocabulary to stitch together answers to questions like why he built "such a great stadium." Virtual Jerry said that when he was in college in the 1960s, his football coach took the team to see the new Astrodome in Houston, and its grandeur inspired him.

"Roll the clock forward thirty years later, I was thinking about a new stadium for the Dallas Cowboys," Virtual Jerry said. "One thing I didn't have to think about was 'could a man do it?' because when I was nineteen, I saw one built that looked like it came from Mars. I didn't know where I was going to get the money, but I got it built. You can put five of those damn Astrodomes inside the one I built."

Virtual Jerry called Cowboys quarterback Dak Prescott "a Pied Piper" for his leadership skills. He said Jimmy Johnson, his former college roommate and coach whom he fired after they won two Super Bowls together, "enhanced our lives by the positive experience we had of winning."

Virtual Jerry, though, short-circuited when he was asked what he thought of Roger Goodell, his occasional foil.

"Roger Staubach would be competing for the number one supporter that I personally—" he said before the emcee cut him off.

"No one thought more of Coach Landry and respected him more than me," Virtual Jerry began again, referring to the legendary coach he fired after purchasing the Cowboys.

The visit with Virtual Jerry left visitors with a lot to unpack as they made their way to the field to take photos, toss little footballs, and use the 15 percent coupon they received for merchandise at the team store. Virtual Jerry was folksy, effusive, and meandering. Yet the twelve-minute show also reeked of his Texas-sized hubris and relentless drive to monetize the Cowboys brand. Each year, about half a million people take tours of AT&T Stadium and The Star, the team's practice facility, generating almost $10 million.[2]

Since buying the team for $140 million, Jones has worked harder than any owner to promote the Cowboys and the NFL. But Jones is also a walking three-ring circus. It takes a special kind of ego to build a digital shrine to yourself, another example of how Jones blurred the line between himself, his team, and the NFL. He negotiated a $50 million deal with Netflix to show a ten-part NFL Films documentary about himself. He also pushed his fellow owners, many of them football men who lacked his appetite for risk, to market, package, and sell their teams more aggressively. In the process, he made them all a lot wealthier.

Decades ago, the NFL was filled with colorful entrepreneurs who weren't shy about promoting their teams, even if they weren't good at running them. Joe Robbie, an avuncular lawyer and politician from South Dakota who worked as a tobacco industry lobbyist, bought the expansion Miami Dolphins in 1966 with the entertainer Danny Thomas. He spent the following twenty-four years scrounging to keep the team afloat. Leonard Tose, a trucking magnate who paid a record $16 million for the Philadelphia Eagles in 1969, was a compulsive gambler who almost lost the team to banks.[3] Al Davis boxed out his fellow owners to take over the Raiders and sued the NFL twice to win the right to move his team.

Jones shared many of their eccentricities, their financial acrobatics, after-hours carousing, and willingness to fight the league. Jones grew up in Arkansas, but he was destined to make his name in Dallas, a city filled with big-talking oil and gas men. Owners regard Jones as a brilliant salesman even as they shake their heads at his methods. His players welcome his enthusiasm, then curse him when their relationships sour. "I stopped, honestly, listening to things [Jerry] says to the media a long time ago," Prescott said a few days before signing a $240 million contract during the 2024 season.[4] "It doesn't really hold weight with me."

Fans blame him for every Cowboys transgression, the most notable being the team's inability to return to the Super Bowl, which it last did in 1996. After the Washington Commanders reached the 2024 NFC Championship Game, the Cowboys became the NFC team with the longest conference title game drought. One fan created T-shirts that read, "Jerry Makes Me Drink."[5] Jones is a rare owner with pop culture cred. He has been roasted on the animated show *South Park* and imitated by Frank Caliendo, the master impersonator.[6] He appeared as himself on the television series *Landman*. Every time the Cowboys play, he is shown on television in his suite, living and dying with his team.

The first time I interviewed Jones, in 2015, he welcomed me to his office in the team's old facility in Irving, Texas. Impeccably dressed, he was gracious and almost solicitous, making sure I had enough iced tea. He leaned into our conversation, flashing a smile as he tried to win me over. His words were another story. He would start new sentences before he finished the prior ones, jamming thoughts together. "To be able to build a building in the NFL, with our game as popular as it is today, to be able to build that building, and arguably in one of the great economic areas of the world, not just the United States, but the world, to build that building as a primary tenant, the Cowboys, who have, uh, the most visibility of any team in the country today, well, we all know that one of the things you want to do when you have something is let everybody know about it," Jones said of AT&T Stadium.

It was mesmerizing and frustrating. I needed to quote full sentences, but the interview was a giant word salad. After our meeting, Jones showed me to the door and said quietly, "Just clean that up."

Reporters and fans trash him, sometimes to his face, yet Jones shows up the next day and answers questions all over again. Most NFL owners—Terry Pegula in Buffalo, Stan Kroenke in Los Angeles, Jody Allen in Seattle—rarely speak to the media. Jones sees the love, the jokes, and even the hatred of the Cowboys as good for the team's brand. For him, the worst sin is to be boring. Being dull doesn't sell tickets, jerseys, or sponsorships.

"I like to be liked, I do," Jones said in court in 2024 when the NFL was sued for conspiring to artificially inflate the price of the Sunday Ticket television package. "But I'm very aware that I'm not liked by a lot in that sense. What is so important is that you are substantive, that you are interesting. The facts are that probably well over half the fans of the NFL don't like the Cowboys and want to kick our you-know-what every time we get out there. But that's the way it is because they don't like me, and they probably don't like me to some degree if they pay that much attention to it. But it makes us interesting."

Most days, NFL owners would prefer Jones not be so interesting. They know he cares deeply about the Cowboys and the league. But they are often flummoxed by his haphazard speaking style and his propensity to see dollar signs around every corner when none needed to be found. For decades, the NFL owners ran the league based on the belief that they were only as strong as their weakest teams, practicing a brand of socialism where most revenue was shared equally.

Then came Jones, a salesman with a Texas-sized appetite. He argued teams should be allowed to keep more revenue from the jerseys and sponsorships they sell. He framed it as a "states' rights" issue, a curious construction coming from a man who grew up in the Jim Crow South. Jones tried to sound like Horatio Alger, extolling the virtues of hard work. But the other owners knew the Cowboys had the best-selling merchandise and believed Jones was trying to grab more of that revenue for himself.

Jones forged ahead anyway. He sold sponsorships worth more than $60 million that competed with the league's agreements, cutting deals with Pepsi when the league's soda sponsor was Coke, with Nike when the league had a deal with Reebok, and with American Express instead of Visa.

"I give Jerry high marks for his entrepreneurship, but the league wasn't built on entrepreneurship," Cleveland Browns owner Art Modell said in 1995.[7] "I wish he would take note of the history of this league and understand we got here by sharing revenue. We can't have 30 teams going around marketing their own soft drinks. What a collective belch that would be."

Jones was driven by the need to pay back the money he had borrowed to buy the Cowboys, and partly to take advantage of the team's sky-high popularity. He said he wanted to show other owners that they could sell more merchandise and sponsorships, too. Ultimately, other teams followed.

"You got to thank Jerry Jones because he force-fed us on the way to make money in the league that we weren't focusing on, or even thinking about," said Carmen Policy, the former president of the 49ers and Browns who often butted heads with Jones. "Jerry felt the more that you can raise the value of the Indianapolis Colts, the higher the value of the Cowboys will grow. And probably his grows exponentially more than Indianapolis."

For all the chaos he created, Jones had the charisma to defang even his biggest critics.

At one cocktail party, Jones "came over to my wife and said, 'Marie, that Carmen, he's like Jesse James: dangerous and good looking, too,'" Policy said. "I mean, he wins you over. He's got that charm that he adjusts. And he would never get down and nasty or mad at you."

Jones learned about salesmanship growing up in North Little Rock, Arkansas. He was born in Los Angeles in 1942, a year after his parents, Pat and Arminta, drove to California to find work in an airplane factory supplying the war effort.[8] (They eloped in Arizona on the way.)

Jerry's sister, Jacquelyn, was also born in Los Angeles, in 1944. When the war ended the following year, the family returned to Arkansas.

Pat had no interest in being a sharecropper again, so he opened a supermarket. A showman, he liked to wear white suits and cowboy hats and put a bandstand in the middle of the store and hold talent shows. When Jerry was nine, his mother dressed him in a suit and bow tie and told him to greet customers at the front door. "I remember her saying, 'Now, when this woman comes in, you might want to push her basket around the store for her,'" Jones recalled.[9] "'She might give you a nice little tip. More importantly, she'll think it's cute and it will be good for our customers.'"

He portrayed his childhood in rosy terms, and for a white teenager in the 1950s, it likely was a good life. But he came of age during the civil rights movement, when white leaders in the Deep South resisted the federal government's desegregation of public schools, including in North Little Rock. Many years later, *The Washington Post* found a photo of Jones on the steps of his high school watching a group of angry white people harass six Black students trying to enter the school for the first time. Jones said he was only there to watch, not to heckle. But his worldview was undoubtedly shaped by these events. Years later, Jones's attitudes toward race became a focus when he acknowledged his team had a poor record hiring coaches of color.[10]

This was one of Jones's many blind spots, along with drinking heavily, being photographed with strippers,[11] and making off-color comments about his players, including quarterback Troy Aikman, who he said "looks good in the shower."[12]

Jones was a running back in high school and went to the University of Arkansas in 1960 on a football scholarship. His family also moved four hours north to Springfield, Missouri, where Pat Jones started an insurance agency. In school, Jerry studied business and went out for the football team, switching from running back to offensive lineman.

His senior year, he roomed with Johnson, his future coach. Jones was cocaptain of the team, which went 11-0 and beat Nebraska 10–7 in the Cotton Bowl to win the national championship.

During summer breaks, Jones sold insurance for his father and shoes out of the trunk of his car to his fraternity brothers. He resold student tickets before games and then raced to the locker room to suit up. Dubbed "the Razorback businessman,"[13] he earned undergraduate and master's degrees in business in 1965. His master's thesis was titled "The Role of Oral Communication in Modern-Day Collegiate Football."[14]

After graduation, Jones's father sent him to Oklahoma to sell insurance. There, he met another salesman who taught him about the oil and gas business. Jones didn't have a degree in geology, but he was a careful listener and quickly found success. He also tried to borrow money from the pension fund of the International Brotherhood of Teamsters, then headed by Jimmy Hoffa, to open Shakey's Pizza Parlors in Missouri, a venture that fizzled.

Jones was determined to own a football team. In 1966, then just twenty-three, he flew to Houston and hung around the lobby of the hotel where the American Football League owners were meeting. He spoke to Lamar Hunt of the Kansas City Chiefs, Ralph Wilson of the Buffalo Bills, and Joe Robbie, who had just bought the Dolphins. Soon after, Jones flew to Miami and helped Robbie move into the team's new office, pushing Robbie's desk up a flight of stairs. Jones told Robbie he wanted to own a team. Robbie told him the San Diego Chargers were for sale and called Barron Hilton, the team's owner. Hilton only wanted to speak to serious bidders who could produce a $1 million letter of credit. Jones told the Teamsters about his ambition to own a team and they gave him a letter of credit from the Central States Pension Plan.[15]

"I was sitting with them going over my dreams when I said, 'Where I really wanna be is in football,'" Jones said he told the

Teamsters.[16] "And they said, 'Well, you know, our union might want to be involved in sports.'"

Hilton wanted $5.8 million for the team, a steep price for Jones. Undeterred, he flew to Kansas City to see Hunt, who said that every team in the league was losing money, but they were going to compete with the NFL. Hunt didn't tell Jones that secret merger talks were underway. Either way, Jones's father persuaded his son that buying the Chargers would bury him in debt.

"He told me, 'I hate to see you start life behind the eight ball,'" Jones said.

Hilton sold the team for $10 million, and for years Jones regretted taking his father's advice.

Several months later, Jones cobbled together another group of investors and borrowed money to buy fifty-one pieces of property worth $3 million. Jones planned to sell the land and divide the proceeds. But he personally guaranteed the loans, and when he couldn't sell the land fast enough, the banks came calling. Jones owed well over $100,000, crushing debt for someone earning $35,000 selling insurance. His credit cards were revoked. One rental car agent cut his card into pieces in front of him. He became so nervous he needed two hands to hold a beer.

He persuaded his bankers to restructure his debts so he could hold on to the land, some of which was turned into a development with a Walmart. He and his father also bought thousands of acres of ranchland outside Springfield and created a drive-through exotic animal park that became a tourist destination in southwest Missouri. They sold the park, which is now known as Wild Animal Safari, in 1995.[17]

Jones hit it big speculating on oil and gas wells. In 1971, he founded Jerry Jones Oil and Gas, which generated tens of millions of dollars that he reinvested in banking, crude oil shipping and refining, and poultry processing. In the 1980s, he struck a deal with

Arkla, a gas company, which was led by Sheffield Nelson, a hunting buddy. The state bought all the natural gas Jones's company produced at a fixed price, which turned into a windfall when gas prices plunged. Bill Clinton pointed to the sweetheart deal to hammer Nelson when they faced off in a gubernatorial race in 1990.

"I have a very high tolerance for ambiguity," Jones said in 2010. "I work best when I don't know that I'm gonna get my check at the end of the week, or I don't know what the answer is at the end of the month."

Jones was still hungry to buy an NFL franchise, and the Cowboys—the self-proclaimed "America's Team"—went on the block in 1988. For decades, coach Tom Landry, general manager Tex Schramm, and player personnel guru Gil Brandt built the country's best team, using computers to scout players and create plays. Starting in 1966, the Cowboys made the postseason eighteen of the next twenty years and advanced to five Super Bowls, winning twice. The Steelers won four Super Bowls in the 1970s, but the Cowboys were more popular because they played in the NFC East against teams in the largest markets, and because of their risqué cheerleaders.

By the mid-1980s, Landry lost his touch. The Cowboys fell to 3-13 in 1988. Seats and suites in Texas Stadium went unsold, and the team was losing more than $1 million a month. Owner H. R. "Bum" Bright had his savings and loan taken over by the federal government, and a chunk of the rest of his money was tied up in the team. In the fall of 1988, Jones woke up with a hangover while on a fishing trip in Cabo San Lucas, Mexico, with his oldest son, Stephen. He opened the newspaper and read about the team's troubles. He knew he had to pounce.

About seventy-five potential investors expressed interest in the team, but five were taken seriously, including Jones, Los Angeles

Lakers owner Jerry Buss, and a mysterious Japanese billionaire.[18] Bright wanted at least $100 million for the team, $60 million for the stadium lease, and $20 million to cover the club's debt.[19] Jones's accountant, Jack Dixon, told him the team "was ridiculously overpriced and buying the Cowboys would be financial suicide. He could have gone dead-dog broke on this."[20]

Negotiations sped up after Bright lowered the price to $140 million. Unlike the other bidders, Jones wanted to replace Landry with Johnson, who was coaching at the University of Miami. It wasn't a deal-breaker—Bright had openly criticized Landry—but Bright wanted to keep negotiations quiet because news of Landry losing his job would spark a backlash.

Jones did his homework. He met Broncos owner Pat Bowlen and 49ers owner Eddie DeBartolo, and Dan Burke, the president of ABC. In January 1989, Jones made the first of a half dozen visits to Dallas to see Bright. By mid-February, Bright decided that Jones was the best candidate even though he only had $90 million in cash—about all the money he had—and needed to borrow the rest. Their negotiations came down to a difference of about $250,000, so they flipped a coin. Jones lost, but he had the Cowboys for $140 million plus $11 million in debt, the first nine-figure sale in NFL history. Jones called Johnson and told him to start putting together a coaching staff. Johnson called Dolphins coach Don Shula to ask for permission to speak with his son David. Oddly, Shula never called his close friend Schramm to ask whether Landry was losing his job.

Bright wanted to close the deal, meet Schramm to discuss Landry's fate, and announce the sale at the beginning of March. Jones hoped Landry would retire on his own. But television reporters in Fort Worth got wind of the deal and the plan to replace Landry.[21] Jones and Johnson flew to Dallas to finalize the details with Bright. After their meeting, they took their wives to Mia's, a Mexican restaurant where they thought they would be left alone. By chance, *Dallas Morning News* reporter Ivan Maisel was eating there with his fiancée. He knew Johnson because he had covered college football. Maisel introduced himself, got a quote, and called the newspaper to tell his boss to send a photographer quickly.

The next day, a photo of Jones and Johnson was splashed on the front page under the headline "Cowboys Sale Near; Landry Likely Out."[22] To compound matters, the men looked like they were celebrating. When they returned to Bright's office to finalize the deal, Jones and Johnson met Schramm, who knew he could not save Landry's job. Jones and Schramm flew to Austin to break the news to Landry, who was playing golf. The only coach in the Cowboys' twenty-nine-year history was out. Jones and Schramm returned to Dallas for a press conference at 8:15 p.m. on a Saturday night.

Jones waved off suggestions that he prepare. It was a mess. Facing a bank of television cameras and intense scrutiny, Jones appeared to stomp on Landry and Schramm, two beloved figures. "This is Christmas to me," he said. Jones said he would be immersed in all parts of the organization, "down to the jocks and socks," a sign Schramm was on thin ice, too. Bum Bright called Jones "as square as a graham cracker" and said new leadership was needed. Jones was quickly branded a "hillbilly buffoon." Hate mail and death threats followed.

His image took another hit when he fired many longtime staffers. Others left on their own. Jones brought his longtime assistant, Marylyn Love, from Arkansas. New to Dallas, she would call Jarrett Bell, who wrote for the *Dallas Cowboys Weekly* magazine, to ask where to get dry cleaning done or find good barbeque. "It was real seat-of-the-pants," said Bell, who became a columnist for *USA Today*. Jones asked Bell for his thoughts on how the Cowboys were run. He wanted to know, for example, why reporters were deferential to Schramm even though the team had missed the playoffs for three straight seasons. Bell told him Schramm got the benefit of the doubt because he was available to the media, even taking calls at home. At the Super Bowl a few years later, Jones introduced Bell to NBC announcer Dick Enberg and said, "This is the guy that got me started."

Jones worked overtime to fix the team's leaky finances, sleeping in the office some nights. He looked for money everywhere, even suggesting scrapping the prohibition on the team's cheerleaders appearing where beer or liquor was served, a rule meant to protect them. After fourteen cheerleaders quit in protest, Jones backtracked and all but one of the women returned. Jones stumbled again, calling the cheerleaders "the pick of the litter."

Schramm left to run the World League of American Football, the NFL's new international venture.

"I'll say this right now," Jones told *The New York Times*.[23] "We'll have change around here from now on, in all phases of it. The people who won that last Super Bowl 13 years ago" for the Cowboys "aren't anywhere to be found."

Everything seemed to go wrong in Jones's first season, in 1989. Johnson had the assistant coaches he wanted, but the team's rookie quarterback, Troy Aikman, lost all eleven of his starts. The Cowboys finished 1-15 and drew about 52,000 fans a game, well below capacity. The team hit rock bottom on Christmas Eve when they were set to host the Packers. Jones received an early morning call. The stadium toilets were frozen. "And I'm sitting there thinking, a year ago, I didn't have a care in the world. We were getting ready for Christmas. My ship had come home a little financially and everything was great. Now here I am, we've won one football game. They just about made me the Darth Vader of the world for changing the coach. I don't know if we're going to live to tell about this financially. And now every damn commode is frozen." It was, Jones said, "just a reminder that life had changed."

"I like to smear that Cowboys peanut butter on everything."

But that offseason, Jones and Johnson selected running back Emmitt Smith in the first round of the Draft. It didn't come without drama. Fred Gaudelli, who produced the Draft for ESPN, asked Jones if he could put a camera in the Cowboys' "war room." Jones said fine, as long as the team's draft board was not shown. However, Jones didn't tell Johnson until the day before, and Johnson freaked out.

"Jones was always great with access," Gaudelli said. "He would play anytime, anywhere, on any day if it would put the Cowboys in the national spotlight. He did not care."

The team finished 7-9 and attendance jumped 15 percent. Jones began filling the suites and selling new sponsorships. Some deals were with companies that competed with NFL sponsors. Jones owned the pouring rights in Texas Stadium, so in his mind, his sponsorship with Pepsi was with the stadium, not the team, and did not conflict with the league's deal with Coke. Tagliabue and the other owners thought Jones was skirting the rules.

Jones pressed on. In 1993, he created a commemorative Super Bowl jacket and had thirty thousand of them produced by Apex One and distributed by JCPenney, with Jones getting 20 percent of every jacket sold.[24] The league learned about the deal and sent Mike Ornstein from NFL Properties to tell Jones to cease and desist. "I go down there and say, 'Jerry, you can't sell these jackets.' He says, 'Mike, I'm going to sell them, so you tell them guys in the league office I'm going to sell them.'" Ornstein was ordered to buy the jackets and destroy them. "We couldn't have them in the market, so I gave Jerry, like, $1 million, $30 a jacket or whatever it was, not to sell them, but to keep it out of the market. And then he decided he was going to do that with everything."

Jones cut more deals to cash in on the Cowboys' Super Bowl titles in 1991 and 1992. He signed other agreements with 7-Eleven,

Frito-Lay, American Express, and Nike. The Cowboys had the most valuable sponsorships, so Jones reasoned he deserved more than the one-thirtieth share that every team received.

"Everything we had, he did the opposite," Ornstein said.

At a meeting in Palm Desert in March 1993, the owners discussed Jones's deal with JCPenney "that would have the effect of allowing a team to directly license its logos," according to meeting minutes. The owners said the league had the sole right to license logos. The issue arose again at a meeting in early 1995, when "a spirited discussion ensued."

Jones argued that sharing revenue evenly didn't motivate owners. "America didn't come along as a commune, where people got out and worked and gained assets and position, then turned around and gave it back to everybody else who's not working," he said.[25]

Many owners viewed Jones as greedy. In one meeting, Jones argued that he deserved a bigger share of jersey sales because the Cowboys were the most popular team. Jets owner Leon Hess sarcastically replied that he wanted a bigger share of the league's broadcast revenue because his team was in the largest television market.

"You go back to when we voted to share our television revenues equally," Giants owner John Mara said of his father, Wellington. "That's why it was so abhorrent to him when Jerry Jones comes in and makes his own deal with Nike. That wasn't a league-first philosophy."

The showdown reached a breaking point in September 1995 when the Cowboys were in New York to face the Giants for the season-opening game. Jones called Al Michaels, the announcer that night, and asked him to come to the St. Regis Hotel a few blocks away in Manhattan. Jones told him about his plan to announce his new agreement with Nike before the game. He would walk on the field with Nike founder Phil Knight and Monica Seles, the tennis star and Nike athlete. The press release announcing the deal included the headline "Cowboys Owner Bucks N.F.L. Again."[26]

"I said to Jerry, 'You're going to create an earthquake on Park Avenue,'" where the league has its offices, Michaels said. "He said, 'I'm ready.'" Michaels admired his pluck. "He's a wildcatter, but he's a smart wildcatter. He's not afraid to make moves that no one else makes or will make."

Two weeks later, the owners in charge of NFL Properties voted unanimously to sue Jones for $300 million. Jones countersued for $750 million.

Jones "drove us nuts," Policy, the 49ers president, said. "We kept saying, 'Jerry, why are you violating these rules? I mean, if they're not going to be honored, how do we run a league?'"

Other owners pushed the envelope, Policy said, but they did so quietly. Patriots owner Robert Kraft signed a similar deal with Pepsi ten days after Jones did, but it raised few eyebrows.[27] "Kraft knew exactly where he wanted to get to, but he would take the time to get there without causing collateral damage," Policy said. "Jerry wants to get there quick. If there's some damage caused along the way, that's the way it is."

Tagliabue publicly upbraided Jones. "Jerry Jones dishonors the agreement he made when he came into the NFL partnership," he said on *This Week with David Brinkley* hours before the Cowboys played the Steelers in Super Bowl XXX.[28] "He takes what does not belong to him. The NFL is what we sell. It belongs to 30 teams, not the Dallas Cowboys."

On December 13, 1996, the two sides dropped their lawsuits after Jones pointed to game-day programs to show that other teams cut deals with companies that weren't league partners. In an agreement brokered by future commissioner Roger Goodell, Jones kept his existing sponsorships and could continue to sign new ones with carveouts.[29] Teams could keep revenue from apparel sales in their home markets, but they had to share revenue from stadium naming rights because those would get national exposure on NFL broadcasts.

"Do you really want to know why I brought this lawsuit? Because the NFL sued me," Jones said in 2024. "It caused all of the principals of the NFL league office, with the help of some other great owners, and we sat down, in two weeks got worked out what we'd been generally working with ever since, successfully."

Some owners were still angry. Ornstein recalled visiting Mike Brown in Cincinnati. Ornstein told him, "'We'd like you to think about start doing some local marketing. You know, Jerry's going to make $5 million this year.' All of a sudden, Mr. Football, he turns his chair around and said, 'How much?!'"

Owners who paid far more than Jones for their teams appreciated how he helped grow the league's revenue.

"When he is committed to a path or road or direction that he feels is the correct one, Jerry is a dog with a bone," Arthur Blank of the Falcons said.[30] "He will not let it loose until either he eats it or it kills him. People respect that with him."

Even as he was criticized as a team-first owner, Jones worked hard on league-wide issues, particularly negotiations with television broadcasters. In October 1993, the Cowboys were in Philadelphia to play the Eagles. At the Cowboys' team hotel, Jones ran into Jim Nantz, the CBS announcer who was there to meet coaches and players. "You know what's going on with these television negotiations," Nantz recalled Jones saying. "He said, 'You better tell your guys back in New York to get with it, because I'm telling you right now, you might lose this package to Fox.'"

What distinguishes Jones is he doesn't hide his insatiable drive to make money or his joy at owning the Cowboys.

"Money is how a businessman measures success," Stephen Jones said.[31] "In a way, accumulating money is keeping score. Jerry may not need more money, but if he doesn't make it, in his mind, he has failed."

When he dines out, he prefers to sit at a table in the middle of a restaurant. When everyone is ready to turn in after a long dinner, he'll ask the group whether they want to go for one more. The answer, at least to Jones, is yes. When the Cowboys visited New Orleans to play the Saints in 2019,[32] Jones was mobbed by fans chanting his name as he walked down Bourbon Street with a drink in his hand.

"If you want to fly with the owls, you better soar with the eagles," Jones was fond of saying. Or, as one associate put it: "There's no stop sign with Jerry, only a yield sign."

At the Combine in Indianapolis each February, Jones sat at a big table each night at Prime 47, a steakhouse where agents, team executives, and the media knock back drinks until 3 a.m. Jones's table was near a corner table reserved by Bob LaMonte, the agent for many coaches and general managers. One night, Jones leaned over to LaMonte and said, "Bob, I love what you do, but I can't get a freaking drink. You have all the cocktail waitresses! I just want a glass of wine." LaMonte grabbed a bottle of his wine and gave it to Jones. "I like how you work, Bob," Jones said.

Jones applauds pluck. At one league meeting, Raiders president Amy Trask went to the microphone to make a point. As she began talking, Tagliabue told her to sit down because he wanted to wrap up the session. Trask kept talking and Tagliabue let her finish. As the room emptied, Jones sidled up to her and said, "What you did, it popped my buttons!"

At an owners meeting in 1994, Jones bad-mouthed Johnson at a late-night drinking session with reporters. The next morning, mayhem ensued when news broke that Jones was going to fire Johnson. When the owners went to lunch, someone suggested sending Jones out first into the sea of reporters and cameras. Jones was instantly surrounded. He looked around and said with a smile, "All this for the two-point conversion," the rule change that the owners had just approved.

Jones follows coverage of the NFL and the Cowboys closely. The televisions in his office are often tuned to ESPN and other sports networks. Every day, he reads *The Dallas Morning News*, *The New York Times*, *USA Today*, and *The Wall Street Journal*. He generates news on his regular radio appearances and postgame gaggles with reporters. The press box at AT&T Stadium has a tap so reporters can grab a beer after the game.

On rare occasions, Jones snaps. In October 2024, he took aim at the radio hosts who interviewed him every Tuesday. Tired of their questions about the Cowboys' slow start, he threatened to have them thrown off the air. The station, after all, was the team's radio broadcast partner. "If I'm going to be grilled by the tribunal, I don't need it to be by the guys I'm paying," Jones said.[33] "I can take it from fans and take it from other people. I take a lot of pride in how fair and how much I try to work with the media, we're brothers and sisters. But I was a little frustrated there today."

Despite it all, Jones showed up to the Super Bowl media party in Dallas in 2011. An ice storm hit the previous night and temperatures plunged. Hundreds of reporters crammed into the House of Blues as Jones and his wife, Gene, weaved their way through the dimly lit club, shaking hands and stopping to chat. Jones could have been schmoozing with VIPs, yet he did a full loop of the club.

Jones doesn't worry much about choreography, at least compared to Kraft of the Patriots. At the owners meeting in 2023 at the

Biltmore Hotel in Phoenix, Patriots spokesman Stacey James alerted the media that his boss would speak during a lunch break. About a half hour before Kraft arrived, several dozen reporters and cameramen assembled in front of thorny red shrubs and an enormous saguaro cactus, which provided an Arizona-themed backdrop. Kraft spoke for about fifteen minutes, then walked across a driveway to an NFL Network television set for another interview. His wife, Dr. Dana Blumberg, handed him their dog, a Shih Tzu named Heisman that Kraft received on his eightieth birthday from Ari Emanuel, the CEO of Endeavor, the entertainment and media agency.

The next day, after the meeting ended, the owners ran for their limos and private jets. On his way to his limo, Jones was surrounded by reporters and television cameras. He spoke carefully, for him anyway, about the fate of Dan Snyder, the owner of the Commanders, who was selling his team. After ten minutes, Tad Carper, his handler, ended the questioning and half the writers left. The other half walked a few more steps with Jones and asked more questions. Jones complied and then jumped in his car.

Jones is always in sales mode, a real-life version of Alec Baldwin's character in *Glengarry Glen Ross* whose philosophy was "Always be closing." In 2006, John Madden and Al Michaels, Dick Ebersol, who ran NBC Sports, and Fred Gaudelli, the *Sunday Night Football* producer, were in Dallas for a Cowboys game. Jones invited them to dinner at the Preston Trail Golf Club, the club that once counted Mickey Mantle and Pat Summerall as members. When the group arrived, the dining room was empty because Ross Perot had rented the club for his fiftieth wedding anniversary.

A couple of hours into a rollicking dinner, Jones showed the group renderings of his new stadium. Out came an easel with images of what would become AT&T Stadium, including the giant scoreboard hanging over the field. Jones said he wanted NBC to broadcast the first game when the stadium opened in three years. "The whole thing goes on and on and on," Gaudelli said. "He puts on this amazing show. We thought we were just going to dinner." Robert McClelland, the doctor who tried to save President John F. Kennedy's life at Parkland Hospital in 1963, stopped by to say hello after the Perot party broke.

Three years later, Ebersol and Gaudelli flew to Dallas, where Jones gave them a tour of the $1.2 billion stadium that had just opened. Ebersol told Jones that before the first regular-season game at the stadium in September, NBC would broadcast the *Today* show from Arlington, Texas, and CNBC would talk about the stadium on the *Power Lunch* show. "To this day, every time Jerry sees me, he says, 'I'll never forget what you guys did for me,'" Gaudelli said.

The night before the first game, Jones gave Michaels and Madden a tour of the stadium. Construction occurred during a recession, and Michaels asked why Jones didn't save $100 million by eliminating some of the amenities and fixtures. "I said, 'Didn't this keep you up at night?'" Michaels recalled. "Jerry said, 'Yes, but I had one time to do it right.'"

AT&T Stadium was a monument to Jones's Texas-sized vision. MetLife Stadium in New Jersey and Lambeau Field in Green Bay have more seats, but Jones packs in more fans because he sells thousands of standing room tickets. AT&T Stadium is a big reason why the Cowboys surpassed $1 billion in team revenue for the first time in 2023.[34]

"I just can't describe the combination of having that 91,000 people sitting there cranking it up and living and breathing and dying and coming back to life," Jones told me.[35] "That was something that you dream about."

Jones knows he owns a franchise that is much more than a collection of players and a stadium. One of Jones's favorite lines is, "I like to smear that Cowboys peanut butter on everything." The manifestation of that philosophy is The Star, the team's headquarters, practice facility, and high-end community in Frisco, twenty miles north of Dallas. In 2015, Jones's daughter, Charlotte, gave me a tour of the site when it was under construction. Afterward, I received a call from the team spokesman. Jerry, he said, wanted to give me a tour. I said Charlotte had done a fine job, what possibly could be different? Jerry, he said, wanted to take me in a helicopter to view the site.

The next morning, we met at a hangar at Love Field that housed several of Jones's private jets. Once aloft, the windows fogged up, and Jones used the sleeve of his suit to wipe the condensation. Hearing Jones in the noisy cabin was impossible because he didn't know how to use his headset. But I could see his ambition for the ninety-one-acre site, which included a twelve-thousand-seat indoor stadium. The Cowboys Club at the Star, a members-only club, would have a dining room overlooking the team's practice fields. The Cowboys Fit at the Star would be a members-only gym where weekend warriors could train near players. After circling the site twice, Jones told the pilot to head north, where he pointed to hundreds of acres of land that he would develop into homes and shops.

"You have to have the juice to make it operate," Jones said of the project after we landed.[36] That juice was the Cowboys.

Years later, Jones's vision became a reality. The Star Boulevard runs south from the Cowboys headquarters to The Huddle, a roundabout, which intersects with Winning Drive, where diners can eat at an Italian restaurant called Lombardi. Signposts and banners honored current and former Cowboys, and a store featured the Charlotte Jones collection. In front of the football stadium was a turf football field where young kids tossed footballs in the shadow of an Omni Hotel. It was a full commercial celebration—and exploitation—of the Cowboys name.

For all his efforts to promote the Cowboys, Jones is forever thinking about how the league can make more money. Years before Shad Khan bought the Jaguars in 2011, Jones encouraged him to pursue a team.

"He was saying that the future of the league was very bright, and what they were going to do, and that they needed more people getting in who were businesspeople and could help the league move forward," Khan said. "He is larger than life. Iconic."

Jones is loyal. He was the only owner to fly to California to attend the funeral of Raiders owner Al Davis. He was also the only owner to testify in person on behalf of the league when it was being sued in the Sunday Ticket case. Jones returned from his vacation in France to prep for the trial in Los Angeles. At the courthouse, Jones paced the hallway before he was called to the stand. Jason Cohen, the Cowboys general counsel, told Jones not to pander to the jury. Just answer the questions from Beth Wilkinson, the league's lawyer. Don't turn to speak to the jurors directly.

Jones did exactly the opposite, trying to win over an eightysomething woman in the jury. Even though he had sued the NFL to win the right to keep revenue from the sales of Cowboys merchandise and sponsorships, Jones insisted it was in the best interests of the league to share its media revenue equally because it produced more parity, which made for more compelling competition.

"You must have competitive balance and a quality so that those teams can be put together so that you have the kind of exciting games that cause our fans to be interested," Jones said on the stand. "Whether it's their town playing each other or whether it's other towns, that lifts all boats."

The next morning, Jones arrived at 8:15 to finish his testimony. As lawyers and reporters milled around the courtroom, Jones, chomping at the bit to get going, sat in the witness chair. No judge, no jury. Jones was by himself for about ten minutes before Cohen told him to come back and wait for the judge and jury to arrive, and for the lawyers to call him as a witness. When he finally returned to the stand, he said the NFL was an important diversion from everyday life.

"Certainly, the experience I've had with the Cowboys and the NFL, oh, it's not the end-all of everything, it's just not," Jones said. "But what it is, it adds just a little bit of a respite for people that really are getting their fannies kicked and really do have some worries."

4.

THE ULTIMATE MIDDLEMAN

Robert Kraft welcomed me into his spacious but cluttered office at his team's headquarters in Foxborough, Massachusetts, on a brisk January morning in 2017. His dress shirt untucked and his silver hair in need of a comb, Kraft looked refreshingly unguarded. In a few days, his team would play in its sixth consecutive AFC Conference title game. It was an unmatched level of success that at times was overshadowed by the simmering tensions between his star quarterback Tom Brady and head coach Bill Belichick, and with the NFL itself. The three of them were still livid about being penalized for allegedly deflating game balls in 2015, a scandal known as Deflategate that became an absurd national topic of conversation. Winning another Super Bowl would be, for them, the ultimate revenge. All their winning bred jealousy and contempt among the many non-Patriots fans. Some fans also despised Kraft, Belichick, and Brady because they supported the political demolition man, Donald Trump, who would take office less than a week later. Kraft, Jerry Jones, and five other NFL owners each donated $1 million to his inauguration, which did not go over well with Democrats in deep blue states like Massachusetts.

At times, Kraft would abandon a thought midsentence and jump to a new idea, something he jokingly called "R.K.K. A.D.D." Then he sprang up from behind his desk—which included a plaque that read "Shalom Y'all!"—and brought a small shopping bag around to me.[1] I peered inside: two plastic cartons of six eggs each. The labels read "Kraft Family Farms." They were laid, he explained, by chickens that his late wife, Myra, wanted so they could eat fresh eggs. Kraft joked that they were the only chickens that spent winters in Boston and summers on Cape Cod. They were great, he insisted. Boston Red Sox owner John Henry visited Kraft's home and had an omelet that he said was the best he'd ever eaten.

My mind wandered. I had only a short while to ask Kraft about the Deflategate scandal—the $1 million fine, the loss of draft picks, and the four-game suspension for Brady—and what he thought of Roger Goodell, whom Kraft had championed for years but now criticized. I also wanted to ask why Kraft, who supported many Democratic causes, stood by Trump, who was taking glee in trashing Democrats. And now one of the most powerful men in sports gave me a dozen eggs. *Could I even carry them on the plane later that day?*

Maybe this was one of the random acts of kindness Kraft was known for. I had heard he would buy coffee for customers when he visited Dunkin' Donuts. In fact, there was a big Dunkin' cup on his desk that day. Perhaps the gift was his offbeat way of currying favor with a reporter at a newspaper he admired. Kraft told me more than once that he and former *New York Times* publisher Arthur "Punch" Sulzberger had helped pay for the Hillel chapter at Columbia University, their alma mater. Or maybe the eggs were just an offering from a man who spent his life trying to connect with people.

Kraft was a bridge builder, someone who could schmooze his adversaries across political, social, and religious borders and find ways to forge a consensus. Time after time in his decades at the NFL, Kraft found middle ground between fractious groups of headstrong owners, between owners and players, and between the league and its business partners, including the television networks.

His diplomatic skills made Kraft a longtime partner of and much-needed counterpoint to Jerry Jones. The men had a lot in common: success as entrepreneurs, instincts for risk and opportunity, a love of football, and children who took an active role in managing their teams. Their fathers both owned small businesses and were influential in their lives. Jones and Kraft bought their money-losing teams for record prices, spent years rebuilding them, and reached Super Bowl glory. They were two of the most engaged owners, worked together to win more lucrative television contracts and labor deals, and built groundbreaking stadiums. They sat on the committee that selected Goodell in 2006.

How they went about their business, though, was a study in contrasts. Jones had a million ideas that he was relentlessly selling. He tried to win over skeptics with a smile and boundless energy. He worked the phones day and night, loved a good time, but got right back to dealmaking the next morning. "Jerry could talk a dog off a meat truck," Kraft told me, adding that Jones's style of selling ideas sometimes got in the way of his objectives.

Kraft was less of a dreamer but expert at sifting through proposals and figuring out how to synthesize them into an actionable plan. He preferred to win people over by making them see the logic on their own, not wearing them down over bottles of Johnnie Walker Blue.

"Jerry's the best salesman in the world," one longtime NFL partner told me. "An incredible storyteller. He's the best drinker in or out of the NFL. I think Jerry has done a great job with the business of the Cowboys. And he likes to have fun. He's living every moment.

"But I think what you see with Robert is, he's always trying to get the right deals for the league because he wants to be the person who helps orchestrate what's best for the league. Jerry is more focused on making his franchise the best franchise in the league."

My interview with Kraft went for more than an hour, and he eventually got around to answering my questions. Goodell and the league, he said, had "really messed this up badly," referring to Deflategate. But Kraft said he took his medicine for the good of the league and chose not to fight back. "I mean, we can, but we're a partnership," he said. "There's jealousy, there's envy, there's stupidity. Sometimes, life is unfair, and you have to suck it up and move on and not use it as an excuse."

He defended his friendship with Trump, whom he met in the late 1990s when Trump invited him to play golf at his course in West Palm Beach, Florida. Their friendship deepened and Trump, always a front runner, became a regular in Kraft's box at Gillette Stadium, where he rubbed shoulders with Jon Bon Jovi, Tommy Hilfiger, Mark Wahlberg, and CBS chief executive Les Moonves. Kraft said he never forgot that Trump offered support after his wife died in 2011 of ovarian cancer. Kraft said he backed plenty of Democrats, including "the other guy," declining to name President Barack Obama. His support of Trump was part personal, part financial, evidence of a fluid set of priorities that allowed a Jewish billionaire to move in and out of business circles in the Middle East, Asia, Africa, and other places where money often speaks louder than religion, ethnicity, or political affiliation.

"Loyalty is important to me, and he has been a wonderful friend," Kraft said. "I think one of the great problems in the country today is the working poor, the middle class, that there hasn't been growth in income on an equal basis, and I really think the policies he's going to bring to bear are going to be great for the economic side of America."

Kraft made the most of his access to the president. Just weeks after we met, he dined at Mar-a-Lago with Trump and Japanese prime minister Shinzo Abe and his wife when North Korea fired a missile toward Japan. Photos showed Trump handling the national security crisis at the table while Kraft and the Abes smiled.[2]

But later in 2017, Trump tested Kraft's loyalty when he lashed out at the NFL owners and Goodell for not firing players like Colin Kaepernick, the quarterback who knelt during the playing of the national anthem. Kraft, perhaps the only owner who was friends with Trump and rapper Jay-Z, said the league needed to stand by the players while also finding a way to make them stop kneeling.

Kraft distanced himself from Trump after the riots at the Capitol on January 6, 2021. But four years later, after Trump took over the Kennedy Center for the Performing Arts, his wife, Dr. Dana Blumberg, was chosen as a new board member.[3]

Playing all sides was not new for Kraft. It was how he bought the Patriots in 1994, parlaying his ownership of the parking lots around the team's stadium into the purchase of the stadium and then the team. It was how he used his experience as a part owner of the CBS affiliate in Boston to become the chairman of the league's media committee, which has negotiated rights deals that supersized the NFL. And it was how he helped push through the approval of an unprecedented ten-year labor contract that ended a 136-day lockout, saved the 2011 season, and created a platform for the NFL to grow even larger.

"He developed these strong relations with some of the media people and a lot of executives and he's a businessman, too," said Carmen Policy, referring to Moonves, Rupert Murdoch, and the other network chiefs. "He really emerged as one of the three most prominent owners in terms of influence in the league."

Kraft's journey to the top of the country's most powerful league began in Brookline, the suburb of Boston where John F. Kennedy spent his early years. Born in 1941, Kraft was the middle of three children. His father, Harry, owned a dress company in the city's Chinatown. His mother, Sarah, was a homemaker. His father was a lay leader at the orthodox Congregation Kehillath Israel, kept a kosher home, and wanted Kraft to become a rabbi. Kraft loved sports but couldn't join school teams because he had to attend Hebrew school four afternoons a week and temple on Saturdays, after which he returned home to discuss the Talmud with his father. He and his older brother, Avram, and his younger sister, Elizabeth, didn't carry money or ride the streetcars on the sabbath.

The family lived modestly in rental apartments and Kraft had a series of jobs, including selling newspapers at Boston Braves games before the team left for Milwaukee in 1953. As a teenager, Bobby, as he was known, rode his bicycle past the house of the dean of the Harvard Business School hoping to pick up work. He won a scholarship to Columbia University, where he finally played the sports he craved as a kid. He joined the freshman and lightweight football teams, which his parents learned about only after they received a call that he was injured in a game and needed surgery.[4]

On a trip back to Boston in 1962 to watch Columbia play Harvard in basketball, Kraft and some friends went to Ken's Delicatessen in Copley Square. There, they saw Myra Hiatt on a date with a student from Bowdoin College. Kraft urged one of his friends to find out her name. When Myra got up to leave, she winked at Kraft, who returned the wink. The next day, Kraft called her dorm at Brandeis, where she was a history major, and was told she was in the library. He headed there and spent an hour looking for her in the stacks. Kraft asked her out on a date, and they clicked immediately. By the end of the evening, Hiatt proposed to *him*. Kraft returned to Columbia, where he became class president and graduated in 1963 with a degree in history and economics. They married soon after and spent their honeymoon in Israel. Their first son, Jonathan, was born before Myra graduated college a year later.

Kraft went to work for Myra's father, Jacob, who owned Rand-Whitney, a packaging company in Worcester, Massachusetts. He also received a fellowship to attend Harvard Business School and earned an MBA in 1965. Kraft believed his father-in-law was too risk-averse, so in 1968, he engineered a leveraged buyout to obtain half the company, then bought out the remaining shareholders to take full control. A few years later, he started International Forest Products and combined it with Rand-Whitney because he believed demand for packaging would grow as global trade boomed. The companies would reside under the Kraft Group umbrella, which in time included a private equity firm, a real estate business, an event management company, the New England Revolution soccer team, and the Patriots.

Kraft rooted for the Patriots from their creation as a charter member of the AFL in 1960. Eleven years later, he bought season tickets when the team moved from Boston to a new stadium in Foxborough about twenty-five miles away. On Sundays, Kraft gave his four sons letters to hand to their Hebrew school teachers so they could leave class early and make it to the stadium by kickoff. Myra, who preferred to stay at home and do the *New York Times* crossword puzzle, only found out years later.

The stadium was one of the worst in the league, with row after row of metal bleachers and little protection from the elements. There were few amenities or signs, a big reason the team was often near the bottom of the NFL in local revenue. After trying to buy the money-losing team, Kraft acquired the money-generating elements of the team, a lesson he learned when he owned the Lobsters, a tennis franchise, in the 1970s. That team played well, but Kraft received no revenue from concessions, parking, or signage. Ultimately, the franchise folded.

The Patriots were a mess. The Sullivan family owned the team, a family trust owned the stadium, and a third group owned the raceway next to the stadium and the three hundred acres surrounding it, which was used for parking. In 1984, Chuck Sullivan, the son of team owner Billy Sullivan, paid promoter Don King $45 million for the rights to the Victory Tour featuring Michael Jackson and his brothers. He pledged the Patriots' stadium as collateral. The tour drew 2.5 million fans and grossed about $75 million, yet somehow lost money. The stadium was put into bankruptcy.

Kraft thought he had a deal to buy the team, stadium, and land for $80 million, but the Patriots made it to their first Super Bowl in 1985 (where they lost to the Chicago Bears). The Sullivans expected better days ahead and took the team off the market. When they defaulted on their stake in the raceway anyway, Kraft signed a ten-year deal to pay them $1 million a year in return for an option to buy the land for $17 million. The deal was a money loser because parking generated only $600,000 to $700,000 a year, but the option would turn out to be a bargain.[5]

Two years later, the Sullivans put the team up for sale and the stadium into bankruptcy. Victor Kiam, the gregarious owner of Remington, a razor company he promoted in popular television advertisements, bought the team for $83 million. But he offered only $17 million for the stadium because he planned to build a new stadium elsewhere, or perhaps move the team to Jacksonville. Kraft offered $25 million for the stadium. He knew that Kiam couldn't move the team without his permission because the stadium lease required the

Patriots to remain the anchor tenant until 2001. Kraft hired Andy Wasynczuk, a Harvard Business School graduate who worked at Bain Capital with Jonathan Kraft, to run the stadium. Soon, Kraft was earning about $2 million a year from parking *and* concessions.[6]

"I felt all along the day would come that I would have my chance, and that the lease I held on the Patriots in the stadium would help me make the deal," Kraft said. "The lease was key."

Kiam cried foul, but Kraft told him he should have done his due diligence. As a largely absentee owner, Kiam had to ask Commissioner Paul Tagliabue for an introduction to Boston mayor Ray Flynn, who felt no urgency to help Kiam get a new stadium.

Without revenue from parking or concessions, Kiam was left with just his team's share of NFL revenue and ticket sales, which weren't good. The team went 21-43 during Kiam's four years as owner, and the team was last in the league in revenue. Kiam made matters worse by defending Patriots players accused of sexually harassing Lisa Olson, a *Boston Herald* reporter. Olson sued the team and settled out of court, but women's groups boycotted Remington. In 1992, Kiam sold the Patriots to one of his creditors, James Orthwein, to get out of debt.

A St. Louis native born into the Anheuser-Busch family, Orthwein was the front man for a group that wanted a team to replace the Cardinals, who had left for Arizona in 1988. He told the other owners in 1992 that if St. Louis was awarded an expansion team, he would sell the Patriots. After an extensive search led by Goodell, Charlotte and Jacksonville were granted new teams, not St. Louis.

Without a new team in St. Louis and Kraft holding the Patriots' lease, Orthwein was boxed in. Uninterested in fighting Kraft, he hired Goldman Sachs to sell the team. Like Jones before he purchased the Cowboys, Kraft did his homework. He spoke to other owners and dined with Tagliabue at the Carlyle Hotel in New York.

Tagliabue was impressed that he understood the importance of a profitable stadium and that the new collective bargaining agreement would provide stability. He also liked Kraft's other business bona fides, including his experience overseas.

"He was the kind of owner I felt we needed," Tagliabue would later say.

Orthwein, though, wanted to sell the team to another group from St. Louis and offered Kraft $75 million for his stadium lease. Kraft's wife thought that getting three times what he paid for the lease a few years before was great, but Kraft turned it down.[7] Stan Kroenke, another Missouri native who later bought the Rams, offered $200 million for the team, but he wanted Orthwein to cover the cost of moving the team to St. Louis, a deal-breaker considering the legal costs if Kraft sued to enforce the team's lease.

In late December 1993, Kraft finally got access to the team's finances that other bidders had already seen. Kraft was told to submit a bid by January 10, but then Orthwein's lawyers moved the date up to January 1, forcing Jonathan Kraft, Wasynczuk, and others reviewing the data to work through the holidays to come up with a $158 million bid. After starting the 1993 season 1-11, the Patriots won their last four games, including the finale, an overtime victory over the Miami Dolphins at home on January 2, 1994. After the game, the fans chanted for the team to stay and Kraft, hearing their enthusiasm, told Jonathan, "There's no fucking way we're not buying this thing."[8]

The key was getting around Orthwein's lawyer, Walter Metcalfe, and appealing to Orthwein directly. In mid-January, the Krafts flew to St. Louis. Orthwein wanted a record $172 million. Kraft went back to Chad Gifford at the Bank of Boston for more money. Despite being stretched financially, Kraft told Gifford, "I'll never let you down." Gifford was convinced: "Ultimately, bricks and mortar and balance sheets don't pay you back," he said. "People pay you back. And I believed him."

The Patriots were a financial basket case, and with free agency and a salary cap about to start, the owners fast-tracked Kraft's application. At the end of January, he flew to Atlanta, where the Super Bowl was being played, to meet the finance committee. Kraft was intimidated meeting owners that he knew only by name. Kansas City Chiefs owner Lamar Hunt put him at ease. "Boston Lobsters, best name in sports history," he told Kraft. "It was a welcome-to-the-NFL moment," Kraft later said.

The entire ownership held a special meeting on February 22, 1994, at the Hyatt Regency in Orlando. They spent forty minutes discussing Kraft's purchase before the Minnesota Vikings proposed approving the deal. Jones seconded it, and the sale was unanimously approved. Kraft was now in one of America's most exclusive clubs.

Like Jones five years before, Kraft entered the league at a pivotal time. Jones joined just as Pete Rozelle was retiring and Tagliabue began work ending years of labor strife. When Kraft came on board, a new revenue sharing system would help the league secure larger television rights and sponsorship deals, which helped Jones, Kraft, and other new owners like Wayne Huizenga in Miami and Jeffrey Lurie in Philadelphia recoup the hefty amounts they paid for their teams.

Still, owning an NFL team wasn't like running a company. Kraft and his family would become celebrities if the team won or goats if the team played poorly. Every major decision would be scrutinized. Kraft also had to explain his purchase to the person who mattered the most, Myra. She didn't care for the sport. Her priority was philanthropy, and she and Kraft had given tens of millions of dollars to charities like the Boys & Girls Club. "We try to do things with little or no publicity," Kraft said publicly in 1991.[9] "Public service gives me psychic income that is vital to me."

Myra thought her husband was nuts to spend so much money on a terrible team. He told her the team was worth about $115 million, yet he ended up paying 50 percent more. "The summer house better be in my name," she said. She made Kraft promise that buying the team would not impact their charitable giving. He said if anything, it would enhance it, given the visibility of the NFL. She was skeptical.

"I'm glad for the players; they're a great bunch of guys," she said before the Patriots lost to the Packers in the Super Bowl in 1997.[10] "But it's...a football game. I mean, God knows what else is going on in the world."

But the Krafts had saved a local team from leaving, which raised their profile in Boston. The day after Kraft was approved as owner, the team sold more than eight hundred season tickets to fans who waited on long lines in a snowstorm. In a few months, the team sold out the season for the first time. Kraft wore his fandom on his sleeve, riding in a golf cart through the parking lots before games to greet fans. Kraft still had to figure out how to turn a profit and settle a pile of lawsuits against the team that he inherited. But things were looking up.

"I've got to tell you, the minute he bought the team, it's like somebody snapped some fingers, the lights went on, and things got better," Policy said. "He started selling tickets. He started getting fan interest back. He started getting people to believe again, and you know the rest of the story."

Still, Jonathan Kraft and Wasynczuk, the chief operating officer, had to learn how to manage the team's roster under the new salary cap. As consultants at Bain, they calculated the fair value of companies, not athletes. Sports fans take for granted analytics-driven roster building. But at the time, their approach created friction with Bill Parcells, the old-school coach Orthwein hired in 1993.

"If they want you to cook the dinner, at least they ought to let you shop for some of the groceries," Parcells quipped.[11]

The team went 10-6 in 1994, led by second-year quarterback Drew Bledsoe, who threw for more than 4,500 yards. The Patriots made the playoffs for the first time in eight seasons, losing in the Wild Card game to the Cleveland Browns, who were coached by Belichick.

Kraft grew close to Bledsoe, inviting him to his home and personally negotiating his ten-year, $103 million contract extension. Bledsoe would tell Kraft about his issues with Parcells and Kraft would try to intervene, which Parcells detested. Relations frayed even as the Patriots went 11-5 and made it to the Super Bowl in 1996. Parcells's contract had a noncompete clause that prohibited him from coaching elsewhere for a year. He told Kraft he wanted out of it, and Kraft said no. The morning after the Patriots won the AFC Championship Game, Parcells woke up Tagliabue at home. He wanted to announce that the Super Bowl would be his last game as Patriots head coach. Parcells said his noncompete clause didn't prohibit him from working for another team, only that he couldn't coach. Tagliabue told Parcells he did not want to talk about his contract and that he shouldn't make any announcements before the game. Soon after the Super Bowl, the Jets hired Parcells as a consultant. Kraft accused the Jets of tampering and demanded draft picks as compensation.

Tagliabue summoned the Krafts and Jets owner Leon Hess and his president, Steve Gutman, to his office. After the teams stated their case, Tagliabue met separately with the owners over lunch. Tagliabue told Hess that offering Parcells a job as a consultant was a sham. Kraft said he was getting screwed and should receive the Jets' first-round draft picks for the next three years, several other picks, and $5 million. It sounded extreme, Kraft said, but the Jets had harmed his family's reputation. Hess responded that he had heard what Kraft was saying, and that if Parcells was so terrible, the Jets would gladly take the coach off his hands if *Kraft* paid *him* $3 million. "I'll free things up for you to pursue a new coach," Hess said. The Patriots ended up getting one draft pick as compensation, and Parcells took over as coach of the Jets in 1997. The bad blood between the teams lasted for years.

Kraft got his revenge in 2000 when he lured Belichick away from the Jets. Belichick had moved with Parcells to the Jets in 1997 with an understanding that he would become head coach when Parcells stepped down. Kraft had fired Pete Carroll and brushed off suggestions by Tagliabue and others to avoid Belichick. Kraft knew Belichick's skills as a defensive coordinator because he coached in New England with Parcells. Kraft also knew that Belichick had a degree in economics and could manage the salary cap.

"Harvard Business School teaches you many things, but not everything," Kraft told me. "Bill had a strong economic background, he understood value, and he had the discipline of knowing when to move on from players. Loyalty is very important to me, and I probably carried people longer in the early years. I supported keeping players we shouldn't. I always try to know what I know and what I don't know, and I was so happy to have someone who understood personnel and economic value, and in my opinion, a good coach in the NFL needs to have some sense of economics given that there's a salary cap, because otherwise you'll want to keep every player."

Eager to emerge from Parcells's shadow, Belichick said he wanted out of New York because the Jets were in flux after Hess died in 1999. But the team learned this only *after* it called a news conference to announce Belichick's promotion. On January 4, 2000, with the media waiting, Belichick left his office with team spokesman Frank

Ramos, walked into Gutman's office, and gave him a shred of paper that read, "I resign as HC of the NYJ." He then turned to Ramos and said: "Let's go. I just resigned. We might as well tell the media."

"I had no idea I had just accepted his resignation," Gutman said. "I was dumbfounded."

The Jets protested to Tagliabue just as the Patriots had a few years earlier. The Patriots gave the Jets their first-round draft pick in 2000 and two more picks in 2001; the Jets sent two lesser picks back.[12] "What we didn't have was the guy who turned out to be one of the best coaches in the history of the NFL," Gutman said. For years, "he beat us like we were high schoolers."

After years of turmoil, Kraft finally had the coach he wanted and, a year later, the quarterback of his dreams in Tom Brady, who emerged after Bledsoe was injured early in the 2001 season. Kraft's search for a new home for the team entered a new phase. He was a hometown owner and a longtime season ticket holder—unlike Jones, who was ridiculed in Dallas as a "Beverly Hillbilly from Little Rock."[13] Kraft was a successful businessman, but he was considered nouveau riche in Boston, where politics were dominated by Irish Americans, Italian Americans, and the city's Brahmins.

The day before he bought the team in 1994, Kraft called Governor William Weld to secure help in getting a new stadium. The governor said he would, but he was no match for Thomas Finneran, the chair of the state's House Ways and Means Committee, who opposed public subsidies for stadiums. When talks stalled, Kraft complained that he had borrowed heavily to buy the team because he thought lawmakers would help him get a new stadium. "The state is not around to immunize people from unintelligent decisions," Finneran shot back.[14] In 1995, the state rejected a plan to let Kraft build a domed stadium next to a convention center by the harbor. Kraft then announced plans for a privately funded $200 million open-air stadium in South Boston. By then, Kraft's honeymoon in Boston was over. Finneran called Kraft a "whining multimillionaire" in search of public subsidies,[15] and residents in the working-class neighborhood said that a stadium would create more traffic. The deal died.

"I don't know if it's anti-Semitism, or anti-Kraftism, or anti-footballism, but it's really strange," Jonathan Kraft told *The Boston Globe*. "If they knew my father and what he has accomplished—I mean, he is a great man. I just don't get it." (Finneran, who was dubbed "King Tom" for his leadership style, later pleaded guilty to obstruction of justice and left politics.)

Kraft didn't want to leave Boston, but he began to look elsewhere. In September 1997, he denied that he was offered $10 million a year to move the team to Providence to play in an as-yet unbuilt, seventy-thousand-seat stadium.[16] About a year later, Kraft agreed to move the team to Hartford, Connecticut, in return for perhaps the sweetest deal in sports history. Connecticut governor John Rowland promised to build the Patriots a $374 million publicly funded stadium, ensure the Patriots' revenue from luxury boxes and club seats grew along with other NFL teams, and let Kraft keep profits from the stadium without paying rent.

This got the attention of Massachusetts lawmakers, who agreed to spend $72 million on infrastructure improvements in Foxboro if Kraft built a new stadium there. At the eleventh hour, Kraft backed out of the Hartford deal. Construction in Foxborough began in March 2000. Kraft repaid the state with money from a fee to park at the stadium and borrowed $150 million from a new NFL stadium fund that he helped create. He did not sell personal seat licenses that fans would have had to buy to purchase season tickets, though club seats had to be leased for ten years. CMGI, which had signed a $120 million naming-rights deal, pulled out after its stock cratered during the collapse of the dot-com bubble, and Gillette stepped in. When construction was halted and financing dried up after the attacks on September 11, 2001, Kraft personally signed for loans.

The stadium opened in time for the start of the 2002 season just a few months after the team won Super Bowl XXXVI. Five years later, Kraft opened a 350-acre mixed-use development adjacent to the stadium called Patriot Place, a real estate model other owners imitated.

"It's the only stadium in America where the land, the financing, and the infrastructure, there's not one dollar of public money," Kraft said. "I've done some nutty things in this business that I wouldn't do in another business, but knowing the equity of the fans has really made a difference."

While Kraft was overhauling one of the NFL's worst franchises, he dove headfirst into league business just as Jones did after he bought the Cowboys. The men inhabited their roles differently. The owners were shown on television in their suites during games. Jones was irresistible because he was also the Cowboys' general manager and often stood on the sidelines at the ends of games. But he never asked to be on television, whereas Kraft kept tabs. The day after one rainy night game, he called the producer of the game to ask why he had not been shown on television. He was told that the rain and the glare from the stadium lights made it difficult for him to be seen.

Jones and Kraft dined together with their wives when their teams played; Jones ate at Kraft's home in 2003 when the Cowboys visited Foxboro. (The Patriots won, 12–0.) They also had their differences and came to blows in 2017 when Jones threatened to sue Kraft and the other owners on the compensation committee over Goodell's pay package. But they also came to each other's defense. In 1996, when

Jones was being pilloried by Tagliabue and other owners for signing his own sponsorship deals, Kraft said Jones was "one of the brightest people I've met in the NFL. The problems come in—and I've said this directly to Jerry—when you don't know when to stop and you go over a certain border." But, Kraft added, "that has to be balanced against the things he does that are very positive."[17]

Kraft and Jones took early stakes in DraftKings, a fantasy sports app that became one of the largest sportsbooks when sports wagering was legalized in 2018.[18] When the company went public in 2020, Kraft netted more than $15 million when he sold 11 percent of his stake.[19]

Both owners embraced Tagliabue's vision for a more expansive league and were critical in helping realize it. "We wanted to pay back the investment and debt on the team, and media was the best way to do that," Kraft said. Tagliabue recognized Kraft's experience owning a television station in Boston and his connections to Mel Karmazin, Les Moonves, and other media executives, and appointed him in March 1997 to the broadcast committee that oversees the largest source of league revenue. Pat Bowlen ran the committee and avoided the spotlight. Kraft, by contrast, became a fixture at the annual Allen & Company media confab in Sun Valley, Idaho. Jones and Kraft wooed executives, drove negotiations, and spoke to the media. "It was always Jerry first and then Kraft second taking credit for having made inroads with the networks and the network executives," said Policy, the 49ers president. "But everybody you talk to, especially Dick Ebersol at NBC, the sun rose and never set on Pat Bowlen."

As another former NFL executive put it: "Pat was just a straight guy, believed what he believed. I think he had humility. He didn't need to see his name in the paper every day."

Kraft made his presence felt in 1998 during talks that resulted in eight-year deals with Fox, ESPN, and CBS for a record $18 billion.

Some owners wanted to move more games to cable television because ESPN was willing to pay more than CBS and Fox. But Kraft believed that most games should remain on over-the-air networks to reach the greatest number of fans, a philosophy the NFL continues to follow even as other leagues move more games to pay-television services.

Bowlen, Jones, and Kraft were also instrumental in the creation of the NFL Network in 2003. The league wanted its own cable channel to appeal to its most avid fans and to collect modest fees of less than twenty cents a subscriber from cable and satellite providers. (ESPN received roughly $3 per subscriber at the time.) The league launched the network on DirecTV, which also carried Sunday Ticket. The league persuaded EchoStar, DirecTV's principal rival, to carry the NFL Network, and the cable companies followed.

In 2007, the league created *Thursday Night Football* and put eight games on NFL Network, which turned the league into a competitor of CBS, Fox, and other networks, and gave it leverage in negotiations. Time Warner and Cablevision fought against the higher fees the NFL wanted. Comcast, on the other hand, tried to buy the network as a backdoor way of obtaining NFL games. The owners turned down the offer because they believed Comcast would bury NFL Network.

With a modest number of games, the NFL Network was an attractive partner. By 2009, the league was in talks with Disney. Jones and Woody Johnson of the Jets were eager to sell the network, but Kraft and Steve Bornstein, who ran the NFL's media division, felt the NFL Network would play second fiddle to ESPN, another Disney company. Retaining NFL Network, they believed, would pay dividends in the long term by allowing the league to speak directly to its fans.[20] They told Jones that if the NFL had sold Sunday Ticket to DirecTV in the 1990s, the league would have received a big, one-time check but given up hundreds of millions of dollars in annual rights fees. "We've got something now because we kept the rights to ourselves," Kraft and Bornstein said. They won the day. It was, as one participant said, "the best deal we never did."

Holding the rights to Sunday Ticket, a $400-a-year service, paid off, too. In 2022, after DirecTV ended distribution of the service, Kraft helped negotiate a new deal with YouTube.[21] Price tag? More than $2 billion a year.

NFL Network was different. Its value fell as the number of cable subscribers plummeted. In 2021, the league hired Goldman Sachs to explore the sale of the network.[22] But the numbers disappointed the owners, a sign the league might have missed its window to secure the windfall Jones had sought.

Kraft spends considerable time in entertainment circles and was particularly close to CBS. After Fox outbid CBS for the rights to broadcast the NFC games in 1994, CBS vowed to return in 1998. Kraft helped convince CBS to pay $500 million for the rights to show AFC games, about twice what it offered four years earlier for the NFC package. CBS's return coincided with the rise of the Patriots, and Moonves was a fixture in Kraft's suite at Gillette Stadium. The men were so close that in 2005, Kraft joined the board of Viacom,[23] which owned CBS, and chaired the compensation committee that determined Moonves's pay. Moonves left CBS in 2018 following accusations of sexual harassment and abuse.

Media deals are critical to the league's economics, and as the top representative for the owners in negotiations with the networks, Kraft was arguably more powerful than Jones. Most NFL media deals have exclusive negotiating periods that are no more than a promise to talk to the networks. The league structures its contracts so it has flexibility to move in a different direction. "We only get a few times to change our trajectory, so having a very clean back end to our contracts allows us to adjust. It's a vital issue with us," said Brian Rolapp, the head of the NFL's media group.

When contract negotiations begin, Kraft, Goodell, and league staffers give the networks a broad outline, like the league's schedule of seventeen games over eighteen weeks, what the playoff bracket will look like, and the windows for games, including Sundays and Mondays and, in recent years, Black Friday in November and Christmas Day. They then invite the networks to provide their best ideas to start more detailed conversations. "Robert and the other members on the media committee are involved in the preparatory and strategic elements," Rolapp said. Once negotiations get more detailed, Kraft and Goodell try to find a balance between maximizing the size of the rights deals and giving the networks what they need without bleeding them dry.

Kraft, Goodell, and the rest of the NFL's negotiating team have a major advantage because they have the most sought-after content—NFL games—and they will be around longer than the network executives, who may be gone by the time the contracts expire.

"The people you deal with, they're just hired guns, they don't have skin in the game," one league executive said. "This is why the owners love guys like the network executives. They're just waiting for them to say, 'I'll do this deal because at the end, it's not going to be my problem.' That's music to Bob Kraft's ears."

Kraft influenced the league's approach in other ways. Frank Hawkins, who worked on rights deals for fifteen years at the NFL, said Kraft had a slogan: "Manage like you own it. Pinch every penny. Roger took it and ran with it."

This approach became Goodell's north star. Take the Pro Bowl, which for years was held in Honolulu and was popular with the players because they could take their families on vacation. But the NFL lost about $4 million a year hosting the event,[24] so Goodell moved the game to Orlando and Las Vegas to save on airfare and hotels, and so more fans could attend.

In 1998, Kraft became the chair of the finance committee. He knew firsthand about the rising cost of building stadiums, so he pushed for the creation of a fund backed by $1 million from every owner's share of their national revenue for twenty years. The fund subsidized the cost of building or renovating stadiums, and Kraft was one of the first recipients.

Like Jones, Kraft used his personal connections to bring business partners to the league. In 2001, he helped negotiate a ten-year, $250 million deal with Reebok to become the league's uniform supplier.[25] Kraft's friend Paul Fireman ran the Massachusetts-based company. Reebok paid a flat licensing fee (albeit a huge one) rather than royalties and fees, like many earlier deals. Reebok also paid for exclusivity as the NFL moved away from its longtime practice of signing agreements with multiple companies in each category.

When Tagliabue announced his retirement in 2006, Dan Rooney of the Steelers and Jerry Richardson of the Panthers cochaired the committee to find his replacement. They were old-school centrists. Two other members of the committee, Al Davis of the Raiders and Lamar Hunt of the Chiefs, were longtime owners of former AFL teams. Jones, Kraft, and Woody Johnson of the Jets represented the new wave of owners who believed Goodell would help them get a faster return on their investment.

They got their man, but Goodell's election was more than a change of leadership; it was a change in how the league monetized its assets. Tagliabue tackled fundamental problems facing the league and in a few short years brokered a new revenue sharing agreement that laid the foundation for more lucrative financial deals. Tagliabue was a skilled litigator who preferred to let the owners work out their own differences. At least in his first years as commissioner, Goodell was more of a politician who listened to the owners and synthesized their preferences.

"He's good at taking in input and trying to steer, but he doesn't have an independent point of view the way Paul did," Hawkins said.

Jones and Kraft had Goodell's ear. They were roughly a decade younger than Rooney, who was seventy-four when Goodell became commissioner, so they were the future of the league. Kraft and Jones ran teams that played in two of the country's largest markets, and their teams were the second and third most valuable franchises in the NFL in 2006.[26] Kraft and Jones were also celebrities. Jones made weekly appearances on local radio shows and met reporters after every Cowboys game. Kraft spoke frequently to reporters, including sitting for a television interview with the Spanish-language network ESPN Deportes in 2018. He obliged the reporter, who called him "Roberto," by eating guacamole and drinking a shot of tequila.

By the time Goodell became commissioner, the Patriots had won three Super Bowls between 2002 and 2005, and coverage of the team was largely positive. That changed in 2007 when the Patriots were caught videotaping Jets coaches during a game. Dubbed "Spygate," the controversy transformed the Patriots from a model franchise into cheaters in many fans' eyes. Goodell had little choice but to penalize the Patriots. In the documentary *The Dynasty*, Kraft said he urged the league's lawyers to fine but not suspend Belichick. The coach missed no games but paid a record $500,000 fine. The team paid $250,000 and lost a draft pick.[27]

Ornery in public, Belichick became Darth Vader after Spygate. Eric Mangini, Belichick's protégé and the Patriots defensive coordinator in 2005, warned Belichick about videotaping and wrote to Ray Anderson, the league's head of football operations, about the practice. Mangini left to coach the Jets in 2006 and was on the sidelines when the Patriots were caught the following year.

Kraft was branded a cheater by association. He took his lumps before, especially during his botched attempts to build a new stadium in Boston and in Hartford. Now, fans and the media were asking whether the Patriots won their titles unfairly.

Kraft foresaw this kind of blowback in 2002 when Arthur Blank, cofounder of Home Depot, bought the Falcons. Blank was in New York for a new owners orientation and Tagliabue suggested he have breakfast with Kraft. Kraft told Blank to apply the same principles he used to build his company to running the Falcons. What would be different, Kraft said, was the media scrutiny. Blank said that he was used to the spotlight, having built a Fortune 100 company.

"He smiled at me and said, 'No, you'll see,'" Blank recalled. "It's like when you have a child and they ask you a question and you can't fully explain it to them, so you kind of give them an explanation. But what you really are saying is 'You'll see.' That's the kind of look I got from Robert."

When he died in 1975, Harry Kraft left his son, Robert, an ethical will that read in part: "Remember, the legacy I'm trying to leave you is a good name. It is a man's most precious asset."[28] Kraft took this seriously. He and Myra gave away tens of millions of dollars to charities and preached the importance of family and loyalty. In 2009, NFL Films spent a year with the Patriots to document Belichick and "The Patriot Way" so people could "see 100 years from now exactly what the team had done."[29]

After Spygate, Kraft and the Patriots were viewed more skeptically, including in 2013 when Patriots tight end Aaron Hernandez was arrested for murder, in 2015 when Brady was accused of deliberately deflating game balls, and again in 2019 when Kraft was charged with two misdemeanors for soliciting prostitution in a spa in Jupiter,

Florida. Prosecutors linked Kraft to "modern-day slavery," and he became a punchline on late-night television. Charities that accepted millions of dollars of his money condemned him. At an owners meeting in March 2019 a month after the story broke, Kraft uncharacteristically avoided reporters.

Like the other two dozen men swept up in the case, Kraft could have cut a plea deal, paid a fine, and done some community service. Instead, he spent millions of dollars on lawyers (including Alex Spiro, who defended Aaron Hernandez, and Jack Goldberger, who helped Jeffrey Epstein reach a plea deal) to fight the case. They argued the police had illegally installed video cameras in the spa and set up a sham traffic stop that pulled over the Bentley that Kraft was a passenger in. Months later, the video from the spa was buried and the prosecution's case fell apart.

Unlike Jones, who made little secret of his carousing, Kraft was sensitive to scrutiny of his private life. Kraft had garnered sympathy when Myra passed away; the team wore "MHK" patches that season, which they dedicated to her. A year later, Kraft was dating a woman half his age. In 2012, a tape surfaced showing Kraft rehearsing lines with Ricki Noel Lander, an actress auditioning for a part in an Owen Wilson–Vince Vaughn comedy. At the end of the video, Kraft can be heard uttering obscenities. Kraft said in a statement that he was trying to help Lander "catch a break" in Hollywood and that "I think we can all agree that Owen Wilson has nothing to worry about. I am going to stick to my day job."[30] Lander, who showed up with Kraft at the US Open tennis tournament and the Allen & Company retreat in Idaho, later had a baby that Kraft said he would support even though he wasn't the biological father.

By NFL standards, Kraft seemed to be everywhere. He wore his own brand of Nike sneakers. He danced with Cardi B at a Super Bowl party. He was friends with musicians like Jon Bon Jovi, Elton John, and rapper Meek Mill, whom he visited in prison.[31] He was close to Michael Rubin, the founder of Fanatics, another company Kraft drew closer to the NFL's orbit.

Kraft took NFL players to visit Israel, including Jerod Mayo, a linebacker who played eight years with the Patriots. On their trip in 2019, Kraft first got the idea to have Mayo replace Belichick, which he did in 2024.[32] After Brady left after the 2020 season, Belichick and the Patriots struggled, making the playoffs just once. Without Brady as a buffer, Kraft's relationship with Belichick soured to the point that he told friends that his coach was "the biggest fucking asshole in my life."[33]

Like Jones a quarter century before, Kraft was grappling with the end of his team's dynasty. By 2024, both teams had losing records and dim prospects. The Patriots' decline did not diminish Kraft's influence in league matters. Goodell appointed him to a committee to recommend which team or teams should move to Los Angeles. Kraft was a key player in negotiations to renew the league's labor deal in 2020 and in talks with the networks that resulted in more than $110 billion of broadcast rights deals—twice as much as the previous agreements. Kraft was on the committee that recommended that private equity firms be allowed to buy up to 10 percent of teams.

"I view Bob like I do Lamar Hunt, one of the founders of the league," Jones said. "I don't know that we have anybody that today has made that kind of contribution to the NFL franchise."[34]

Like Jones, Kraft is firmly in his eighties and handing more tasks to his sons, particularly Jonathan. Both men will be almost ninety years old when the next round of labor talks and broadcast deals come up for renewal. For now, they're busy burnishing their images. While Jones worked on a ten-part documentary about his ownership of the Cowboys, Kraft has focused on getting inducted into the Pro Football Hall of Fame. Jones entered in 2017, more than twenty years after the Cowboys last went to the Super Bowl. Kraft's Patriots won six championships, yet Spygate, Deflategate, and the prostitution case in Florida appear to have hurt his candidacy.[35]

Those were certainly legitimate reasons. But if an owner's eligibility is based solely on Super Bowl trophies his team had won and how much money he generated for himself *and* the league, Kraft would have been inducted long ago.

5.

GREAT ESCAPES

Art Modell's exit from an owners meeting in the spring of 1996 was right out of the Martin Scorsese film *Goodfellas*. After buying the Cleveland Browns in 1961, Modell was beloved in the city. But by 1995, he was undone by expensive contracts and an aging stadium. After the city refused to help him build a new home, Modell did the unthinkable: He planned to move the team. Baltimore offered him a new, $200 million stadium rent free for thirty years plus a $50 million signing bonus.[1] By that November, word of the move leaked, forcing Modell into exile. He received death threats and traveled with bodyguards. He never returned to Cleveland.

The owners formally approved his relocation plan in February 1996. Angry Browns fans snuck into the hotel in Chicago where the meeting was held and affixed stickers of Modell's face in the urinals in the men's room so the owners would have to pee on his image. Spooked, Modell was wheeled out a back door in a laundry cart.

To settle a lawsuit with Cleveland, Commissioner Paul Tagliabue offered the city the NFL's next expansion team. But Modell was still dogged by Browns fans. Some of them picketed outside his high-rise apartment in Florida and yelled, "Jump, Art, jump." In an episode of *The Drew Carey Show*, whose star was a rabid Browns fan, a character who went to the bathroom was told, "Don't take a Modell." And at the league's annual meeting in March 1996, Browns fans returned. To avoid them, Modell arrived and left through the hotel's kitchen.

NFL teams have been relocating for as long as there's been an NFL. In 1921, when the league was still known as the American Professional Football Association, the Decatur Staleys moved two hundred miles north to Chicago and renamed themselves the Bears. In those early years, teams moved from Toledo to Kenosha, from Pottsville to Boston, and from Dayton to Brooklyn. During World War II, teams merged, including the Steelers and Eagles, who played as the Steagles.

In the 1950s, the NFL absorbed the Cleveland Browns, Baltimore Colts, and San Francisco 49ers when the All-America Football Conference folded. In the 1960s, new teams were added in Minnesota, Atlanta, and New Orleans. The NFL absorbed all ten AFL teams in 1970.

By then, cities were building new stadiums to keep teams from moving, so owners began looking for the best deal they could get, even if it meant abandoning their fans. Roger Goodell often talks about the importance of fans. But he means all fans, including the tens of millions who watch on television. Since the 1970s, media contracts have been the largest share of the league's revenue, and keeping broadcasters and fans at home happy takes priority over fans who tailgate and buy tickets.

The growth of media money accelerated in the 1990s and 2000s when the NFL began playing on Thursday and Sunday nights. By the time the NFL's revenue from broadcast rights surged past $10 billion a year, fans in stadiums looked more like props on television. Less than 5 percent of fans who watch NFL games do so in person.

Don Ohlmeyer, who produced *Monday Night Football*, understood that broadcasters needed to look for new fans to appeal to advertisers. "You know, our approach was, screw the football fan; he's going to watch anyway," Ohlmeyer told NPR.[2] "We need to attract other people to make this a successful show in prime time."

The introduction of fantasy football and the Sunday Ticket subscription service, which lets viewers watch every out-of-town game, made it easier for fans to follow teams around the country. Trudging to a stadium and paying hundreds of dollars for tickets, parking, and beers became less appealing than sitting on the sofa in a man cave.

For years, though, owners moved in search of fans and cheaper stadiums. Al Davis moved the Raiders from Oakland to Southern California so he could play in the far larger Los Angeles Memorial Coliseum. Davis had a second motive: He wanted to start a pay-per-view business that would charge fans to watch out-of-town games in movie theaters. That business never got off the ground, but a decade later, the NFL created Sunday Ticket.

When the league tried to block Davis from moving, he sued, claiming that the NFL was a monopoly. While the league fought the case in court, it couldn't stop other teams from moving, lest it prove Davis's point. Robert Irsay, the volatile and unloved owner of the Colts, saw an opening. When Baltimore mayor William Schaefer refused to pay for improvements to Memorial Stadium, Irsay cut a deal with Indianapolis, which built the RCA Dome to lure a team.

Schaefer "could have had us for $10 million for a 25-year lease, that's all," said Jim Irsay, who took over the team when his father died in 1997. "That move was not on my father. That was on Schaefer."

The final straw came in March 1984 when the state legislature passed an eminent domain law designed to prevent the Colts from leaving. Irsay called Jim at the Colts' offices in Owings Mills, Maryland.

"The trucks are coming in," Irsay recalled his father saying. "I'm giving you a short list of a dozen people who are going. Get everyone else out of the building except those people. And when it's dark, I'll tell you when the Mayflower trucks are coming."

A few hours later, during a snowstorm, fifteen moving vans hauled away the team's equipment under the cloak of darkness. Faithful Colts fans never forgot the betrayal. Cardinals owner Bill Bidwill was next. He moved his team to Arizona in 1988 after the city of St. Louis refused to help him. A few years later, Davis moved the Raiders back to Oakland because the authority that ran the Coliseum in Los Angeles would not build new suites. Davis convinced the city of Oakland to add a wall of suites in the Oakland Coliseum that was dubbed "Mount Davis."

But no move prompted more outrage than Modell's departure for Baltimore. The Browns were deeply intertwined with Cleveland's psyche. The team was a powerhouse in the 1950s and early 1960s, exemplified by running back Jim Brown, meshed with the city's gritty image. The Browns' demise in the 1970s mirrored Cleveland's fading fortunes. The "Mistake by the Lake" described both the city and the team's crumbling stadium.

By the 1990s, the team, led by Belichick, made the playoffs just once and finished 5-11 in 1995. Through it all, Modell remained a hands-on owner with a sense of humor. At one league meeting,

Hugh Culverhouse, the bombastic owner of the Buccaneers, wore a red suit. When Modell finished speaking, he ceded the floor to the "Bloody Mary from Tampa." Yet Modell, whose money was tied up in the team, was competing against younger, wealthier owners.

As the longtime chair of the broadcast committee, Modell negotiated television rights deals that generated far more for the owners than revenue from ticket sales. But teams still relied on game-day revenue to turn a profit, and money from luxury boxes and club seats did not have to be shared with the other owners.

Modell's Browns, though, played in Municipal Stadium, which had been built to lure the 1932 Olympic Games. Modell took control of the crumbling building from the city in the 1970s and spent $54 million on upgrades, Jim Bailey, Modell's lawyer, told me. Still, it was built for the Indians, the incumbent baseball team, and had few of the revenue-generating features like newer stadiums in Miami and Detroit.

Modell asked the city to help him pay for a new home. Instead, the city helped the Indians build Jacobs Field, which left Modell without a tenant. Then the city helped the Cavaliers build a downtown arena to lure them from suburban Richfield. Even the Rock & Roll Hall of Fame received public funding. Cleveland mayor Mike White promised Modell he would help him build a new football stadium if he didn't lobby the city council. He later backtracked.

Perhaps White believed Modell could afford to build his own stadium, or that he would never leave. Modell complained to Tagliabue that city officials were anti-Semitic, and that he really didn't have the money. Among other things, his son, David, who worked in the front office, had lavish appetites. One year, he checked into the Breakers two weeks before an owners meeting and was enjoying himself so much the hotel manager called the league to make sure he could cover his bill. (The manager was told to call Modell.)

Modell had set up a holding company that included the team, and he borrowed against the company's receipts. This gave him cash to sign free agent wide receiver Andre Rison to a $5.6 million deal, with most of the money paid as a signing bonus.

Rison made the Pro Bowl four of his first six seasons with the Falcons, but he was a bust in Cleveland, with career lows in receptions, yards per game, and touchdowns. Chris Berman of ESPN dubbed him Andre "Bad Moon" Rison after the Creedence Clearwater Revival song "Bad Moon Rising." He became a target of fans and returned the bile.

"We didn't make the fucking move," Rison said after an ugly home loss to the Packers late in the 1995 season, after word of the team's departure leaked. "So, for all the booers, fuck you, too. I'll be glad when we get to Baltimore, if that's the case. We don't have any home field advantage. I've never been booed at home. Baltimore's our home. Baltimore, here we come."

If Rison was disliked, Modell was hated.

"We got a deal done in forty days," Bailey said. "Baltimore had a place and the finances. It was a state agency but independent enough it could act autonomously. They had money from a special sports lottery" to build a new stadium.

Modell and Bailey wanted to announce the move after the season. But the media in Baltimore discovered that the team had filed an application with the league to relocate. Modell skipped town and missed the last few home games, which included fistfights and flying trash.

"I had to go back to Cleveland once because the city sued us, and I had bodyguards take me to the airport and pick me up," Bailey recalled. "Off duty cops."

Already dealing with the Rams and Raiders leaving Los Angeles, Tagliabue settled with the city: Cleveland could keep the Browns' logos and records, which would be assigned to a new team.

"To the fans of the Browns, I can say very simply, you can count on us, the Browns will be there by 1999," Tagliabue said in February 1996, even though the new team had no owner or stadium.

Modell, appearing publicly for the first time since word of the team's departure leaked, called the episode "a very, very tough experience for a lot of people."

A month later, the owners met at the Breakers, where Modell had to slip out through the kitchen. The once-jilted fans in Baltimore got a new team, the Ravens, and the Browns eventually returned to Cleveland. But Modell's mad dash from Cleveland convinced Tagliabue and the owners that they needed a way to keep teams from moving without violating antitrust laws. The answer was to enhance the league's relocation guidelines.

From then on, teams needed the approval of three-fourths of the other owners before they could move. Owners also had to do everything possible to maximize "fan support." And "no club has an 'entitlement' to relocate simply because it perceives an opportunity for enhanced club revenues in another location." In other words, teams couldn't simply run for the money.

Still, the lure of new stadiums remained. St. Louis, which lost the Cardinals in 1988, built a domed stadium that became the home of the Rams, which were owned by Missouri native Georgia Frontiere. The Rams moved to St. Louis a year before the Browns left Cleveland.

In 1997, Bud Adams, the owner of the Oilers, left Houston, where his team was a tenant in the Astrodome. The newly minted Tennessee Oilers played in Memphis in the Liberty Bowl with the intention of moving to Nashville when their new stadium was ready in two years. But fans in Memphis had no interest in supporting a club that was destined for a rival city, so the Titans moved to Nashville a year early and played a season at Vanderbilt University.

The moves were tough on the fans, and they tested the league's relationship with its sponsors and broadcast partners. The NFL no longer had a team in Los Angeles, the country's second largest city and its entertainment capital, or in Houston, another top-ten market. The new relocation guidelines, though, slowed the merry-go-round, at least for a decade or so.

The relocations did not solve every problem. Despite moving into a publicly financed stadium in Baltimore, Modell still had substantial debts. When he couldn't repay his loans, the NFL secretly covered for him. The league did not want to run the team, so it told Modell to find a partner within 180 days.

"The scripted message was 'Look, you screwed up. You got in over your head and we've stepped in,'" said Frank Hawkins, the league lawyer who worked on the bailout. "'We can't take a piece of your team long-term. You need to take us out by bringing you a new partner.'"

In March 2000, Modell sold 49 percent of the Ravens to Steve Bisciotti, who also had an option to buy out Modell. He exercised it in 2004, paying $325 million for the other half of the team.

Few people at the league office knew about Modell's bailout. The NFL was trying to create a $1 billion stadium fund that Kraft pushed for. If the bankers knew that a team was effectively insolvent, the league's borrowing costs might have risen. Owners were kept apprised of the bailout only by phone. No communications were in writing.

After years of tumult, the relocation guidelines added some order, and owners began borrowing up to $150 million from the new stadium fund. They also sold the naming rights to their buildings, some more than others. The Dolphins' home in South Florida has been renamed eight times, including once as Land Shark Stadium.

Owners also sold personal seat licenses to defray construction costs. Carolina Panthers owner Jerry Richardson is credited with being the first to require fans to buy these licenses, which were needed to purchase season tickets. Yet of all the owners' moneymaking schemes, their most audacious was their dance with lawmakers. Year after year, they claim they need fancier stadiums to keep up with their peers. Never mind that every team turns a profit thanks to the league's ever-growing media deals. Never mind that the NFL's salary cap limits the owners' largest expense, player contracts. The owners—many of whom complain about government getting in the way of industry—demand subsidies and tax breaks to help pay for their stadiums, socializing their costs and privatizing their profits.

With few exceptions, lawmakers pony up because they don't want to endure the wrath of voters if a team leaves. To politicians, being an "NFL City" means every Sunday your city is showcased on television. The stadiums are sold as linchpins to redevelopment, even though NFL teams only play a dozen or so home games a season. The taxes generated by stadiums *rarely* cover the public subsidies.

Some governments do pay off their debts. In Minneapolis, the Vikings received nearly $500 million from Hennepin County, which also agreed to as much as $280 million in maintenance. In June 2023, the Minnesota Management and Budget office announced that the state had paid off $377 million in bond debt for U.S. Bank Stadium, twenty years ahead of schedule.[3]

But more often, the politicians who cut these deals leave stadium subsidies for their successors. In Cincinnati in 1996, voters approved a half of 1 percent increase in the sales tax to help build and maintain stadiums for the Bengals and Reds, pay for Cincinnati's public schools, and give homeowners an annual property tax rebate. The stadiums were also meant to revive the city's waterfront.

The sales tax receipts fell so fast during the recession of 2009 that Hamilton County had to shore up the sales tax fund. The Bengals and Reds refused to renegotiate their leases, and the county cut basic services and drained a bond reserve fund. The county commissioners who approved the deal lost their seats.

"Anyone looking at this objectively knows it's a train wreck," Dusty Rhodes, the county auditor, told me. "I told them they were making a big mistake, but they didn't want to hear me."

Teams routinely threatened to move to Los Angeles as leverage. Rams owner Stan Kroenke, who married into the Walton family and made a fortune in commercial real estate, bought a stake in the Rams before they returned to St. Louis in 1995. He increased his position to 40 percent in 1997. He also acquired the right to buy the rest of the club, which he exercised after Frontiere died in 2008.

Soon after he took over, he pushed the St. Louis Regional Sports Authority to upgrade the Edward Jones Dome, pointing to a clause in the team's lease that required the building to be in the top tier of NFL stadiums. In February 2013, an arbitration panel ruled in favor of the Rams' proposal to spend $700 million on improvements, and gave the stadium authority, which proposed spending $120 million, thirty days to find the money for the plan. The authority rejected the plan, which allowed the Rams to break their lease in early 2015.

Kroenke then purchased the Hollywood Park Racetrack in Inglewood, California, which he planned to knock down to make way for new homes. He also bought a sixty-acre plot next to the track for a stadium. The NFL wasn't surprised. A few days before the Super Bowl in 2014, Kroenke sent Goodell an email about his plans, but urged discretion.

"We're going to try very hard to stay under the radar screen and nobody will know we bought it," Kroenke told Goodell.[4] "We'll stay hidden, which is what we want, for as long as we can."

Speaking to reporters, Goodell claimed that he did not know about any plans by Kroenke to develop a stadium in Los Angeles.

The league's relocation guidelines required teams to make a good faith effort to succeed in their home market. The Rams looked for ways to sidestep them. In December 2013, Kevin Demoff, Kroenke's top lieutenant, wrote to his boss and said the Rams could get the league's permission to move the team if, among other things, it focused on the "downward trend" in the St. Louis market. Since the Rams returned to St. Louis, the city had lost some of its largest companies and was the country's twenty-second largest media market and slipping.

Documents and emails released in 2022 as part of a settlement to compensate the city and county of St. Louis for the Rams' departure showed how Kroenke, Demoff, and NFL executives worked behind the scenes.[5] In late 2014, the *Los Angeles Times* reported on Kroenke's plans to build an eighty-thousand-seat stadium in Inglewood. Kroenke, advised by the league, had his real estate company issue a bland statement that said no decision had been made about what to do with the property. Fans in St. Louis sensed doom. At a half-time ceremony in 2014 for the Rams' Super Bowl–winning team from 1999, fans cheered Marshall Faulk, Kurt Warner, and other members of the Greatest Show on Turf. When their coach, Dick Vermeil, thanked Kroenke, he was booed.

Civic leaders in St. Louis unveiled a plan to build the Rams a new outdoor stadium next to the Mississippi River.[6] They secured a naming rights sponsor, National Car Rental, which is based in St. Louis.[7] Dave Peacock, a former executive at Anheuser-Busch, cochaired the stadium development group. He spoke often with Goodell and other league executives to emphasize that the city was doing everything possible to keep the team, as per the league's relocation guidelines.

As he did, Kroenke quietly tried to convince his fellow owners that staying in Missouri was hopeless and that he could build a marquee stadium in Los Angeles. Kroenke briefed Houston Texans owner Bob McNair and Steelers owner Art Rooney II. Jerry Jones talked up Kroenke's vision. In January 2015, he told me Kroenke didn't need league approval to move. "Keep in mind that teams have moved without the permission of the league," he said. "They just have."

Jones's comments set off alarm bells because Chargers owner Dean Spanos and Raiders owner Mark Davis, who were unable to win stadium subsidies in San Diego and Oakland, also wanted to build a stadium together in Carson, California, twenty miles from downtown Los Angeles. Goodell set up the Committee on Los Angeles Opportunities that included Kraft, McNair, Rooney, Giants owner John Mara, and Chiefs owner Clark Hunt.[8]

But it was clear to those owners that Richardson, who ran the league's stadium committee, was in charge and he favored the Chargers and Raiders' project. Their proposal was not as flashy as Kroenke's, but it would solve two problems at once. Bob Iger of Disney was brought on to promote it.[9]

"I wasn't going against Jerry Richardson at the time and I wanted to help," Mara told me. "I wanted to help Dean, I wanted to help Mark, because they were in lousy stadiums and there was no hope for either one of them. At least the Rams had a backup plan [in St. Louis]. These guys had no backup plan."

Richardson was friends with Spanos—they both helped negotiate the 2011 labor deal—but their friendship might have blinded Richardson to the advantages of Kroenke's plan backed by a far wealthier owner. Richardson only had about half the owners on his side, far less than the twenty-four votes needed to approve the Chargers-Raiders joint plan.

Some owners were willing to help the Chargers, who played in a city the NFL loved. They were less enamored with the Raiders, who had a messy tenure in Los Angeles in the 1980s and 1990s. Davis inherited the team from his voluble father, Al, and owners thought little of his business acumen.

A bunch of owners wanted to see where the winds were blowing before casting their vote, and on this issue, Jones was the league's weatherman. He said that if the NFL returned to Los Angeles, it had to be in a big way. LA was the entertainment capital of the world, and the NFL was the country's premier entertainment product. The Carson project would not make the needed splash.

Jones had a bloc of reliable votes: Dan Snyder in Washington, Terry Pegula in Buffalo, Jimmy Haslam in Cleveland, and, of course, Kroenke. But the Committee on Los Angeles Opportunities voted 5–1 in favor of the Chargers-Raiders plan, which would keep both teams in their home state.[10] The Raiders still had many fans in Southern California as well. Chiefs owner Clark Hunt cast the one nay vote because he was unsure if Los Angeles could sustain two teams. He effectively endorsed Kroenke moving the Rams.

"The four of us that voted along with Jerry [Richardson] were not going to cross him at that point, quite frankly," Mara said. "Clark, I guess to his credit, felt like Stan's proposal was the best fit for the league."

The next day, the full ownership met in the Azalea Ballroom in the Westin Houston, Memorial City. Richardson explained why his committee voted in favor of the Carson plan. Iger showed up and endorsed the plan.

Then Demoff presented the Rams' plan for Inglewood. The stadium would be three-quarters underground, have a translucent canopy for shade, and open concourses. The presentation was a knockout. Seattle Seahawks owner Paul Allen, who almost never attended league meetings, endorsed Kroenke's plan, which carried weight with the other owners.

The first vote was 20–12 in favor of the Rams' project, a rejection of the Richardson committee. In the next round, the owners voted 21–11 for Kroenke after Jeffrey Lurie of the Philadelphia Eagles switched sides. Spanos saw his hopes fade with each vote.

"It's very rare that the owners would vote contrary to a pretty strong committee recommendation," Mara said. "But the Rams presentation was so strong, so impressive."

As the debate continued into the afternoon, Jones asked Goodell for a recess, confident that he could pick off a few more owners in private. Goodell rejected the idea, so Jones asked if a bar cart could be wheeled into the conference room, a suggestion Detroit Lions owner Martha Firestone Ford seconded. Cocktails were served.

Jones made a second request: a secret ballot. Jones knew that many owners did not want to *publicly* oppose Richardson and the committee. But privately, they might choose Kroenke's plan. Around 6 p.m., a compromise was worked out to give the Chargers a one-year option to move in with Kroenke if their quest for a new stadium in San Diego failed. If Spanos stayed in San Diego, Davis could move in with Kroenke. The owners approved the plan, 30–2.

"Thank you for your trust," Kroenke told the owners. "I won't disappoint you."

Spanos emerged from the meeting shell-shocked. The press conference was more like a funeral than a celebration. Kroenke tried to look happy and restrained at the same time. Spanos, who trusted Richardson, looked mortified that he had to go back to San Diego and beg for public funding again. Davis seemed giddy to be left out because, as it turned out, he was already talking with officials in Las Vegas.

Kroenke said the process was "bittersweet" and he understood "the emotions that are involved of our fans and it's not easy to do these things." He never apologized to them, though, and quickly shifted back to blaming public officials.

Afterward, Jones met reporters in the hotel lobby. Grinning ear to ear and holding a tumbler of scotch, he said Kroenke's stadium was "absolutely the greatest plan ever conceived in sports, as far as how to put the show on."

The celebration continued at a steakhouse next door where Jones, his son Stephen, Snyder, Pegula, and a few others toasted Kroenke.

The vote underscored the NFL's money-first ethos. Fans in Oakland, San Diego, and St. Louis were tossed aside so the owners could make even more money. Oakland and St. Louis spent hundreds of millions of dollars to help their NFL teams only to see them leave.

Goodell paid lip service to the idea that the NFL cared about its fans. But the league's priority in 2016 was to appeal to broadcasters and sponsors by returning to the country's second-largest television market.

Spanos limped back to San Diego and pleaded for funding again. But having shown he was willing to leave town, voters were even less inclined to help him. In November 2016, they rejected a referendum that would have steered millions of tax dollars toward a stadium the Chargers wanted to build in downtown San Diego.[11]

Spanos knew a sweet deal when he saw it. In January 2017, he said the Chargers would move to Los Angeles and become a tenant in Kroenke's $5 billion stadium. No begging politicians, no debt to take on. The other owners weren't happy the NFL would leave San Diego. But they couldn't turn their back on Spanos.

They didn't abandon Davis, either. In late 2016, Jones, Kraft, Goodell, and league officials visited Las Vegas. Davis had teamed up with Sheldon Adelson, the casino magnate who lobbied lawmakers in Nevada to approve funding for a new stadium on The Strip. The NFL had long shunned Las Vegas because the city's sportsbooks could corrupt players and coaches. Yet over lunch at the Wynn, Steve Sisolak, the chairman of the Clark County commissioners who spearheaded the effort to lure the Raiders, noticed that the owners were more concerned about the region's ability to host a team than about gambling.

"I don't think we had to sell them" on Las Vegas, Sisolak, who later became governor of Nevada, told me. "They were pretty anxious to move here."

Clark County approved $750 million in subsidies for a new stadium that Davis planned to build. Cash-strapped Oakland could not match the offer, and in March 2017, the owners voted 31–1 to let the Raiders move to Sin City.

Over the years, the NFL has angered fans by moving teams, yet most of them kept watching games anyway. A few season-ticket holders and cities have sued departing teams, but the cases are almost always dismissed.

But the NFL met its match in St. Louis. Soon after Kroenke moved the Rams to Los Angeles, the city, county, and regional sports authority sued the NFL,[12] alleging the league misled the city by sidestepping its own relocation guidelines. They sought more than $1 billion to offset the loss of future tax revenue. Goodell, Kroenke, Demoff, and owners on the Los Angeles Opportunities committee were deposed. Emails were unearthed that appeared to show Kroenke and Demoff working with Goodell and other league officials to help the Rams leave town.

The city and county filed their case in Missouri state court, where judges were more likely to be sympathetic. The Rams lost decision after decision, and after the U.S. Supreme Court declined to hear the case, the team agreed to pay $790 million.[13]

The league wired the money to St. Louis with the expectation that Kroenke would cover the tab. But Kroenke told the other owners he expected them to help him cover the cost. After all, he had spent $5 billion on a new stadium in Los Angeles, which quadrupled the value of the Rams and increased other team valuations.[14]

The owners were furious.[15] As part of his relocation agreement, Kroenke agreed to cover the costs of the move. Mara said that if Kroenke had not agreed to indemnify the league, he and other owners would never have supported his plan.

Goodell asked Mara to find a way for Kroenke to repay the league. When he couldn't, Jaguars owner Shad Khan stepped in. Nearly a year after the settlement, the owners agreed to waive the league's debt limit so Kroenke could pay $571 million, or about three-quarters of the total settlement. Kroenke paid another $22 million to cover the league's legal bills. The owners covered the rest, each forgoing $7.5 million from their share of league revenue.

In the end, the settlement was the cost of doing business for a league whose revenue was growing by about $1 billion a year thanks partly to the new stadiums being built.

"To be honest with you, what he built out there is amazing, and it ended up working out well," Mara said of Kroenke's stadium. "The Chargers moved in there, a great stadium was built in Las Vegas. So, all's well that ends well."

NFL fans in Oakland, St. Louis, and San Diego felt otherwise. Rafael Alvarez, a San Diego native, was the cofounder of Bolt Pride, the largest Chargers fan group.[16] For more than twenty years, he sat with fellow diehards behind the end zone at home games, tailgating before and afterward. He helped raise thousands of dollars for local charities. He implored Spanos to stay in San Diego.

When the Chargers left, Alvarez was torn. He did not want to give Spanos any money, but he was devoted to the team and his friends. So, for each Chargers home game, he would drive up from San Diego to tailgate and head home before kickoff. "At the end of the day, it's the Bolt Pride Family I'm there for," he said. "I'm still a Charger fan for life. But you have to make business decisions just like the Chargers did."

6.

THE SENATOR'S SON

"The only thing I want to do in life, other than to be the commissioner of the NFL, is to make you proud."[1]

—Roger Goodell, in a letter to his father, Charles Goodell, 1981.

Steve Underwood clearly remembers Roger Goodell's declaration in 2010. The longtime general counsel for the Tennessee Titans, Underwood was at the Ritz-Carlton Orlando, Grande Lakes for the NFL's annual meeting. Speaking to a ballroom of owners, team executives, coaches, and their families, Goodell gave a state-of-the-league address that laid out the league's business opportunities.

The NFL was by far the most lucrative league in the country, but it was facing headwinds. Stories about the long-term impact of head injuries were scaring parents and raising questions about the viability of the game. Goodell had laid off staff at the league's office to steer the NFL through a recession. Most of all, the owners were eager to claw back $1 billion in revenue that the players had won in the 2006 collective bargaining agreement. Kraft, Jones, and other owners hoped to reach a deal before that agreement expired in March 2011. But they were prepared to lock out the players if necessary.

Goodell knew how to read the room. The son of a congressman and senator, he had spent his entire professional life at the NFL. Goodell was elected commissioner in 2006 because he helped the owners solve big problems, like strong-arming local governments into subsidizing their stadiums. He knew the owners regretted signing the 2006 labor deal and were committed to undoing it. So that night in Orlando, he spoke to them in a language they understood: He promised to make them a lot richer.

Anthony Noto, the league's chief financial officer, fed Goodell an audacious financial target: The NFL would generate $25 billion in revenue by 2027.[2] Underwood recalled a few gasps and sideways glances among the executives in the room. The NFL brought in about $8 billion in 2010, double what it made seventeen years earlier, in 1993. Now Noto and Goodell suggested that the league would more than *triple* its revenue in the next seventeen years.

"You know, Roger always speaks confidently, and him saying it not all that far into his reign as commissioner, I have to admit, it was quite a statement," Underwood said. "I didn't see how he could achieve that, to be deadly blunt."

For years afterward, when Goodell was asked about whether the league was on pace to meet his target, he emphasized that any revenue-generating deals the league cuts must burnish the NFL's brand, not just line the owners' pockets.

"I don't know whether we'll get there, but we're working towards that goal," Goodell said before the Super Bowl in 2015.[3] "It's something that we think is practical, but we want to do the growth the right way. The most important thing is everything we do has to become high-quality. It has to be done in a way that reflects well on the NFL."

By 2025, Goodell's goal didn't just look practical, it looked achievable. The league's revenue had grown on average by more than $1 billion a year to pass $23 billion. The NFL's media rights contracts, its largest source of revenue, were a big reason. In 2014, the league secured $55 billion in rights fees over the following eight years. In 2021, the NFL doubled its rights fees to more than $110 billion.[4] In 2011, the owners' share of total revenue grew by roughly five percentage points, albeit based on total revenue, not net revenue. In 2020, the league convinced the players to accept a seventeenth regular-season game on top of the extra playoff games they'd already added. New revenue poured in from stadiums opened in Atlanta, Las Vegas, Los Angeles, and beyond.

According to *Forbes*, the average NFL team in 2023 was worth $5.1 billion, almost twice as much as teams in the NBA, the next most valuable league.

Goodell was doing fine, too. About 90 percent of his compensation was based on bonuses linked to a host of benchmarks, such as landing favorable labor agreements and lucrative commercial deals. He received $63,900,050 per year, or just under $128 million for fiscal years 2019–20 and 2020–21, making him one of the most highly paid executives in the country.[5]

Many of America's sports leagues are run by lawyers. NBA Commissioner David Stern and his successor, Adam Silver, both worked at

Proskauer Rose. So did Gary Bettman, NHL commissioner, who learned the ropes from Stern. Rob Manfred, the commissioner of Major League Baseball, was the league's labor lawyer before he replaced Bud Selig.

Then there is Goodell, who never earned an MBA or a law degree. Instead, he studied on the job, which prepared him to become commissioner, a job he'd coveted for decades.

Goodell is perhaps the only commissioner who looks like he could play the sport he governs. More than six feet tall with a broad chest, Goodell for years showed up before sunrise at NFL headquarters to work out in the basement gym. He has the mentality of a football player, too. In the words of one associate, he is "a grinder" who works long hours and makes sure he is prepped before every meeting. Owners, league staff, and network executives recount getting texts and calls from Goodell at all hours. He gives his phone number to players, including Tom Brady and Peyton Manning. His circle of insiders included Lamar Hunt's widow, Norma, and John Madden, whom Goodell called "Coach."

Goodell watches most prime-time games, often in his man cave in Bronxville, New York, where he will critique the officiating and television production. The league took a wholesale look at broadcasts to partly address one of his pet peeves—too many commercial breaks. He wants to know what technology networks are developing. He is not a big notetaker, but he listens closely and will ask associates about small details weeks later. In meetings, he doesn't lead so much as facilitate.

"He has a big office and there's a table, and you'd sit at the table—sort of more informal than him sitting behind the desk," Paul Hicks, the league spokesman from 2010 to 2015, said in a deposition. "And he'd say, 'You want to start with your list or you want to start with my list?' And so you'd work the list. But it was informal. It was never a presentation or a thing. It was a conversation. You were advocating for what you wanted him to do. And he was really good at the Socratic method, and he'd make you defend your position—you know, until he was satisfied that whatever you were suggesting was a good idea or not."

Another former staffer said that Goodell "thrives on debate" and "that makes going in front of him tough." He doesn't scream in meetings, but "silence means he's pleased. Or he'll give you a little 'good.' Or he'll cross-examine you. That made me stronger. This is big boy sports."

Goodell makes mental notes about how his staff dresses and how they deal with stress. He expects his deputies to have opinions and follow through on tasks.

"Some people tell him what they think he wants to hear, but he sniffs out BS better than anyone," one former executive said.

Many veterans of the Tagliabue era spoke glowingly of him. He was, they said, the smartest man in any room he entered and at times let subordinates know it. He could be short-tempered and imperious and had an intellectual disdain for some owners. But executives appreciated that he was strategic, didn't micromanage, and wasn't afraid to ask questions about topics he didn't understand. He would ask executives for reports, absorb the details, and synthesize them into his own speeches to the owners and others. Some executives said this took the heat off them but also left them overshadowed. Still, the NFL was growing, and for many it was a fun time to be at the league.

Goodell was a very different boss. He held his cards close to the vest and was wary of challengers. He was a 24/7 boss, and he expected his staff to work all hours. Staffers said Goodell could be intimidating, intentionally or not. He recruited and wanted to be surrounded by top-notch executives. But one former executive said that attending an NFL alumni gathering was like being with "one of the unhappiest groups of successful people."

Owners were focused more on results than process.

"What he does, which is what really good leaders do, he'll be the last one to talk," Falcons owner Arthur Blank said. "He'll get everyone else's opinion in the room and listen to all the conversation and then he'll inform, with that knowledge that he's just picked up and his own inherent thinking about something, that we ought to do this."

In many ways, Goodell is more like a Senate majority leader than a CEO, constantly trying to build a supermajority. "Eight of the owners can stop any great idea, so that's his kind of mentality," one former associate said, referring to the twenty-four votes—a three-quarters majority—it takes to pass major initiatives.

Many meetings have no written agendas or minutes taken, perhaps so they cannot be found in discovery, though Goodell might scribble notes on a piece of paper or Post-it note.

"Generally those—he'd watch you rip it up and throw it away, and if it was part of a bigger thing, he'd put it on a piece of paper," Hicks said. "Sometimes it was in a folder."

By all accounts, Goodell loves his job and has no other professional ambitions. A knee injury ended his playing career before he entered college, but Goodell seems to get a similar dopamine rush from being commissioner.

"I personally know he works at this seven days a week, all day," Patriots owner Robert Kraft said. "There's a uniqueness to the NFL that I think some managers from the outside wouldn't fully understand. I mean, think about it. You've got a board of directors of thirty-two people. You have so many different dimensions of the business."

Fans jeer Goodell at the Draft and mock him as a sanctimonious bully for his heavy-handed player suspensions, which led sportswriter Drew Magary to dub him the "Ginger Hammer."[6] Podcaster Bill Simmons, without evidence, called Goodell a liar for denying that he had seen a video of Ray Rice knocking out his fiancée.[7] Barstool made shirts with Goodell's face and a red clown's nose after he suspended Brady during the Deflategate scandal.

Goodell's friends said he was frustrated by this portrayal and felt like he could not win in the media. But one area that Goodell could control was helping the owners make money by, among other things, embracing Kraft's mantra to "manage like you own it."

"We worked together on the media contracts over the last twenty-five years, and he really has a touch and feel and adaptation to the marketplace, knowing when to be very strong and knowing when to back off," Kraft said.

Many executives doing business with the NFL have a different view.

"There was a coldness and a 'that's it' tone in Roger's voice that was chilling," said Dick Ebersol, the longtime chief of NBC Sports.[8] "At his heart Roger can be a cold son of a bitch.

"I think the people on the other side of the negotiating table are going to hear that in the coming months," Ebersol added, referring to the then-upcoming labor talks. "He's going to show mettle, and he's going to do what he thinks is best for the National Football League. It's what he's always done."

Goodell has long wanted the NFL to transcend sports. In his office, he kept a framed cover of a magazine with the names of the biggest corporate brands in the country, a reminder that he wanted the NFL to be among them.

"Roger doesn't view the other leagues as competition," a league staffer said. "He wants to be mentioned with Disney and the Vatican, these massive institutions."

The middle of five sons, Goodell was infatuated with football and the Redskins growing up in the Washington, DC, area. He was so smitten with the game, he slept with a football at night. His mom, Jean, a nurse, was a central figure in his life, and she taught him the importance of hard work.

Goodell also looked up to his father. Charles Goodell represented House districts in New York as a Republican for a decade until 1968, when he was appointed to fill the remaining two and a half years of Robert F. Kennedy's Senate term following his assassination. The Goodell boys worked on their father's campaigns. The great-grandson of an abolitionist, Goodell was fiscally conservative and generally progressive on social issues. Members of the Goodell clan attended the Chautauqua Institution,[9] a nonprofit humanistic group southwest of Buffalo, and a relic of an era when artists, educators, religious leaders, and the wealthy met in genteel settings to explore "the best in human values."

At times, the senior Goodell seemed like a killjoy. While much of the world celebrated the Apollo 11 moon landing in 1969, he called the space program wasteful and dangerous.

"I just don't think it's worth the cost we put into it," Goodell said.[10] "We have too many other programs in this country that urgently demand money."

In other ways, he was a progressive leader. In 1970, Goodell cosponsored a bill calling for an end to the war in Vietnam. President Richard Nixon, previously an ally, put him on his enemies list. Vice President Spiro Agnew called Goodell the "Christine Jorgensen of the Republican Party," a reference to the former soldier who became a woman after a sex change operation.[11] Goodell said his father knew his antiwar stance might cost him a chance at a full six-year term, but he stood by his convictions. Roger kept a copy of the Vietnam Disengagement Act, a proposed bill that his father authored, in his office.

In an interview with *Time* in 2012, Goodell said his father was never the same after leaving the Senate. He died at age sixty, in 1987.[12]

Goodell has offered few details about his life before the NFL. But one of Goodell's younger brothers, Michael, said that Roger protected him from neighborhood bullies when they were younger.

"Absolutely, he would beat the crap out of people," said Michael Goodell, who later came out as gay and called his brother a "hero figure."[13] "Roger was not Atticus Finch."

Goodell's oldest brother, Bill, went on to run a hedge fund.[14] His second oldest brother, Tim, became a lawyer at the Hess Corporation,[15] while his youngest brother, Jeff, was a school administrator.[16]

The Goodell family split their time between Washington and Westchester County. Roger attended Bronxville High School, where he was cocaptain of the football team and not much of a student. "He was a big dumb jock," Michael Goodell said. "He played that up. He was walking around in his letter jacket, with his girlfriend on his arm and stuff. He was big man on campus."

He was also something of a hard-ass. Athletes at Bronxville had to sign pledges that they wouldn't drink or get into trouble. As team captain, Goodell kept an eye on his teammates at parties. "All of a sudden it was like an alarm went off," Michael Goodell said. "They were running out of the back door as he was coming in the front door. It was like Prohibition."

Goodell injured his knee before he arrived at Washington & Jefferson College in Pennsylvania and never played football there. But he became a more serious student and earned a degree in economics. While some of his classmates went to Wall Street or joined the Peace Corps, Goodell had a very precise job in mind. After he graduated in 1981, he wrote to his father, "The only thing I want to do in life, other than to be the commissioner of the NFL, is to make you proud."[17]

Goodell wrote to Commissioner Pete Rozelle and every NFL team, looking for work.

"Being an avid football fan, I have always desired a career in the NFL," Goodell wrote to Rozelle.[18] "Consequently, as a great admirer of you, it would be both an honor and a pleasure to work for you in any position that may be available."

Goodell received fifty-three rejection letters. But Don Weiss, executive director at the league, wrote to say that Goodell should stop by if he was ever in the area.[19] Goodell was working in a management-trainee program at a steel company in Pittsburgh, but he called Weiss and said he was in the area. Then he drove all night to get to New York the following morning. Six months later, in 1982, the NFL offered him an internship.

It is possible Weiss recognized Goodell's last name and decided that hiring a senator's son was a good thing. Still, Goodell did not waste his opportunity. After his four-month internship in Rozelle's office, he took a one-year internship with the Jets. He was impressive enough that the team's defensive coordinator, Joe Gardi, offered him a full-time job.[20] But Goodell returned to the league office to work as an intern in the public relations department clipping newspaper articles. Rozelle was his idol, and getting his job was Goodell's goal.

"I was the lowest of the low, let's put it that way," Goodell said in a deposition in 2022.

Goodell quickly took on more consequential tasks. One included trying to persuade college recruits to sign with NFL clubs, not the fledgling United States Football League, which had lured stars like Herschel Walker and Reggie White.[21] Goodell manned a hotline that college players could call to get information about the NFL.

In 1987, Goodell became the assistant to the president of the American Football Conference, a ceremonial position that counted votes when the owners chose Super Bowl cities. It brought Goodell closer to Lamar Hunt, the creative and powerful owner of the Kansas City Chiefs who, among other things, had an interest in growing the game overseas.

Tagliabue tapped Goodell to help with the league's international expansion. In 1990, Tagliabue wanted to play a game in Berlin to celebrate Germany's reunification and help publicize the World League of American Football, which would start playing the following year. On a flight to Berlin, Goodell sat near the East German Olympic gold medal figure skater Katarina Witt. Goodell chatted her up and began a long-distance relationship, which became a source of amusement at the NFL. Co-workers bought Goodell a set of skates as a joke.

Goodell was an eligible bachelor and a rising star at the NFL. The staff in the early 1990s was chummier. Goodell was friends with Greg Aiello, who came to the league from the Cowboys, and was best man at his wedding. Some staff recalled a Christmas party where two women began fighting after they discovered they were *both* dating Goodell. Goodell met Jane Skinner, a former anchor on Fox News and the daughter of Sam Skinner, a chief of staff for President George H. W. Bush, at a mutual friend's wedding. They began a long-distance relationship while she lived in Milwaukee. They married in 1997.[22]

Many of Goodell's co-workers from that period viewed him as political and ambitious, at times willing to push them out of the way to get ahead. Others appreciated Goodell's pluck and said he understood that the owners were the power brokers and that helping them was critical to his career. One longtime NFL executive recalled how at league meetings, groups of employees would go out to dinner together. When they returned to the hotel, they would sometimes see Goodell arriving, too, but with an owner or two.

Goodell didn't walk around telling people that he wanted to be commissioner, but it was clear to those around him he did.

"I spent enough time with Roger to know that was his ultimate goal, what he really wanted to do," said Neil Austrian, the league's president in the 1990s. "I mean, whatever you gave Roger to do was done well, including watching my daughter." Being ambitious, Austrian added, was "not all bad."

The path to the commissioner's job ran through Tagliabue. For years, Tagliabue commuted to New York because his wife, Chan, remained in Washington, DC. Tagliabue was a bachelor during the week and often dined with Goodell, sometimes at the Yale Club or the 21 Club, Rozelle's old haunt. Goodell went jogging in Central Park with Tagliabue's wife when she was in town.

Tagliabue gave Goodell bigger tasks, like helping run the lottery for two expansion franchises. Baltimore and St. Louis, which had lost the Colts and Cardinals, expressed interest. So did Oakland, which lost the Raiders, as well as Nashville and San Antonio. Charlotte and Jacksonville were granted teams in 1993. During the process, Goodell met mayors and business leaders across the country.

Tagliabue was wary that the league would be sued by cities that did not win a new team. As Goodell was fielding offers, Jodi Balsam, a league lawyer, did prep work just in case.

"Think about it, you have a national beauty pageant that ended up with Carolina and Jacksonville" as the winners, she said. "So, what happens after none of the other parties are satisfied?" The solution, she said, was not to block a team from moving, but to force the team to pay a relocation fee. In some cases, teams tried to foist the fee on cities, like when the Rams told St. Louis to cover the $29 million fee the league wanted.[23]

For several years in the 1990s, Goodell and Frank Hawkins crisscrossed the country trying to persuade officials to subsidize stadiums.

Hawkins recalled one trip to Cleveland, where the city threatened to sue the league after the Browns left for Baltimore. Hawkins flew home from the Super Bowl in Arizona and circled back to Cleveland with a change of winter clothes. Goodell went from Arizona to Hawaii for the Pro Bowl, then to Ohio.

"We had to cross Terminal Square in Cleveland in early February," Hawkins said. "He was wearing a white tropical suit."

A month later, Goodell and Hawkins returned to Cleveland with Tagliabue, who told the Cleveland City Council that Cleveland would get the NFL's next expansion team.[24] On the way back to the airport, the driver took a wrong turn and headed past a demonstration of angry Browns fans. Everyone in the car ducked as they rode past.

Goodell was given other problems to solve. In 1993, Tagliabue ousted John Bello, who ran NFL Properties, the league's for-profit arm. Tagliabue wanted to bring the division in-house because, among other things, Bello had cut trading card deals with the players that helped them pay for their lawsuits against the league. Goodell took over on an interim basis, but some Properties executives felt he did not give them credit for signing big sponsorship deals with Coke and other companies. Goodell, though, won points with Jerry Jones because he backed his push to let teams control their own local marketing rights. In 1999, Austrian left in part because some owners felt he took too corporate an approach to running the league's business operations. He butted heads with the owners who for decades had made most of the key decisions that affected the league.

"The primary reason for the meteoric rise of the NFL is the direct, extensive involvement of the team owners themselves," said Marc Ganis, a consultant to the league and teams. "That changes the mindset of decision-making. You look much more into the future as opposed to: What is it worth today? What can I trade it for?"

With Austrian gone, Goodell's stature rose. He did not take Austrian's title, but in 2001 was named chief operating officer. His relationships with the owners deepened. At the annual meeting in 2004, for instance, he attended eight out of the nine owners sessions.

It was at this meeting, which took place at the Breakers in Palm Beach, that the owners voted unanimously to start talks with Tagliabue about extending his contract, which was expiring in May 2005. Former NFL executives later said that Goodell expected Tagliabue to retire, not have his contract extended. Tagliabue announced his retirement in March 2006, after completing his last labor deal with Gene Upshaw. Goodell finally could apply for the job he'd sought for twenty-five years.

The search for a new commissioner was less complicated than in 1989, when Tagliabue was chosen on the twelfth ballot. The NFL was in a far stronger position in 2006. Tagliabue's bond with Gene Upshaw produced seventeen years of labor peace, which helped the owners win larger media and sponsorship deals, generating revenue that helped them build new stadiums. As Tagliabue's protégé known to every owner, Goodell was the favorite to replace his boss. That was apparent to Jim Barlow, a Broncos executive. Well before Tagliabue stepped down, Barlow's boss, owner Pat Bowlen, introduced him to Goodell.

"I remember standing next to Pat at an owners meeting when Roger walked up," Barlow said. "Pat is like, 'Jim, I'd like to introduce you to the next commissioner of the NFL.'"

Tagliabue didn't overtly lobby for Goodell, but he laid the groundwork for him. Goodell's main opponent was Gregg Levy, an outside counsel from Covington & Burling, Tagliabue's old firm. Levy was popular with some of the less hands-on teams, including the Lions and Titans.

The election took place at a hotel outside Chicago in August 2006. On the third ballot, Goodell was ahead 17-14-1. On the next-to-last ballot, Goodell secured twenty-three votes, more than the two-thirds majority he needed. The owners ultimately chose Goodell by acclamation.[25] Goodell, forty-seven, was the NFL's commissioner, just the fourth since World War II. Steelers owner Dan Rooney went to Goodell's hotel room to tell him.

"When I saw Dan smiling, I knew it wasn't bad news," Goodell said, adding that he was lucky he had just put his pants on before Rooney knocked on the door.

Goodell's only regret was that he couldn't tell his father. "My dad was not alive to see me become commissioner," he later said.[26] "But I know that, wherever he is, he is smiling."

Rooney, Richardson, and the other owners who worked closely with Goodell had gotten their man. He lacked Tagliabue's prodigious legal mind, but he had a deep understanding of the inner workings of the NFL and knew how to listen to the owners.

"Roger got his MBA from Pete Rozelle and Paul Tagliabue," Kraft said. "That's not a bad education."[27]

Like many leaders, Goodell promoted some of his confidants, while a few of Tagliabue's lieutenants left. Joe Browne, the longtime spokesman and one of Goodell's first bosses, saw his role overshadowed by Aiello. Hawkins departed after a couple of years.

Goodell never replaced himself because he was familiar with every corner of the NFL. To keep abreast of what the owners were thinking, Goodell called each one at least once a month, keeping track of the calls on a card he kept in his desk. When an owner wanted help, say, getting Broadway theater tickets, Goodell would take care of the request himself. In this way, he made himself indispensable.

When Tagliabue became commissioner in 1989, the NFL was in crisis. The game was popular, but the league was at war with its players. The television deals signed in 1987 would soon be up for renewal.

Without the labor strife or financial peril, Goodell could focus on matters like enforcing the league's personal conduct policy to "clean up" the game. During his seventeen years as commissioner, Tagliabue suspended twenty-eight players for a total of forty-eight games. Two other players were suspended for entire seasons and one, Rae Carruth, was suspended indefinitely. Goodell, who fixated on protecting the NFL's brand, surpassed Tagliabue's totals in just his third season as commissioner. Albert Haynesworth, Adam "Pacman" Jones, and other stars received hefty penalties. Steelers quarterback Ben Roethlisberger was suspended for six games—later reduced to four—amid allegations he raped a woman. Falcons quarterback Michael Vick was suspended indefinitely after he was arrested for his role in a dogfighting ring.

Some players felt Goodell was capricious, and the union tried to dilute his authority in contract talks in 2011 and 2020. Fans turned Goodell into a punching bag. Owners felt his wrath, too, like in 2007, when the league found that the Patriots broke rules by videotaping the Jets coaches from their sidelines during a game.

Fans of all stripes took aim at Goodell because he served as judge, jury, and executioner when it came to player discipline. This came to a head in 2012 during an investigation into a bounty system that involved Saints coaches paying players who hurt opponents. After four players appealed their suspensions, Goodell appointed Tagliabue to oversee their appeals.

Tagliabue turned on his successor. He confirmed Goodell's finding that the Saints ran a bounty program, and that the players engaged in conduct detrimental to the league. But he vacated the players' suspensions, instead blaming the Saints and "broad organizational misconduct."[28]

The rebuke was a prelude to the biggest crisis of Goodell's tenure, in 2014. As commissioner, he believed in second chances if the accused showed contrition. Players and coaches who didn't bow received harsher penalties. This approach backfired when video surfaced of Ravens running back Ray Rice dragging his fiancée out of a hotel elevator in Atlantic City. In June that year, Goodell met Rice and Janay Palmer together, something that women's advocates say was misguided because a victim is less likely to speak their mind when their abuser is present. Both showed remorse, and Goodell gave Rice a two-game suspension.

The uproar was instantaneous. Critics noted that penalties for taking steroids were worse. In August, Goodell admitted that he mishandled the case and tightened league rules so that any NFL employee, not just a player, who engaged in assault, battery, domestic violence, or sexual assault would be suspended for six games without pay for a first offense and banished for at least a year for a second offense.[29]

"My disciplinary decision led the public to question our sincerity, our commitment, and whether we understood the toll that domestic violence inflicts on so many families," Goodell said in a letter to the owners.[30] "I take responsibility both for the decision and for ensuring that our actions in the future properly reflect our values. I didn't get it right. Simply put, we have to do better. And we will."

Two weeks later, TMZ published a second, more graphic video that showed Rice knocking out Palmer in the elevator,[31] igniting questions about whether the NFL had seen this tape and still went easy on Rice. The video became national news in the worst way. For years, the NFL had tried to attract female fans who often decided what sports their children played. Now, the country was openly discussing whether football might lead to violence against women.

Doctors wondered whether football players who inflicted pain on the field could control that impulse off the field. Women's advocates called for boycotts of the NFL and its sponsors. Senators considered calling Goodell to testify about domestic violence in the league. Even players, typically reluctant to comment about controversies, recognized how the issue threatened the league.

"They want people to watch the game, right?" Jets linebacker Jason Babin said.[32] "If they let things go that are not socially acceptable, people are going to get turned off."

The crisis was a turning point. Soon after TMZ published the second video, Goodell, at Kraft's urging, went on CBS to answer questions from Norah O'Donnell.[33] He appeared defensive and nervous. Two weeks later, Goodell held his first news conference at the Hilton in Manhattan, where he was peppered with questions from CNN and ABC reporters who rarely covered the NFL.[34]

Goodell said he would be accountable but not resign to take responsibility for the fiasco. Adept at spinning negative questions into positive answers, he said he was "proud of the opportunity we have to try to make a difference here and do the right thing."[35]

The NFL gave a seven-figure donation to a crisis hotline for women in distress, and Goodell toured their call center in Texas. The league also strengthened its rules of conduct and hired former prosecutors who specialized in crimes against women to work in a new investigative unit. But the damage to the league's brand took years to undo. The NFL looked callous and more concerned with money than with the people associated with the league. The questions continued through the season, including at the Super Bowl, where I asked Goodell whether he would take a pay cut to accept responsibility. (He punted, saying the decision was up to the owners.) He repeated that he would not resign.

"It's been a tough year on me personally," he said. "It's been a year of what I would say is humility and learning. We, obviously as an organization, have gone through adversity. More importantly, it's been adversity for me. We take that seriously. It's an opportunity for us to get better. It's an opportunity for us, for our organization, to get better. We've all done a lot of soul searching, starting with yours truly."

Goodell, once lauded by the media, felt he couldn't get a break from reporters, and he sometimes lashed out at his communications team in frustration. Outside consultants were hired to help him and the league navigate the media, but every season, a new scandal emerged. Incognito, Rice, Brady, Kaepernick. The league spent millions of dollars on lawyers to fight cases in court and conduct investigations. The drumbeat of bad news diverted attention from the games and dented one of the league's most important benchmarks, television viewership.

Goodell did have one stealth defender: his wife. Writing under the Twitter handle @forargument, Jane Goodell fired back at reporters over stories she thought were unfair to her husband.[36] After one ESPN story about how Goodell dealt with players kneeling during the playing of the national anthem, she wrote: "Reads like a press release from the players' union. You can do better reporting."

Goodell was paid handsomely to resolve crises and deflect criticism of the owners. They weren't happy about the controversies, but they largely backed Goodell because he continued to make them money.

"It's like the old saying," Texans owner Bob McNair told my colleague Mark Leibovich. "The higher up the palm tree the monkey climbs, the more of his ass is exposed."

But the owners recognized that Goodell was spread thin. In 2015, Goodell hired a COO, Tod Leiweke, the former president of the Seattle Seahawks. Soft-spoken and affable, he bonded with Goodell when they climbed Mount Rainer in 2009 to raise money for United Way.[37] (The Sea Gals cheerleaders greeted them when they returned to base camp.) Critically, Leiweke had no ambition to replace Goodell.

Leiweke left quietly less than three years later and was replaced by Maryann Turcke, a Canadian executive who had worked briefly at NFL Media. Like Leiweke, she never upstaged Goodell, though she did make a brief, cringeworthy speech introducing Goodell and Jay-Z when they announced a social justice initiative. Turcke said that as a Canadian, she understood what it meant to be an outsider. Few noticed her departure, either, in 2020.

With or without a COO, Jones blamed Goodell for the drumbeat of off-field distractions, particularly players kneeling during the national anthem. John Schnatter, the chief executive of Papa Johns pizza, was an NFL sponsor and friends with Jones, who owned dozens of Papa Johns franchises in Texas. Schnatter told investors that the protests damaged the company's sales, and later he claimed that Jones and Snyder urged him to attack Goodell.

"Goodell is a coward, and he is incompetent and he's just lucky," Schnatter said.[38]

Jones was also livid that Goodell suspended Cowboys running back Ezekiel Elliott for six games after he was accused of domestic violence against his ex-girlfriend the prior year. Elliott was never criminally charged, and the alleged events happened before he signed an NFL contract. But chastened by the Rice case, Goodell suspended him. Elliott appealed but a league-appointed arbitrator sided with Goodell. The players union won an injunction, and Elliott played the first half of the 2017 season. An appeals court reinstated the suspension, and Elliott sat out six games, three of which the Cowboys lost. They finished 9-7 and missed the playoffs.

Jones then tried to derail Goodell's contract extension. The compensation committee, which included Blank, Kraft, McNair, Mara, Rooney, and Hunt, worked for months on the deal. Jones was not a member of the committee, but he urged the group to make more of Goodell's pay contingent on the league hitting financial targets. To smooth the contract's passage, Blank included Jones in meetings.

"Because I knew he was going to be an issue, I'd rather have the enemy in the tent than outside, so we made him an ad hoc member of the committee just so he's heard," Blank said.

The committee met one night in a private room at a restaurant in midtown Manhattan. Jones couldn't make it, so he called in. They went through the elements of the deal and the committee members recall Jones being on board.

Then Goodell suspended Elliott, and Jones exploded. In a subsequent meeting, Jones asked for a vote on a proposal. Mara suggested that they discuss the issue further before voting on a "half-assed" measure. Jones shot back: "It's only half-assed if it's your ass!"

As the committee tried to finalize Goodell's contract, Jones said on a conference call that he had hired David Boies, the famous antitrust lawyer, because he was contemplating suing everyone on the committee. "All I heard was like, click, click, click, click, click," one committee member said. "Nobody said anything, they just hung up the phone and all the other owners hung up the phone."

Jones and Al Davis had sued the league before, but not other owners. This crossed a red line.[39] The owners approved Goodell's five-year extension worth as much as $200 million.[40] About 90 percent of the commissioner's compensation would be based on a basket of factors, including the league's relationship with sponsors, fans, and the media; the health and safety of the game; and the league's financial performance.

Goodell ordered Jones to pay about $2 million for conduct detrimental to the league, which helped cover the cost of defending the owners on the compensation committee.[41]

"Jerry was pretty tough with Roger, but Roger very easily turns the page and has a short memory," Mara said. "He still deals with Jerry all the time. And that's in the past."

As Goodell's compensation grew, so did the barbs from fans and the media. The league became so defensive about his eight-figure pay packages that it spent millions of dollars to remove its nonprofit status so it no longer had to release annual reports that included the compensation of its top officers. Goodell was lampooned on *South Park*, where he was portrayed as a malfunctioning robot working for the owners.

At times, Goodell's security detail shielded him from the media. In February 2023, the owners held committee meetings in Palm Beach. Reporters rarely attend, but the fate of the Washington Commanders was in the balance, so I flew to Florida and sat in the lobby for two days. Mark Maske of *The Washington Post* and I occasionally spoke with owners and league executives.

At the end of the second day, a hotel security guard asked us why we were in the lobby. We were waiting for friends, we said. The meetings ended and the owners and Goodell were heading to their limousines, so I moved closer to the front door in case an owner left from a different direction. The security guard asked Maske to leave, saying that the hotel did not allow reporters on-site. Moments after he was thrown out, Goodell emerged from an elevator surrounded by his bodyguard; Mara; Joe Siclare, the league's financial officer; Jeff Pash, the league's general counsel; and Goodell's executive assistant. Security guards and local police hustled them into a waiting limousine. The police vanished as soon as Goodell left.

Goodell did fewer interviews, and his public appearances became more curated, including his news conferences at the Super Bowl. In 2016, Goodell drew laughs when he claimed he was "available to the media almost every day of my job, professionally."[42] When Goodell did sit for interviews, it was often with ESPN, NFL Network, and other league partners, or CNBC when he attends the annual Allen & Company media finance conference. He also speaks at industry conferences, including the annual convention of the American Association of Neurological Surgeons.

Goodell helped kick off the 2023 event by participating in a fireside chat entitled "Concussion in Sports: What Every Neurosurgeon Should Know." The panel included Dr. Allen Sills, the NFL's chief medical officer and a brain surgeon, and Dr. Margot Putukian, the chief medical officer of Major League Soccer, who advised the NFL. Dr. Ann Stroink, the president of the association, lobbed questions about the identification and treatment of concussions and the need for more resources for youth sports. She asked no uncomfortable questions about the long-term effects of head trauma.

Goodell has tried to improve the safety of the game, pushing for rules changes, more aggressive policing of concussions, and better equipment. But he and the panelists treated football-related head trauma as a necessary evil. Goodell repeated the well-worn trope that there's risk in everything, including not playing sports, which is a false choice because athletes can play many sports—basketball, tennis, and so on—with far lower risk of head injury.

"I don't really know anything that's completely safe," he said. "I think we all live in a world where there are risks and there are rewards."

Goodell said the league had made progress teaching athletes how to spot a concussion, and padded helmets for each position were being developed. "Those hits accumulate," he said. "You all know better than I do that it can create long-term damage."

Then he leaned into his own experience.

"There's so many things that I've learned through my journey playing youth sports, that there really wasn't medical care when I was playing," Goodell said. "You know, the coach was actually the doctor and that's not a good place to be. Just like me being up here speaking to neurosurgeons. I'm out of my element here."

The following summer, in June 2024, Goodell was back in Los Angeles, this time as a witness in federal court, where consumers in a class action antitrust suit had accused the NFL of colluding with CBS and Fox to overcharge them for Sunday Ticket, a subscription service that showed out-of-town games on Sundays. The case was about more than damages. It was a challenge to a linchpin of the NFL's business, the ability to sign exclusive deals with networks.

The trial was in June, the one sleepy time of year on the NFL calendar. Goodell spent a weekend prepping with Beth Wilkinson, the lawyer defending the league. Dressed in a blue suit with a blue tie, Goodell mingled with league staff and reporters outside the courtroom. If he was nervous, he didn't show it.

During his four hours on the stand, Goodell justified the league's agreements with CBS, Fox, and DirecTV, which sold Sunday Ticket, saying the companies needed exclusivity to justify investing in their products. Goodell said Sunday Ticket costs hundreds of dollars a season because it was designed for hardcore fans. He denied that the league wanted the price to be high to limit the number of subscribers and protect CBS and Fox, whose telecasts of the game were rebroadcast on Sunday Ticket.

"I think we've been very clear, not just today but throughout our period of time, that this was a premium product," Goodell said during cross-examination. "And not just on pricing but on the quality of the product itself."

There was plenty of evidence—including memos from network executives—that suggested Sunday Ticket's price was kept artificially high to limit its distribution. The jury agreed, ordering the NFL to pay almost $5 billion in damages. "It's a great day for consumers everywhere," said Bill Carmody, one of the plaintiffs' lawyers.[43]

Wilkinson argued that the plaintiffs' case was flawed. On August 1, a month after the verdict, Judge Philip Gutierrez agreed and took the unusual step of dismissing the case. It appeared that the NFL had colluded, he said, but the plaintiffs' experts failed to show that consumers were harmed, undermining the jury's calculations of damages. Goodell and the NFL had won again.

The owners, who could have been on the hook for hundreds of millions of dollars each, exhaled, and Goodell got back to what he did best: promoting the league. In August 2024, he went to Paris to watch the Olympics, which, thanks to NFL lobbying, would include flag football for the first time in 2028. He visited CBS's offices for a meet-and-greet with network executives. A few days later, he dropped by the Fanatics fan fest at the Javits Center in New York, where he mugged for the cameras with Tom Brady and pretended to bury the hatchet with him over Deflategate. At the end of August, he flew to Minneapolis, where the owners held a one-day meeting to approve changes that would let private equity firms for the first time buy up to 10 percent of teams.

Team valuations had soared so high during Goodell's tenure that it was getting harder to find buyers for even minority stakes in teams. Now the owners could raise hundreds of millions of dollars to help pay for stadiums, buy out partners, or rearrange their estates without giving up control. The Bills and Dolphins quickly cashed in. The Giants began looking into it, too.

The new rules were the latest financial milestone in Goodell's stewardship of the NFL. Back in 2010, many inside the NFL wondered why Goodell made his bold $25 billion revenue target. Now he looked like Jack Welch and Jeff Bezos rolled into one. The escalating value of the league's media deals would help the NFL hit $25 billion, but Goodell wasn't stopping. At the Draft in Detroit in 2024, he floated the idea of an eighteenth game that would push the Super Bowl into Presidents' Day weekend, further expanding the NFL's grip on the entertainment world. Players weren't happy about the idea. "Until you're the one going out there and putting a helmet on for eighteen of those games, yeah, then come talk to me," said Indianapolis Colts center Ryan Kelly, a member of the union's executive committee.[44]

But in time the NFL would likely work out a deal with the union. There was too much money at stake. New stadiums were opening, and the league was eager to find new fans overseas. International expansion was so important Goodell skipped the opening game of the 2024 season in Kansas City, where the Chiefs started the defense of their latest Super Bowl title, and flew to São Paulo, Brazil, for the NFL's first-ever game in South America.

"I thought the target was aggressive, but to be honest, achievable," Kraft said of the $25 billion goal. "I'm proud of Roger for putting it on the table to motivate everyone in the league office and the business management of teams that we all had to pull it together and try and make that happen."

The owners know Goodell will eventually retire, but they're in no rush to contemplate a world without him. He has a one-of-a-kind résumé finely tuned to running what is essentially a Fortune 500 company masquerading as a sports league.

"He's at the top of his game, he's healthy, why would he want to go anywhere else?" Khan of the Jaguars said.

The NFL has talented executives like Brian Rolapp, who began working in the league's media group in 2003 and helped the owners secure mammoth broadcast deals. He's polished and smart. But whenever his name surfaces in stories as a potential successor, other stories pop up suggesting that Goodell is in no rush to leave. And why would he? He earns gobs of money to do a job where he is in total control. He's told friends that he wishes he could leave, but he can't find a suitable replacement, something his friends doubt.

"Roger has always been good at marginalizing the marginal and exaggerating the role of the cool kids," one former league executive said. "He recognizes that he works for individuals who aren't used to hearing no and are used to being flattered, and he knows how to deal with that."

If Goodell ran a big corporation, he would have a larger, more disparate set of constituents, including millions of shareholders who would use the company's share price to measure his progress. Running the NFL is more about keeping the owners, the networks, and other business partners happy, and he knows most of them personally.

"He's more of a politician than a CEO," one executive said. Politicians often lead from behind, pleasing allies, placating enemies, and bending their values to fit the situation, something Goodell has done well. Take sports gambling. In 2012, he said a gambling scandal "could be very damaging to the NFL and very difficult to ever recover from."[45] He held that view until May 2018, when the Supreme Court overturned restrictions on sports wagering outside Nevada. Suddenly, Goodell said betting on sports was a way for fans to "engage" with the game.

By the time his contract expires in 2027, Goodell will be sixty-eight and the league's revenue will likely surpass the $25 billion revenue target he set seventeen years earlier. If Goodell succeeds in getting an eighteenth regular-season game, he'll be able to celebrate his birthday two days before Super Bowl LXI in Los Angeles. The owners will be there to celebrate with him.

"I mean, $22 billion is great, but it's just the tip of the iceberg," Colts owner Jim Irsay said. "Our brand is as great of a brand that there is. The supersizing has just begun and people younger than me that'll be there when I'm gone will be taking this thing to dimensions that you can't even imagine."

Goodell isn't paid just to make money for the owners. He's also paid to deflect criticism and solve problems, perhaps none bigger than the dangers of playing the sport itself.

7.

"ONE OF THOSE RARE EXISTENTIAL THREATS."

On a warm April day in 2013 at the federal courthouse in Philadelphia, the essence of the NFL was on trial. In the packed courtroom was a battle not over whether the league was a monopoly or whether teams can move cities, but whether football was destroying the men who played it—and whether the league had to compensate them for it.

More than four thousand former players had joined a class action lawsuit, alleging the NFL lied to them for decades about the dangers of repeated hits to the head. Untold numbers of them had cognitive and neurological problems. The suits were a profound threat to the league. Everyone knew football was a violent game. But was it *killing* players?

There would be no answers in the one-hour hearing, only arguments. The league claimed, as it often did, that the players' cases were governed by the collective bargaining agreements they signed and an arbitrator, not a judge, should hear them. The players said their claims were outside the bounds of those labor deals because they included allegations of fraud dating back to at least since 1994. That was when Commissioner Paul Tagliabue created the Mild Traumatic Brain Injury Committee—a name that underplayed the seriousness of the injuries—after New York Jets receiver Al Toon and other players retired because of concussions. Stuffed with team doctors and NFL sycophants, the committee, led by Elliot Pellman, a rheumatologist with no expertise in brain disease, repeatedly denied any link between head hits and brain damage. The group published studies with incomplete data and shoddy conclusions in the journal *Neurosurgery*, which was edited by a doctor who worked for the Giants.

The league's front began to crack in 2002 after Hall of Fame Steelers center Mike "Iron Mike" Webster died at age fifty, his body and mind shattered. A little-known pathologist in Pittsburgh, Bennet Omalu, found that Webster had chronic traumatic encephalopathy—or CTE—a brain-wasting disease linked to repeated head hits and whose symptoms included memory loss, uncontrollable anger, depression, and suicidal thoughts. The finding shook the league and the players. If banging your head in practices and games caused brain damage, then CTE might become football's version of black lung disease.

This would undermine the NFL's future. Youngsters who played football were far more likely to buy tickets and jerseys when they got older. If their parents believed their children might get brain damage playing the game, they might steer them toward baseball, soccer, and other sports. Fewer kids playing football would lead to fewer fans, which over time could erode the league's finances.

An experienced lawyer, Tagliabue knew liability when he saw it. So did the owners, who in 2002 approved the purchase of "catastrophic loss" insurance from Lloyd's of London that covered up to $1 million per player. In a deposition in 2022, Tagliabue denied orchestrating the committee's work. But he didn't need to. The doctors on the committee did the league's bidding, attacking Omalu's findings and the work of other researchers who began to detail the cognitive and neurological damage to football players. The committee even ignored the NFL's own disability board, which in 1999 ruled that Webster's rattled brain was caused by years of playing football.[1]

Bad-mouthing Omalu backfired. Alan Schwarz at *The New York Times*; Peter Keating, Steve Fainaru, and Mark Fainaru-Wada at ESPN; Jeanne Marie Laskas at *GQ*; and other reporters exposed the committee's flawed research. They also wrote about players suffering from dementia and other illnesses, as well as the families who cared for them. The stories attracted the attention of lawmakers on Capitol Hill, who in 2009 called in Commissioner Roger Goodell to explain the league's questionable research and disregard for former players.

"The NFL sort of has this blanket denial or minimizing of the fact that there may be this link," Representative Linda T. Sánchez (D-Calif.), said to Goodell at the hearing.[2] "And it sort of reminds me of the tobacco companies pre-'90s when they kept saying, 'Oh, there's no link between smoking and damage to your health.'"

In 2011, players by the hundreds began suing the league seeking damages. A year later, Junior Seau, one of the league's most beloved players, shot himself in the chest with a .357 Magnum.[3] Just forty-three, he left behind four children, a mountain of debt, and a pattern of bizarre behavior. His brain was sent to the National Institutes of Health, where scientists determined that he, too, had CTE.[4]

Webster, Andre Waters, and other players found with CTE were known to football fans, but Seau was adored throughout Southern

California, where he grew up and starred for thirteen seasons. Charismatic, generous, and handsome, he was one of the greatest linebackers ever. His suicide shocked the nation and brought CTE into the mainstream.

Goodell and the owners were being forced into a corner. They pushed to have the hundreds of cases consolidated and moved to Philadelphia, where Anita B. Brody, a senior judge appointed by George H. W. Bush in 1989, took over.

In April 2013, she called a hearing on the league's motion to move the cases to arbitration. Both sides hired lawyers who had argued in front of the Supreme Court. Paul Clement, a former U.S. solicitor general, represented the NFL and David Frederick, who won billions of dollars in settlements with Merck and Pfizer, represented the players.

Brody began by trying to cut the tension in the courtroom.

"Please take off your ties and jackets," she said.[5] "I don't want anyone fainting."

Brody never ruled on the league's motion. She wrote an opinion and put it in her desk, then suggested to both sides that one of them would be angrier than the other if she ruled. If she agreed with the NFL's argument, most of the cases would have been thrown out. But the claims brought by players who played part or all of their careers between 1987 and 1992, when there was no labor agreement, might continue. There would be far fewer players—maybe just a few hundred—but their cases would remain in the news.

In the past, the owners took a hard line in court, and Goodell was driven by what the owners wanted. But publicly he had to tread carefully between defending the league and not belittling the players.

The league and owners knew it would be a public relations disaster if players with dementia took the stand. Packers president Mark

Murphy, a lawyer and former NFL player, didn't think the players' lawsuits had a lot of merit, but continuing to fight them could backfire. "A lot of the players could be very sympathetic plaintiffs," he said in a deposition. "You go to jury trials in some favorable venues in cities where NFL teams have left and gone to other cities. You know, I saw that there was a pretty big risk for the league."

In 2018, Brad Karp, the lead outside counsel for the NFL in the concussion cases, reflected on the league's thinking years earlier. The NFL, he said, "has historically engaged in scorched-earth litigation."[6] But the stakes in the concussion case were far higher because "the risk of cognitive impairment as a result of playing professional football is one of those rare existential threats."

Four months after the hearing in Philadelphia, just before Brody said she would issue her ruling, the league and former players announced a landmark settlement. The league would set aside $765 million to compensate players with ALS, Alzheimer's disease, and other illnesses. Every former player could get tested to establish a baseline that could be used later to determine if his cognitive functions had slipped. Critically, the players would not have to prove that football caused their ailments.

In return, the players relinquished their rights to sue the NFL for concussion-related issues, giving the league "global peace." This peace came cheap: Each team would pay about $24 million over the life of the sixty-five-year settlement, and the owners would get some of that money back from their insurers. The owners paid star quarterbacks more than that for just one season.

It was the NFL at its most bloodless, sidestepping a major controversy by throwing money at a problem. No player or owner would have to testify, and the league would not have to admit fault. Before the settlement was announced in August 2013, Goodell stopped by the office of Paul Hicks, his chief communications strategist, to ask what he thought of the proposed deal.

"I said, 'Well, I believe that we can win legally on the merits, but we'd be losing public opinion because we'd be litigating for multiple years and it would be a distraction to the league and it would damage our growing player health and safety reputation, and so I'm all for settling," Hicks said in a deposition in 2022. "Then I remarked, 'It's not my money.' He laughed and left."

Chris Seeger, the lead plaintiff's attorney, wanted to settle, too. Brody could have thrown out many players' claims. What's more, no sports league had ever agreed to pay so much to settle, and that money would be available soon, not after lengthy trials. The players wouldn't have to prove that their problems were caused by hits absorbed while playing in the NFL. The players, though, would discover years later that the NFL pushed for more rigorous definitions of dementia that made it harder for them to be compensated.[7]

When the settlement was announced, most players were not worried about the fine print. They were angry that Tagliabue, Goodell, and the owners would not have to take the stand. Some players felt Seeger and the other lawyers settled quickly because they wanted to divvy up the $112 million in legal fees the NFL agreed to pay. Still other players felt the settlement was too little, too late.

"You can't buy your brain back," said former running back Thomas Jones, who was thirty-five and worried about the effects of the concussions he said he suffered.[8] "That's the problem. Everybody looks at the money—not the actual issue. There are family members dealing with these players that have problems walking, that don't even remember their names."

Jones planned to donate his brain to Boston University, the leading CTE brain bank. He was also producing a documentary called *The NFL: The Gift or the Curse?*

The announcement of the settlement was just the beginning of a new, torturous phase before players could be paid. Some plaintiffs' lawyers said the $765 million would quickly run out and leave sick players with nothing. Actuarial studies commissioned by the NFL to justify the $765 million estimated that nearly a third of the twenty thousand or so retired players would develop cognitive problems and that their conditions would likely emerge at "notably younger ages" than in the general population.[9] The figures were eye-opening, considering the league had for years denied any links between football and brain damage.

Karp said the projections deliberately overstated injury rates to prove there would be enough money. But Judge Brody pushed both sides to revisit their deal and "uncap" the potential damages. An open-ended settlement was a major ask of the NFL, particularly when Jones and other owners questioned whether football might cause brain damage.

"We don't have that knowledge and background and scientifically, so there's no way in the world to say you have a relationship relative to anything here," Jones said in 2016 after Jeff Miller became the first NFL executive to publicly admit that there was a link between football and brain disease.[10] "A big part of this is prevention. But the other part of it is to basically understand that we don't know or have any idea that there is a consequence as to any type of head injury in the future."

Karp reassured the owners new provisions would be added to allow the league to challenge claims in the name of preventing fraud. Brody signed off on the revamped settlement.[11] Now the players had to vote on it.

Most class action settlements are approved because many claimants do not vote and by default, they are deemed to have accepted the deal. In the NFL settlement, about two hundred retired players opted out so they could continue to sue the league. (Almost all of them eventually settled.) Another seven players opposed the deal because, among other things, players who died after 2015 and were found to have CTE would be excluded, excluding potentially hundreds of claims in the future.

"At the end of the day, players just want a fair shake," said Sean Morey, a wide receiver for nine seasons and one of the seven objectors.[12] Thoughtful and passionate, Morey wanted his fellow players to get paid. But the deal, he felt, let the league off the hook. "In my mind, this is everything the N.F.L. wanted."

In some ways, Morey wasn't wrong. In October 2014, Robert Stern, a neuropsychologist at Boston University who was part of a team studying CTE, submitted a sixty-one-page declaration to the court that said players suffering some of the most disturbing symptoms associated with CTE would receive no money because the tests to evaluate them focused primarily on changes in cognition, or knowledge and understanding.

The settlement did not test for other symptoms, he said. Many former players "have significant changes in mood and behavior (e.g., depression, hopelessness, impulsivity, explosiveness, rage, aggression), resulting, in part, from their repetitive head impacts in the N.F.L., that have, in turn, led to significant financial, personal, and medical changes, including, but not limited to: the inability to maintain employment, homelessness, social isolation, domestic abuse, divorce, substance abuse, excessive gambling, poor financial decision-making, and death from accidental drug overdose or suicide," Stern wrote.

But many players backed the deal, flawed as it was, because they were eager to apply for payments of up to $5 million. Former fullback

Kevin Turner was at the front of the line. Turner, who was friendly with Morey, was one of the two named plaintiffs in the suit. At just forty-five, he had ALS and needed twenty-four-hour care. He wanted to live long enough to get a payout to help his three children.

In 2014, Turner left his family in Alabama and moved to Florida to receive treatments designed to slow the advance of his disease. Each day, he stood in a shower that rinsed him with water that had the chemical content of the water in his body. This gave him a shot of energy even though he could barely use his arms, and his speech was so slurred that the Siri software on his iPhone could no longer understand him.

"I can empathize with players," Turner told me that summer. "But for me and people like me, time is a luxury we don't have."

Turner said that he was reluctant to sue the league that had given him so much. But he sustained more concussions than he could count and was convinced that they contributed to the ALS that was killing him. The NFL should have warned him.

"I remember times when I went back into games when I shouldn't have," he said. "I wasn't given all the information to make that decision for myself."

Turner, who stopped his two sons from playing football, was receiving money from two NFL disability plans. But the bills were piling up—doctors, nurses, treatments, equipment. Five million dollars from the settlement might seem like a lot, but it can cost tens of millions of dollars to keep someone with ALS alive.

"Everyone is focusing on the number and how much am I going to get," he said. "But I am looking at it as how it would help me live longer."

Turner never saw the money he fought for. He died in 2016 while the settlement was being appealed.[13] Turner's family filed a claim on his behalf after the spigots finally opened in 2017. Players quickly discovered dozens of new hurdles: difficulties getting tested, getting preexisting diagnoses approved, and surviving the challenges and appeals by the league. In the first year, only about 10 percent of the roughly 1,400 claims were approved.[14] Those who were paid had money deducted by Medicare for services already provided; lawyers took fees of as much as 35 percent.

In time, more players had their claims approved and, as Judge Brody suspected, the original settlement of $765 million was not enough. By the spring of 2024, 1,863 players or their families had been awarded $1.4 billion.[15] About 20,500 players, or well over 90 percent of all retirees or their families, registered for the settlement. The small number of cases with the clearest diagnoses—ALS and CTE found posthumously—were approved quickly.

But the largest basket of players filed claims for Alzheimer's disease and dementia and were approved at far lower rates. Grant Iverson, a neuropsychologist at Harvard skeptical of the links between CTE and repeated head trauma, was one of several experts hired to develop the baseline tests and protocols for evaluating players.

In 2020, lawyers discovered that Black players who filed dementia claims were denied more often than white players. The root cause, they said, was algorithms designed to estimate a player's cognitive abilities years before he joined the NFL. The algorithms known as "race norming" assumed that Black players were less intelligent before they entered the NFL, so in theory a Black player with dementia would look less demented than a white player later in life.[16] As a result, many Black players were not considered demented under the settlement.

Two Black former players, Najeh Davenport and Kevin Henry, whose dementia claims had been denied, sued the NFL in September 2020. The NFL insisted the algorithms were widely used and there was no intent to discriminate against Black players. But the NFL was sensitive to accusations of racism. Less than two years earlier, the league paid several million dollars to former 49ers quarterback Colin Kaepernick, who had accused the owners of blackballing him. The NFL agreed to eliminate race as a factor when evaluating dementia claims, and many Black players refiled their claims and were approved.

Still, one lawyer who has litigated against the NFL on behalf of players many times said the NFL had plenty of other tools to deny claims.

"We know the NFL doesn't need to use race to screw over players," said Brad Sohn, a Miami-based trial lawyer who was a candidate for the NFLPA's executive director position.

The NFL had a long history of denying benefits to retired players, some of whom cynically claimed the league's mantra was "delay, deny, and hope you die." The league's disability plan is jointly administered by the league and the players union and is funded from the players' share of the league's revenue. In 2007, union chief Gene Upshaw and Goodell were hauled in front of Congress to explain why so few players received benefits. The NFL said just 317 players qualified for benefits worth about $20 million, a pittance to a multibillion-dollar league. Upshaw was criticized for stating that the Players Association didn't represent retired players.

"The NFL is trying to distance themselves from liability for all the carnage left behind by our NFL concussions—just as tobacco companies fought like hell to deny the links between smoking and cancer," Brent Boyd, an offensive lineman with the Minnesota Vikings, said at the hearing. Boyd, whose claims were denied, said the disability plan administrators were "using their tactics of delay, deny, and hope that I put a bullet through my head to end their problem."[17]

Over time, the disability plan loosened its restrictions and doled out more than $300 million in 2023. But when claims are approved, most players receive a lower tier of benefits because the plan deemed their injuries not *directly* suffered on the field. The problem is that unlike, say, a factory worker who loses an arm, most football-related injuries emerge years after players retire.

"The money is already promised to the players, so why does the board go out of its way to make it more complicated?" said Paul Scott, who handled claims at the disability board before starting a company to help players apply for benefits. "It's easier to deny a guy. They didn't look at the big picture."

For many players, disability benefits are not enough. David Lewis was a hard-hitting linebacker for seven seasons, and by his forties he qualified for disability payments and the 88 Plan, a benefit for players with dementia, Alzheimer's, and Parkinson's.

"I've had sprains, broken knuckles, hyperextended elbows, nerve problems in my neck, shoulders," Lewis told me in 2018, when he was sixty-four.[18] "I'd be guessing how much concussions I had."

I met Lewis through a friend who told me not to visit him before 11 a.m. because his medications needed time to kick in. Lewis said he had type 2 diabetes, a kidney ailment, and a congested heart from hypertension. Weighing more than three hundred pounds, he was unable to exert himself much.

"As time went on, all the sickness started to add up," he said. Lewis died less than two years later.

Other players leave the league with addictions. Aaron Gibson, an offensive lineman drafted in 1999, first took painkillers in his rookie year after undergoing shoulder surgery. The pills were readily available from team trainers and doctors. He believed he could stop once he left the league. But after he washed out of the NFL, he played in an indoor football league, where pills were even easier to obtain. His habit got so bad he took as many as two hundred pills a day.

"If I didn't play in the NFL, I know I wouldn't have been in this situation," he said, referring to his life as a "full-on pill addict." While he ran a company that provided bodyguards, he would search for doctors willing to write prescriptions. After pharmacies cut him off, Gibson went to pain clinics and even senior centers, where elderly residents sold him their pills.

Gibson kicked the habit in 2016 with the help of his wife, Brigitte, a sports massage therapist who helped address the pain that drove him to take so many pills, stretching the muscles and tendons in his neck, back, and legs. As the pain subsided, so did his intake of opioids. He had surgeries on his hips, feet, and mouth, but was so fearful of a relapse he took only Tylenol. I visited Gibson after one surgery and was led to his bedside. He was dizzy with pain but determined to ride it out.

"They are a road that I will never go down again," he said.[19]

The NFL tried to counter accusations that it did not care about retired players by trying to change the narrative. In 2010, Goodell hired Paul Hicks to help create a coherent strategy. Rather than defend the NFL, as his predecessors had done, Hicks focused on the future. The league would "not wait for the science" to decide if head hits caused brain damage. It would be proactive.

"I didn't spend one ounce of effort on anything that happened before 2010," Hicks said in a deposition in 2022.

In November 2010, Hicks sent Goodell a twenty-eight-page presentation entitled "The Gathering Storm," a plan to "begin the process of thinking about all that is ahead in a holistic fashion." It started by acknowledging how the issue of brain damage and football, previously a dispute between scientists, was now national news. *Sports Illustrated* ran a cover story on concussions in football, and *The New Yorker* wrote about the "state of football." Hicks urged Goodell and his staff to "embrace the crisis rather than minimize or deflect it."

"Becoming known as a 'dangerous and unworthy' enterprise is a unique and sustained threat capable of doing significant brand damage," one slide read. He cited James Collins, author of *How the Mighty Fall*, who said that institutions failed because of hubris and denying risk. Hicks pointed to boxing as an example of a sport that had become irrelevant.

At the time, the league was negotiating to extend its collective bargaining agreement. Hicks urged the league to take the "high road" with the union, which had been pushing for more player safety.

"If you are going to eat shit, don't nibble," he wrote.

With concussions, the league should "hit back very aggressively" but not "try the case in the media." The league, he said, "cannot be seen as hiding behind a legal strategy as it implies guilt." The league shouldn't "underestimate the cultural impact."

Goodell disbanded the Mild Traumatic Brain Injury Committee and created the Head, Neck and Spine Committee, which sounded like it was staffed by orthopedists, not neurologists. New doctors and researchers were brought in, including a few, like Kevin Guskiewicz, who had been critical of the old committee. The league focused on making the game "safer" by changing rules to reduce or eliminate dangerous plays. The league invested in "solutions" like new helmets. Neurologists were hired to help spot concussed players during games. The league donated tens of millions of dollars to researchers at Boston University, Harvard, Michigan, and other institutions.

Remarkably, Elliot Pellman, the former chair of the committee that pumped out fake science, still advised the league. In 2009,

Lance Lopes, a lawyer for the Seattle Seahawks, wrote to Ray Anderson, the head of football operations at the NFL, to ask why Pellman was still around.

"You need to know that I am told he has little respect around the league from the team physicians," Lopes wrote. "Our doctors can't understand why the N.F.L. continues to use him, and they represent to me (though hearsay) that most of their peers feel the same way. Frankly we feel the NFL needs to look elsewhere for expertise in areas of head trauma, turf injuries, and a host of other areas."

The concussion crisis was so acute, the NFL began to worry about the pipeline of young players. At a league meeting, Charlotte Jones, Jerry's daughter, presented the president of USA Football, a nonprofit group that focused on youth football, with a giant cardboard check for $45 million. This would pay for clinics to teach moms how to tackle without using their heads, a somewhat comical effort to assure them that their sons could play football safely.[20]

"I mean, the NFL is the professional league at the top of the food chain," Hicks said in a deposition. "It was our responsibility to do the right thing for ourselves and also do the right thing for the game at every level. That was Commissioner Goodell's mantra to all of us."

The "safe tackling" program wasn't quite Joe Camel, the mascot used by tobacco giant RJR to get kids hooked on cigarettes. But critics said the program was fantasy. Kids as young as six years old would still be involved in collisions that scientists believed contributed to cognitive and neurological problems later in life. Even Goodell acknowledged this. "It doesn't take a lot to jump to the conclusion that constant banging in the head is not going to be in your best interest," he told *Time*.[21]

But as always, Goodell toggled back to fuzzy phrases that suggested prudence and practicality. The "science was not settled" and "more work needs to be done," he told *Time*. These statements were not untrue, but they were deflection. Science is never "settled," but that doesn't mean slamming your head at high speeds is recommended.

Goodell became practiced at telling audiences, like he did at the Harvard School of Public Health in 2012, that the NFL could have it both ways, focusing "relentlessly on player health and safety, while also keeping the game fun and unpredictable."[22]

Every so often, the commissioner would slip. Speaking to reporters before the Super Bowl in 2016, he offered an array of bromides. "Our agenda starts with focusing on growing and improving the game in every area," he said. "It always starts, and there is no higher priority, than player safety."

But then he was asked about high school players dying from injuries suffered on the field. "In light of that, do you still feel comfortable encouraging parents of teens and preteens to play tackle football through initiatives like USA Football and Play 60?" a reporter asked.

Goodell said the league, through USA Football, was teaching the "right kind of techniques." Then he freelanced.[23]

"From my standpoint, I played the game of football for nine years through high school," he said. "I wouldn't give up a single day of that. If I had a son, I'd love to have him play the game of football. I'd love to have him play the game of football because of the values you get. There's risks in life. There's risks to sitting on the couch."

While Goodell publicly tried to convince fans and parents the game was safer, he privately urged his staff to push back against what they considered inaccurate stories and research that undermined the league's mission. In February 2012, Goodell sent an email to Pellman, Hicks, and other executives and told them that a doctor on the *Charlie Rose* show said that if a person had a gene that made them predisposed to developing dementia, a concussion in football would raise the likelihood of getting dementia by 15 percent. Goodell cited a different study showing that NFL players got dementia at rates consistent with the broader population.

"We should get tape and challenge this," he told them. "We are going to engage in the ground war to eliminate these irresponsible comments."

The NFL's campaign to question the media and scientists at times went too far. In 2015, Junior Seau was to be inducted into the Pro Football Hall of Fame. He was not the first player to enter the Hall posthumously, but he was the first to commit suicide and later be found with CTE. When his family was told about his selection in February that year, Seau's daughter Sydney said that her dad wanted her to introduce him if he was ever inducted.

A few months later, officials from the Hall told the Seaus that Sydney would not be able to speak on her father's behalf, and that a video tribute would be played instead. Sydney and her mother, Gina, felt the Hall, and by extension the NFL, were afraid that she would bring up Junior's death, something Sydney insisted she had no intention of doing.

For months, I had been asking lawyers for the Seaus for an interview with his family and was politely rebuffed each time. Just weeks before the induction ceremony, I flew to San Diego to make one last appeal. The day before I was set to return to New York, the lawyers told me to visit their offices the next day. When I arrived, Gina and Sydney were waiting. They quickly got to the point: The Hall was blocking Sydney from speaking.[24] For the next three hours, we talked about Junior's love of football, his children, and San Diego, as well as his chaotic decline. Through tears, Sydney said she only wanted to tell fans about her dad's life, not his death.

"I just want to give the speech he would have given," she said. "It wasn't going to be about this mess."

The Hall of Fame told me Seau's death had nothing to do with its decision; it was about time management. In the past, presenters on behalf of deceased players often repeated what was in the video tributes, so the Hall eliminated the speeches to save time.

The Hall, while nominally independent of the NFL, would not want to embarrass the league, though. David Baker, the Hall's leader at the time, was close to Goodell and once said that he and his executive team were "the Knights Templar of the holy game of football."[25] He said the Hall had no plans to acknowledge the issue of concussions, unlike baseball's Hall of Fame, which has confronted the topic of steroids. Baker suggested that the concussion-related lawsuits against the NFL were a money grab.

Sympathy for the Seaus forced the Hall to compromise: Sydney would be interviewed live on stage by Rich Eisen of the NFL Network just as her father's bronze bust was unveiled.[26] As she spoke to Eisen, *The New York Times* published her entire speech online.[27] In it, she made no references to her father's brain damage.

"The reason why this honor is so hard to accept is because we had always envisioned him still being here to accept it," Sydney wrote.

The NFL's attempts to shape the public's perception of football included donating tens of millions of dollars to groups studying different aspects of concussions and CTE. One of the largest grants was a $30 million pledge to the National Institutes of Health. In 2013, $14 million of that money paid for an investigation of CTE led by Dr. Ann McKee, a neuropathologist at Boston University who found the most cases of the disease in football players. McKee, who grew up a Packers fan in Wisconsin, believed that CTE would likely be found in many more players. Still, the NFL said its pledge came with no strings attached, and McKee got her grant.

About six weeks before Junior Seau's induction ceremony in 2015, though, Pellman wrote to Maria Freire, who ran the foundation at the NIH that handled private donations. Pellman told her he had heard that the National Institute of Neurological Disorders and Stroke, a division of the NIH, was "close to signing off on awarding Boston University" the remaining $16 million for a long-term study of CTE. "There are many of us who have significant concerns re BU and their ability to be unbiased and collaborative," he wrote. Pellman asked Freire to "slow down the process until we all have a chance to speak to figure this out."

The NFL said it would not influence how its money was spent, yet one of its medical advisors was trying to block a study that was already vetted and awaiting final approval. The grant was not to Boston University but involved about fifty researchers at about a dozen institutions, including BU.

Stern, the neuropsychologist at BU who'd submitted the declaration criticizing the proposed settlement with the retired players, was the main contact for the research group. It was later disclosed that the NFL was trying to steer some of the $16 million to another group of doctors that included Guskiewicz, the former critic now advising the NFL, and Richard Ellenbogen, a neurosurgeon who was cochair of the NFL's Head, Neck and Spine Committee. Their study was less focused on CTE.

Freire forwarded Pellman's email to Walter Koroshetz, the head of the National Institute of Neurological Disorders and Stroke, which was overseeing the CTE studies.

"Yes we knew this was coming," he wrote. "Lot of history here. But our process was not tainted and all above board. The grant will go to a multisite ground around the country. NINDS will manage it. The data will be believable and unbiased. Trouble is of course that the group is led by the people who first broke the science open and NFL owners and leadership think of them as the creators of the problem."

After ESPN broke the story months later,[28] the NFL denied it tried to influence how its grant money was used. By then, a congressional investigation began to look at whether the NFL, an outside donor, tried to tamper with a confidential process at a government agency. The investigation found that the "N.F.L. improperly attempted to influence the grant selection" and that members of the Head, Neck and Spine Committee "played an inappropriate role in attempting to influence the outcome of the grant selection process."

The NIH decided to pay for the grant on its own, and the NFL ended its partnership without its $16 million being spent.[29] Pellman finally left the league quietly.[30] Ellenbogen left the committee, though he was cleared by his university of any wrongdoing.[31]

A year after the debacle, Roger Goodell went to the Jets practice facility in New Jersey during training camp for a town hall with season ticket holders. These events were typically controversy free. But that day, a fan asked Goodell about CTE. Jamal Adams, the Jets' rookie defensive back sitting next to Goodell, jumped in.

"I'm all about making the game safer," Adams said. "But as a defensive player...I'm not a big fan of it. But I get it.

"But I can speak for a lot of other guys that play the game," he continued. "We live and breathe it and this is what we're so passionate about. Literally, I would—if I had a perfect place to die, I would die on the field."[32]

Goodell and the NFL had spent a decade trying to counter allegations it didn't care about the dangers of football. This wasn't just a public relations strategy; it was a legal and financial imperative. Yet Adams showed that some young men who played the game were not getting the message. The league had a lot more work to do.

8.

"THE SMARTEST GUY IN THE ROOM AND HARDLY ANYONE KNOWS HIM."

Baseball fans think their sport is complex because they can understand it. Football fans know their sport is complex because they can't.

—David Plotz, *New Republic*

Joel Bussert looks like a computer programmer from when floppy disks were a thing in the 1970s. Soft-spoken and shy yet confident and precise in everything he says, he could pass for a stern librarian. And for four decades, Bussert was one of the NFL's most influential yet largely unknown employees.

Squirreled away in the football operations department, he was senior vice president of player personnel and football operations and oversaw the NFL's rule book, though his job was far more than that. Bussert had a freakish knowledge of how and why rules were introduced, revised, and eliminated, and he knew the data and reasoning behind each move. He was the guy whom coaches, general managers, and owners consulted when they wanted to tweak rules to produce more scoring, speed up the game, or eliminate dangerous plays. Like the Wizard of Oz, Bussert seemed to live behind a curtain yet oversaw one of the league's most important levers.

"So many times, you got the smartest guy in the room, and hardly anyone knows him," John Madden said.[1]

After he left the league in 2015, Bussert started writing a history of the NFL's rules. When we met in 2024, he had written four hundred thousand words (four times more than in this book) and said he had more to write. He intended the book to be a culmination of his life's work and an encyclopedia that football nerds would cherish.

I wanted to know how the changes to the game contributed to the growth of the NFL as a business. Bussert shared a formula he developed, which summed up the NFL as we know it: Plays plus passes plus penalties equals points.

Bussert said his formula was informed by Hugh "Shorty" Ray, a diminutive teacher and referee who a century ago tinkered with high school rule books.[2] Ray caught the attention of Bears founder George Halas, who hired him as a consultant in 1937. The Bears won four NFL titles over the following decade. Ray was the NFL's supervisor of officials until 1952, and he was voted into the Pro Football Hall of Fame in 1966 for his role in streamlining rules, improving the tempo of the game, and increasing safety.[3]

Ray "believed in plays, plays, plays and devoted his time to creating more plays," Bussert said. "That always drove my thinking."

Bussert's formula, which he called The Four P's, encapsulated what fans think of as the modern game. For the first dozen years of the NFL's existence, starting in 1920, the league used the same rules as college football, which was primarily a running game. In those days, NFL teams averaged fewer than twenty points a game *combined.* Tie scores were routine. The Chicago Bears, who won the league title in 1932, played three scoreless ties and finished 7-1-6.

Joe Carr, the commissioner from 1921 to 1939, understood that professional football needed to be more entertaining to draw fans. Colleges had built-in audiences of students and alumni that the NFL lacked. Starting in 1933, the league overhauled its rules to speed up the game and produce more scoring. The major vehicle for doing that was to enable the passing game. Players were allowed to throw passes from anywhere behind the line of scrimmage, as opposed to at least five yards behind the line. More passes meant more plays, which led to more points. It's the strategy the league has followed ever since.

"In terms of the game we wanted to create, plays drive everything," Bussert said. "We've passed for more yards than we've run for every season but three since 1939, and I assume forever after. You have to protect your skill position players like receivers, and the only way to do that is by calling fouls. And the only way you are going to achieve player safety is likewise calling fouls. Penalizing violence. Those three things produce points."

As Bussert put it in 2019 in an essay, "Offense vs. Defense": "The N.F.L. did not become America's Game by staging low-scoring exhibitions between punters and kickers."

The notion that more points lead to more compelling football is self-evident to anyone who's watched the NFL in the past forty years. Aerial duels are exciting, like the overtime thriller between the Buffalo Bills and Kansas City Chiefs in January 2022 when the lead changed hands three times and twenty-five points were scored in the final two minutes of regulation time.[4] Quarterbacks Patrick Mahomes, Josh Allen, and Joe Burrow can sling the ball to speedy receivers so effortlessly that fans and gamblers (now often the same people) remain glued to the television until the final whistle, which means more viewers for advertisements and action for sportsbooks.

These must-see games are a big reason that CBS, Fox, and other networks pay billions of dollars a year to the NFL to show games, which are the most watched programs on television.[5]

"Live sports in many ways is what it's all about right now in television programming," Sean McManus, the former head of CBS Sports, said. "It's the best way to attract a large audience."

The NFL and the networks can thank the league's founding fathers. After the NFL broke free of the plodding college game, scoring surged. From 1934, average points scored surpassed twenty per game and sometimes jumped by more than two points a season for several years after that. During World War II, when many players were in the military, scoring rose even faster. By 1947, total scoring blew past forty points per game on average and remained there with one exception until the 1970s.

The faster game drew more fans. In 1932, the year before the NFL revamped its passing rules, teams drew an average of fifty-eight thousand fans for an entire season. By 1939, attendance more than doubled to 123,000 per club.[6] In 1950, when the NFL absorbed the Colts, Browns, and 49ers from the All-America Football Conference, attendance jumped another 30 percent. By 1958, the year the Colts beat the Giants in the NFL's first sudden-death overtime game, attendance had grown another 60 percent.

Television networks took note, and broadcast rights grew as a share of league revenue. Bussert's formula became the NFL's catechism and one of the keys to unlocking its financial success.

"Our game all the way back into the 1930s and '40s has been different than the colleges," said Bill Polian, who was general manager with the Bills, Panthers, and Colts. "The passing game was predominant, and it's made for a much, much better product for television and for the fans. No one in the community makes any bones about the fact that's the way we want it to continue."

Polian spent nineteen years on the NFL's Competition Committee, a group of owners—including, at one time, Jerry Jones of the Cowboys—coaches, and general managers who propose and consider rule changes. Some are designed to speed up the game, like tinkering with the number of seconds between plays, and the use of radios in quarterbacks' helmets so coaches can call plays more quickly. Other changes were designed to protect quarterbacks and defenseless ball carriers or to recalibrate the balance between offenses and defenses.

The biggest recalibration began a few years into the Super Bowl era. Scoring began to slip in 1966 and dipped below forty points a game in 1970, the first year of the AFL-NFL merger. Defenses like the Steel Curtain in Pittsburgh and the Purple People Eaters in Minnesota were the stars. Sacks were sexy. Mean Joe Greene of the Steelers starred in a Coca-Cola commercial. On offense, the running game dominated. O. J. Simpson became the first player to rush for 2,000 yards in a season, in 1973. The Dolphins had two 1,000-yard rushers in 1972. Franco Harris and Tony Dorsett were glamour boys.

The Super Bowls of this era were low-scoring slugfests, which irked Pete Rozelle. The Packers won the first two Super Bowls in blowouts. None of the next eight Super Bowls topped forty points combined. Super Bowl IX between the Steelers and Vikings was a 16–6 snoozefest. Something was needed to reinvigorate offenses.

The Competition Committee—led by Cowboys general manager Tex Schramm; Dolphins head coach Don Shula; and Paul Brown, the head coach and owner of the Bengals—pushed through a wave of changes to promote more scoring. Starting in 1972, holding and other offensive fouls committed behind the line of scrimmage were marked from the spot of the previous play, not where the foul was committed, to reduce the impact of penalties. The hash marks were moved closer to the center of the field to give ball carriers more room to run.

In 1974, the goalposts were moved from the goal line to the end line to make it easier to throw and catch touchdown passes. Kickoffs were moved back five yards to the 35-yard line to encourage more kickoff returns. Offensive penalties for holding, illegal use of the hands, and tripping at or behind the line of scrimmage were reduced from fifteen yards to ten yards.

The biggest change was penalties for defenders who shoved receivers more than once three yards beyond the line of scrimmage. In the AFL, defenders used the "bump and run," a technique mastered by the Steelers in the early 1970s, to disrupt a receiver's timing. Scoring fell. Starting in 1977, defensive backs could push a receiver once within three yards of the line of scrimmage or after that point, but not both. The committee also banned defensive linemen from slapping the heads of offensive linemen to stun them.

In 1978, the committee revised the illegal contact rule again to allow a defender to hit a receiver within five yards of the line of scrimmage but not beyond except to protect himself from contact caused by a receiver. Shula championed this change because he felt five yards was easier to officiate.

"It took a while for us to figure it out," Bussert said. "The final version was the five-yard rule in 1978, and that got it done. That liberated the passing game and restored the traditional relationship between the receiver and the defender, and it started us on the way to a more traditional offense-versus-defense balance and, I would say, a more appealing game."

By 1980, 47 percent of all plays were pass plays, up from 38 percent in 1977.

Coaches like Sid Gillman, who led the San Diego Chargers in the 1960s, developed the "Vertical Stretch" passing scheme. One of his acolytes, Don Coryell, took that idea and created pass-happy "Air Coryell" offenses with the St. Louis Cardinals and the Chargers in the 1970s and 1980s. Bill Walsh, who coached at Stanford and led the San Francisco 49ers to three Super Bowl titles in the 1980s, built on their work and created the game most fans recognize today.

Bill Walsh's West Coast Offense was a catch-and-run offense that featured short, high-percentage passes quarterbacks could quickly throw to counteract pass rushers. Walsh spread his receivers and running backs across the field so quarterbacks could read the defense more easily. Walsh scripted plays regardless of the down or distance, rather than starting a fresh set of downs with a running play, the way most teams did.

"The thing that Bill understood is how difficult the quarterback position was and how difficult it was to execute on a high level," said Pete Carroll, who coached the Jets, Patriots, and Seahawks and, as a defensive backs coach with the Bills and Vikings in the 1980s, faced Walsh's high-powered offenses. "He was way ahead of everybody. There were a lot of guys who threw the ball really well, but it wasn't the same. Bill took guys like Joe Montana who did not have a great arm and formulated a system where he could be a great player."

Walsh developed the offense in the early 1970s when he was an assistant coach for Paul Brown's Bengals, and fully deployed it in San Francisco when he took over as head coach in 1979. San Francisco's offenses under Walsh featured Jerry Rice, Dwight Clark, and Freddie Solomon, and finished in the top ten in scoring eight times.

In Miami, Don Shula built a passing game based on speed. Though he championed the running game in the first half of the 1970s, Shula knew where the league was headed. Just months after losing Super Bowl XVII, he drafted Dan Marino and paired him with Mark Clayton and Mark Duper, speedy receivers who averaged 15.7 and 17.4 yards per reception in Miami. In his second season, Marino threw for more than 5,000 yards and 48 touchdowns, both single-season records, and led the Dolphins to the Super Bowl, where they lost to Walsh's 49ers, 38–16.

The Dolphins' pivot led some NFL insiders to question whether Shula crafted rules on the Competition Committee that he could take advantage of. The committee studies endless amounts of game film, so they understand the nuances and implications of rule changes better than most coaches. Bussert, though, said there was nothing underhanded.

"Some of the rules may have coincided with what was good for the Dolphins, but it coincided with what was good for the league," he said.

Years later, Shula and Polian were together on a flight and Polian asked Shula how he overhauled his offense so quickly.

"He said, 'What are you talking about? I had Marino!'" Polian recalled. "'What the hell am I going to do, run the ball?'"

Years later, Polian was also accused of using his influence on the committee. The claim stemmed from the AFC Championship Game in January 2004. The Colts had scored seventy-nine points in their two playoff games before facing the Patriots at Gillette Stadium in Foxborough, Massachusetts. They were stopped in their tracks by the freezing temperature and snow, and the Patriots defense, which harassed Peyton Manning's receivers, grabbed their jerseys, and pushed them out of bounds.[7] The Patriots intercepted Manning four times and sacked him four times in a 24–14 victory.

Polian and others at the Colts complained after the game that the referees should have called penalties for pass interference, illegal contact, and holding. Years later, Polian acknowledged that Patriots coach Bill Belichick saw that referees were not calling penalties on his defensive backs, so he encouraged them to play even more aggressively.

After the season ended, the Competition Committee, which included Polian and Colts coach Tony Dungy, approved a "point of emphasis" for defensive holding and illegal contact more than five yards from the line of scrimmage. This directed referees to strictly enforce existing rules. It was dubbed "the Ty Law Rule" after the Patriots cornerback who intercepted Manning three times in that game.[8]

Dungy denied that the committee pushed for stricter enforcement because the Colts lost. "It wasn't just them, and it wasn't just that game," he said. "We threw interceptions. We blew coverages. We missed tackles. They forced some things and took advantage of mistakes we made."

Bussert added that enforcement of the illegal contact rule had been a problem that entire season. Passing yards in 2003 fell to 401 yards a game, an eleven-year low.

"Enforcement had been on my radar long before the championship games, and it was going to be at the top of the committee's agenda, regardless of the championship games," he said. "A nationally televised game always helps to bring a problem into focus."

Passing yards per game jumped to 421 in 2004, he said.

Scott Pioli, vice president of personnel with the Patriots at the time, remains unconvinced.

"There's a small group of people who steer the direction of what the rules become and what teams they're with and what their team's strengths are," he said. "I'm not mad at Bill Polian at all. I like and respect him. I'd do the same thing. But don't tell me that they're doing things that are for the good of the game. They're doing things for the good of the game while your team is in it."

The following season, with the referees calling more penalties on defensive backs, the average passing yards per team jumped ten yards per game.

More than a decade before, Polian helped popularize another innovation, the "No Huddle Offense," to wear down defenses by making it harder for them to bring in substitutes. The Bengals deployed it in 1988 to beat the Bills in the AFC Championship Game that year.

The following season, the Bills faced the Browns in Cleveland in the playoffs and were losing by ten points in the fourth quarter. Coach Marv Levy told his offensive coordinator, Ted Marchibroda, "We're not going to wait till the end of the game to go to our two-minute drill. Let's go to our two-minute drill right now."[9] Quarterback Jim Kelly led the Bills on two scoring drives and almost won the game before he was intercepted at the goal line.

Afterward, Levy told Marchibroda and offensive line coach Tom Bresnahan, "Why don't we make that our offense next year?" No team used a no-huddle offense as the basis of their *entire* offense. In the offseason, Levy, his coaches, and backup quarterback Frank Reich created a shorthand for plays that would be called at the line of scrimmage. In 1990, the Bills' "K-Gun Offense" led the league with 428 points. The team finished 13-3 and went to their first Super Bowl.

"We averaged around eighteen seconds per play and our practices were an hour and twenty minutes not because we cut out plays but because we ran them so quickly," Polian said.

That offseason, the Competition Committee studied the K-Gun because Shula thought the Bills' offense was not coming to the full set position before snapping the ball. "We went over tape after tape and it got pretty intense," Polian said. "Finally, it was the committee's consensus to leave it alone."

Sometimes, the NFL tinkered too much. In 1988, the league changed the play clock from thirty to forty-five seconds from the time the ball was signaled dead until it was snapped on the next play. This led to a decline of about seven plays a game between 1988 and 1992. Scoring dipped every year from 1990 to 1993.

In December 1993, a cover story for *Sports Illustrated* caught Tagliabue's eye. In the issue titled "Can the NFL Be Saved: 10 Ways to Revive a Boring League,"[10] King argued there weren't enough good quarterbacks, kickers were *too good*, and there were too many substitutions and a lack of "big personalities."

"No question about it, a malaise has settled over the NFL because, very simply, the game is not as good as it used to be," King wrote. "The problem: Parity is a monster unleashed."

The league trimmed the play clock to forty seconds in 1993, and scoring rose again. King was wrong about parity, though. The new labor deal signed in 1993 ushered in revenue sharing, free agency, and a salary cap, which created *more* parity, which made the game more compelling. The Cowboys, Giants, 49ers, and Redskins, the dominant teams in the years before free agency, now had the same amount of money to spend on players as the Bengals, Bills, and Browns. Starting in 1994, sixteen different teams have won Super Bowls, and eight other teams made it to the Super Bowl but lost. Three teams—the Rams in 1999, the Patriots in 2001, and the Saints in 2009—won the Super Bowl after finishing last the year before.[11]

The league's new financial framework changed how teams were constructed, and the salary cap became the most direct connection between the game on the field and the money it produced.

"There's a link between the business of the league and the game on the field," said Pioli, who also worked with the Browns, Chiefs, and other teams. "But it's like the chicken-or-egg thing. Was it the business that made the game change? Or was the game changing what made the business change? Either way, the answer is absolutely, they're intertwined."

Leigh Steinberg, one of the top agents in the 1990s, saw how the cap changed the business of football, leading teams to shift money from unproven rookies to proven starters, particularly quarterbacks. Steinberg represented Troy Aikman, Warren Moon, and Steve Young, three of the top quarterbacks of the era. When the salary cap was introduced, agents pushed for bigger signing bonuses, and to absorb those bonuses, owners offered longer deals. Wanting to preserve flexibility for his players, Steinberg introduced what he called "voidable years," which were triggered by performance targets that would allow a player to become a free agent before his contract expired.

Quarterbacks were (and still are) the most important players on the field, but money had to be allocated to other positions. In Buffalo, Polian tried to determine which players had to be kept at all costs—Jim Kelly, Thurman Thomas, Andre Reed, and so on—and which positions could be filled through the Draft, like guards, who were not as critical as centers or tackles, who had to block edge rushers. "It was really kind of a yin-yang," Polian said. "On the one hand, that position wasn't critical. On the other hand, you can find more of them in the Draft."

When he worked with Belichick in New England, Pioli helped develop a new grading scale that essentially said, "All starters are the same because the market dictates different dollars for different positions." A backup corner, for example, was not the same as a backup guard because the game changed. To defend Drew Brees and Peyton Manning, teams added fifth defensive backs—nickel backs, in parlance—to cover receivers. In New England's system, a backup defensive back was more of a hybrid. Not a classic starter, but someone who played enough that he was not a bench player, either. "Nickel corners play over 60 percent of the snaps, so how can you say that's a backup?" Pioli said. Rodney Harrison, a defensive back who played six seasons in New England, was particularly valuable because he was a safety who, when needed, could play linebacker to defend the run. "Players' values changed not just based on talent but playing time."

There was a learning curve for owners. When the salary cap was introduced, Jones and the Cowboys had won two Super Bowls with Aikman, Emmitt Smith, and Michael Irvin. Signing them to new contracts was not easy. After Dallas won its first Super Bowl, Smith's $2.8 million rookie contract expired, and he became a restricted free agent. No team offered him a contract, so he didn't report to Cowboys camp. After Dallas started the 1993 season 0-2, Smith agreed to a four-year, $13.5 million contract, the highest for a running back at the time. The Cowboys won a second Super Bowl.

Things got more complicated after the salary cap kicked in. Jones allocated nearly half his roster money to Aikman, Smith, and five other players. The remaining money went to the other forty-six players on the roster.[12]

"Jerry Jones kept backloading everything, so now he's screwed," said Charles Haley, the defensive end who won five Super Bowls with the 49ers and Cowboys.[13] "So, now the bill came due and he doesn't have the money to be able to do that."

Robert Kraft faced a similar problem when he took over the Patriots in 1994. Kraft formed a bond with some players, clouding his ability to clearly weigh the impact of their contracts on the chemistry of the team. In his second season as owner, Kraft gave Drew Bledsoe a seven-year, $41.8 million contract, then a ten-year, $102.8 million extension in 2001, the year Bledsoe got injured and his backup, Tom

Brady, took over the starting role. Kraft meddled less when Bill Belichick took over as coach and shadow general manager in 2000.

The salary cap spawned a cottage industry of experts who tried to "optimize" team rosters. Thomas Dimitroff, a scout with the Patriots and general manager of the Falcons from 2008 to 2020, was hired by Paul Tudor Jones, the hedge fund billionaire, to run SumerSports. The company uses NASA-level computer power to help teams build rosters by synthesizing a player's physical attributes like speed and mobility with their medical data and psychological metrics. The technology, he said, is designed to help coaches and general managers who often don't have time for long-term planning. During the season, coaches push their data analysts to help them prepare for the next game rather than building a more sustainable roster.

"Those data people, the majority of their time is spent with the coaches," Dimitroff said. "It is all about game planning and projections regarding the opposition. Very few of these teams hire people or have the time to focus on roster optimization. By the time they get around to free agency and the Draft, they can't get their heads above water."

Coaches became high-priced free agents, too. In the late 1980s, Bob LaMonte was the first agent to represent coaches in negotiations with owners. This created its own arms race as newer owners who came into the league with deeper pockets were willing to spend their own money to sign top-shelf coaches, much to the consternation of the more fiscally conservative multigenerational owners. "Once the billionaires took over the league, there were no boundaries," LaMonte said, adding that the average coach's salary went from around $300,000 in 1988 to about $8 million in 2024.

Free agency and the salary cap affected the Competition Committee, too. For years, the committee went to Hawaii in early March to watch game film and debate proposed rule changes. In between, they ate dinners and played golf. As a rookie on the committee, one of Polian's jobs was to drive Paul Brown's golf cart.

Tagliabue pushed the committee to move its meetings to Florida or New York because Hawaii was too far to travel. And with the introduction of the salary cap and free agency, coaches and general managers on the committee had to keep in touch with their teams about signing free agents and other personnel changes, something made harder by the time difference between Hawaii and the mainland.

"At the time that the Competition Committee was meeting, you were at the fulcrum of free agency," Polian said. "We had a lot more breaks in meetings. Somebody would get up and walk away and have to take a phone call and you knew full well what it was: some negotiation or some player movement."

With a limited number of dollars to spend on players, injuries became more costly. Bussert said the committee's "player safety era" began in 1995. Penalties for hitting defenseless players were adjusted five times during the decade to cover players beyond punt returners, quarterbacks, and wide receivers. Penalties were introduced for blindside blocks and the use of the helmet as a weapon. In the 2000s, rules were tweaked to create more touchbacks and fewer kick returns, both dangerous plays.

Rich McKay, who has been on the Competition Committee for three decades, said by the 1990s the committee had more data to analyze to determine what blocks caused injuries, or which injuries were most prevalent during kickoffs.

"We were having discussions about it in the past, but we didn't have the data," he said. "We only had video and folklore."

To owners, player injuries equal dollars lost. A sidelined star—particularly a quarterback—can send a season spiraling. Injuries can also derail a career. In 2015, more than 450 players—roughly one-quarter of the league—missed at least one game because of injury, costing the owners $400 million in salaries to players out of uniform. That number grew to more than 550 players in 2022, and their salaries lost topped $600 million.[14]

McKay said the changes to emphasize safety opened the middle of the field for receivers, and quarterbacks could stand in the pocket longer. "It allowed quarterbacks to throw the ball and go to bed at night not worried about what happened to the receivers," McKay said. "You didn't have to live on the perimeter. Now, you run all these routes in the middle because he's not getting hit in the head."

McKay said the Competition Committee didn't manipulate the rules to increase scoring, but coaches and many defenders were unhappy with the changes. Steelers linebacker James Harrison, who was fined six times and suspended once during his fifteen-year career, criticized the efforts to make the game safer.[15] On a podcast in 2024, Harrison recounted a meeting with Commissioner Goodell after he was fined $75,000 for hitting the head of Browns receiver Mohamed Massaquoi in 2010. Harrison told Goodell and others at a disciplinary hearing that the hit was unavoidable because Massaquoi had ducked his head just before impact.

"So they're fining me because he just changed the rules on where you can hit someone," Harrison said.[16] "So we go into this meeting and there's Roger Goodell and a bunch of other cats, a ref, Merton Hanks, long neck, shaky self. And they're going through my hits, like 'What happened here, what happened here?' And Roger Goodell sitting off in the corner like the King Dookie on Turd Island."

Harrison was told that he was still responsible for a head hit even if the offensive player lowered his head.

"You don't care about anything other than the NFL looking like they're worried about player safety, and you just wanna fine [me] so it looks good," Harrison said he told Goodell. He added, "So we had nothing else to talk about. So I left."

Harrison continued taunting Goodell. After the league was plunged into crisis following the release of a video showing former Ravens running back Ray Rice knocking out his fiancée in a hotel elevator, Harrison tagged the commissioner on X (formerly Twitter) and quoted lyrics from a Cash Box Kings song: "[It] ain't no fun when the rabbit got the gun."[17]

The NFL's emphasis on safety, though, led to a decline in concussions and scoring hit a record of 49.6 points per game in 2020. Television ratings rose as well.

"Beginning around 2008, you can see we're back in the forty-four, forty-five range, which I always argued was the sweet spot for the NFL," Bussert said. As receivers became faster and more agile, defensive backs were recruited for their speed and finesse, most notably the "Legion of Boom," the nickname given to the defensive backs on the Seattle Seahawks.

In the 1990s, passing teams were in vogue, led by the St. Louis Rams, who were dubbed the "Greatest Show on Turf." The top passer each year in the 1990s threw for an average of 4,342 yards. In the first decade of the 2000s, the average jumped to 4,609 yards. In the 2010s, the average hit 5,069 yards. In 2007, the New England Patriots became the first team to run a majority of their plays out of the shotgun.[18]

The game became so fast that referees botched calls, particularly judgmental ones like defensive pass interference. But the league knows that fans—and gamblers—must believe that what they're watching is real and fair, so instant replays are used to get it right.

The NFL's traditionalists like Paul Brown and George Young, the general manager of the Giants, were adamantly against replays. Shula, on the other hand, supported it.

"Replay was the most contentious issue I've ever witnessed in the league," Polian said. "People who were longtime friends and associates were on opposite sides of the issue."

The NFL tested instant replay in seven preseason games in 1978 but went no further. In 1986, the owners adopted its limited use. During the strike-shortened 1987 season, 490 plays were reviewed, and fifty-seven calls were reversed. In 1988, the owners voted 20–5 to continue using instant replay for a third season. But support waned because of the clunky technology and delays, and in 1992, the owners voted 17–11 to discontinue using it.

Browns owner Art Modell defended the instant replay in a losing cause. "It's there, everybody can see it, and we're not using it," he said.

Then on December 6, 1998, the New York Jets faced the Seahawks in a game with playoff implications. The Jets were tied with the Miami Dolphins for first place in the AFC East and in the hunt for their first division title in nearly three decades. Optimism—that rarest of emotions at Jets games—was in the air that day.

At 6-6, Seattle was vying for a wild card berth to end their decade-long playoff drought. The Seahawks had a 31–19 lead in the third quarter. In the fourth quarter, Jets quarterback Vinny Testaverde found rookie receiver Keyshawn Johnson for a touchdown to narrow the deficit to 31–26. Testaverde then drove the Jets to the 5-yard line. With thirty seconds remaining and the Jets facing fourth and five, Testaverde took the snap and charged up the middle. He fell just at the goal line. Head linesman Earnie Frantz signaled touchdown. The Seahawks defenders waved their arms frantically to show that the ball failed to cross the goal line. Kevin Harlan and

Sam Wyche on CBS agreed. A replay showed that Testaverde's knee touched the ground a yard or so short of the line.

Yet when the referees converged to discuss the call, they reaffirmed that Testaverde scored and, because the NFL had ditched the use of instant replay, there was no way to dispute the ruling. The Jets won, 32–31.[19]

"God's playing in some of these games, and He was on our side today," Jets coach Bill Parcells said afterward.[20]

Asked whether he scored what became known as the "phantom touchdown," Testaverde said: "It doesn't matter. It's what the ref thinks."

A debate over instant replay ignited overnight. Owners, coaches, and league executives worried that a blown call could affect a postseason game. Some suggested bringing back instant replay for that year's playoffs, but that was considered too hasty.

"Everyone's greatest fear is what happened yesterday happening in the Super Bowl," league spokesman Greg Aiello told *The New York Times*,[21] which ran an editorial calling on the NFL to reinstate instant replay. "We acknowledge today again that Testaverde hadn't scored."

In the offseason, the owners reinstated the instant replay for big plays that could change a game or season. By then, newer high-definition televisions helped referees make calls, and the league, like the millions of fans watching at home, quickly became addicted to it. It didn't stop the never-ending debates over contentious calls even as the percentage of plays reversed doubled to 58 percent between 1999 and 2022. The NFL now has robotic cameras in every stadium to speed up the time it takes to confirm whether a player is out of bounds or scored a touchdown. The league, though, had no plans to use high-speed cameras to make calls like holding or pass interference.

"I think the game needs to be officiated on the field because there does need to be the element of judgment," McKay said. "Otherwise, when you take the officiating out of the game and try to put it in a different place, I'm just nervous about what that leads to. You'd have to rewrite all the rules."

9.

A HIGH SCHOOL CAFETERIA FOR BILLIONAIRES

Amy Trask was not yet thirty when she joined the Los Angeles Raiders as a lawyer in 1987, "a man's job" in a man's league. Back then, few women outside of an owner's family held executive positions within NFL teams. But Raiders owner Al Davis had a reputation for making groundbreaking hires, including coaches of color such as Tom Flores and Art Shell. Trask had been an intern with the team a few years earlier and impressed the boss, who cared little about NFL orthodoxy. He was, as someone once quipped, as popular as income tax.[1]

Davis was forever embroiled in lawsuits, including with the NFL, so Trask had plenty to do. But one task that she sweated more than most was ensuring that Davis got his favorite seat at owners meetings. For reasons no one could remember, the NFL did not assign seats in the ballrooms and conference rooms where the owners met every few months. One owner reckoned that Commissioner Pete Rozelle thought the owners should mix and mingle. But the owners were creatures of habit and liked to sit in the same place each time, near owners who were friends and allies. Putting small plaques with each owner's name at their seats would have been simple. But for years, no one did. So underlings like Trask raced to meeting rooms hours in advance to make sure the boss had his regular spot.

"The league meetings in the room were very much like a high school cafeteria," said former league lawyer Frank Hawkins.

The rooms where the thirty-two owners and their top executives meet have had the same layout for decades. The commissioner and his staff sit at a dais with screens on both sides for presentations. When not in use, the NFL "shield" is on the screen, like a national flag. Three long tables perpendicular to the dais form the letter *E*, with four or five owners sitting on each side of the tables. The owners sit in cliques—the Maras and the Rooneys over there, Jones and Snyder over here—that serve as proxies for their status, their alliances, and their beefs.

Davis, a lone wolf, was one of the smartest readers of the room and could spot weaknesses and opportunities to exploit. He liked to sit in the last seat at the table to the commissioner's right so he could swing his chair around to the head of the table and get a full view of the meeting in front of him. It also made it easier to grab a cup of coffee.

NFL meetings aren't as formal as the U.S. Senate, but they have their traditions and quirks. The owners follow Robert's Rules of Order. There are committee meetings, quarterly gatherings, and occasional special meetings to consider urgent issues, like the sale of a team. The largest meetings are in March and alternate between Arizona and Florida at exclusive hotels like the Frank Lloyd Wright–inspired Biltmore in Scottsdale and the Breakers in Palm Beach, the marble palace built by Henry Flagler.

These annual meetings are the NFL in full. Owners and team presidents are joined by head coaches and general managers. Spouses and kids frolic by the pool during the day, and everyone is invited to the commissioner's state-of-the-league address, which for a time included guest speakers like President Bill Clinton and David Brooks, the *New York Times* columnist who spoke about the role of football in American culture.[2]

The next day, the owners get down to business in the main meeting room, where each club typically has two representatives. For the most important votes, the owners go into "executive session," where each club has only one representative present. Owners like Paul Allen of the Seattle Seahawks almost never attended meetings and dispatched his team president as his proxy. But most owners, from Rooney of the Steelers to Jones of the Cowboys to Kraft of the Patriots, are almost always there.

To the outside world, the NFL is a powerful sports league. Yet NFL owners are an idiosyncratic bunch who insist on sitting in the same spot every time, including Davis.

"There's hilarious get-the-chair stories, everybody racing to get there to put our names on the chairs," Trask said. "I would get there at five in the morning and sneak through the kitchen to put our names on chairs. I mean, getting the chairs was a big deal."

There was often a notepad left near the door so that Trask and others could scrawl their team's names. About a decade ago, the league finally started to leave small plaques with the logo of the owners' teams at their seats.[3]

For all their bravado in the business world, few owners had the temerity to take another owner's seat. The owners didn't build the world's premier sports league by throwing caution to the wind. They did it by playing the safe odds, and they took no chances when it came to their seats, too. What did they care if an assistant lost an hour of sleep? Billionaires are used to having others do things for them.

For years, the Raiders sat next to the Chargers, and near the Browns and sometimes the Broncos. Kraft of the Patriots and Jaguars owner Wayne Weaver sat facing each other at the front of the middle table, closest to the dais. Jones of the Cowboys and Snyder sat a few seats back in the middle of the middle table. Bud Adams of the Oilers sat in the front of the left table near Mike Brown of the Bengals. Dan Rooney of the Steelers and George McCaskey, the son of Bears owner Virginia McCaskey, as well as Richardson from the Panthers, sat near the Maras. Rooney would sometimes roam the room to keep tabs on mavericks like Brown of the Bengals. "He felt like if Mike wasn't sitting next to him, Mike would do something crazy," one former NFL executive said of Rooney.

For years, Broncos owner Pat Bowlen sat across from Lamar Hunt of the Kansas City Chiefs because he admired Hunt's modesty and smarts.

"Pat wanted to be in the middle, not right up front, but in the middle of the middle section," said Jim Barlow, the Broncos' finance chief in the early 2000s, who was dispatched to get his boss's seat. "He told me, 'Look for Kansas City's place holdings. I want to be across from Lamar.' I used to see those two interact quietly, two veterans who knew what was going on."

Barlow recalled how he would hear comments from the back of the room and when he turned to see who was talking, "Pat would say, 'That's just Rooney going off on some tangent.'"

When Leon Hess owned the Jets, he sat next to Wellington Mara of the Giants. Buffalo Bills owner Ralph Wilson was often on his own. Wilson sometimes groused that Hunt and Adams were celebrated as the driving forces behind the AFL even though he bankrolled other owners to keep their teams afloat.

Friendships were important, of course. But the seats represented power and status. Snyder approached Shad Khan after he bought the Jaguars from Weaver in late 2011. They knew each other because

Snyder had visited Khan's yacht in the South of France years before. Snyder wanted Khan to sit with him and Jerry Jones.

"You need to hang with us or otherwise they're going to screw you," Snyder said, without specifying how Khan might get screwed.

Khan instead followed the only advice Weaver gave him. At the meeting in Dallas where the owners approved the sale of the Jaguars, Weaver told Khan to continue to sit in the front row of the middle table.

"We got done with the meeting and Wayne said to me, 'You know where we sat?'" Khan recalled. "He said, 'Okay, now I've spent a long time getting to that spot. So, at the next meeting, you need to get here a couple of hours ahead and put your briefcase and your stuff on those seats because people are going to start messing with you.'"

Khan didn't ask Weaver why sitting there would stop anyone from messing with him. But one of the benefits of sitting in the middle was its proximity to Kraft, one of the most powerful owners in the league. Kraft led the broadcast committee and was on the finance and compensation committees, and Khan learned from watching him wield his influence.

These days, Jonathan Kraft, the oldest of Kraft's four sons, frequently represents the team, with Robert Kraft coming in and out of the meetings for discussions of topics he cares about. When he's there, Kraft plucks away on his iPad, surfing the web. Jonathan is the heir of the Patriots, but when his father is in the room, "there's no question who's number one, it's Robert," Khan said.

Microphone stands are placed between the rows for owners or executives who want to speak. Khan takes a less-is-more approach, preferring to speak only when necessary. If two people have already made a point, he doesn't want to waste time repeating it. Khan said he does most of his negotiating in smaller committee meetings.

Jones speaks—and sometimes shouts—more than anyone else. He got in battles with Alex Spanos from the Chargers, and would shout down Brown, who was often at odds with the more money-focused owners. Jones is known for his circular references, allergic reaction to punctuation, and folksy idioms. Though he could take time making his point, as the ultimate alpha male with the most valuable team, he was given a wide berth.

"Where he's going to go and how long he is going to ramble, no one knows," Khan said. "I mean, he definitely has a hall pass."

Like any high school cafeteria, there is plenty of whispering. David Modell, the son of Browns and then Ravens owner Art Modell, often cracked jokes that made Trask giggle. At one meeting, Bowlen arrived clad in black from head to toe. "Sub-Commander Marcos has entered the room," Modell whispered, a reference to the Mexican revolutionary Subcomandante Marcos, who wore black and rode horseback. Davis heard them snicker and told them to knock it off.

At another meeting, 49ers president Carmen Policy debated Jets president Steve Gutman in what Trask called a professional business dispute. At one point, one man said to the other, "You, sir, are alarmingly disingenuous."

Jack Donlan, who was representing the Tampa Bay Buccaneers, asked Trask in his Boston accent, "I heard you're pretty smart. Is 'alarmingly disingenuous' the same thing as a fucking liar?"

Donlan was a pugnacious lawyer who represented the owners' Management Council for years, so she took his question seriously. "Well, yes, I think it is, because if you wanted to call someone a liar, you would simply say they are disingenuous," she said. "But if you say you're alarmingly disingenuous, it's like saying you're a fucking liar."

Davis groused: "He didn't ask for a fucking grammar lesson."

Some disputes turned into verbal food fights. In October 2021, at the InterContinental hotel in New York, Rams owner Stan Kroenke dropped a bomb: He wanted every owner to share the cost of a $790 million settlement he was negotiating with the city and county of St. Louis, which had sued Kroenke and the league for failing to follow their own relocation guidelines.

The owners were livid. Kroenke had agreed to cover the cost of the move to LA. Now he wanted the other owners to spend hundreds of millions of dollars to bail him out. Jones, who pushed for Kroenke to move to LA, came to his defense.[4] But Mara and Kraft were not having it. They had been deposed in the lawsuit and fined for not providing financial records the plaintiffs sought.

"It was a big shouting match," one owner said.

Blowups like this are rare, but meetings can get frosty. Owners can be abrasive and have mammoth egos. During his more than two decades in the league, Snyder was so abusive that one owner who sat near him found a new seat.

"He was just a jerk over and over," the owner said, adding that Snyder was the only person he had seen put his feet on the table.

Snyder sold his team for $6 billion in 2023 to a group led by billionaire Josh Harris, who now sits near Jones.

10.

"GREED IS A GREAT SIN."

Jerry Jones has a unique way of speaking. Colloquialisms morph into mixed metaphors. Sentences run on and on—then on some more. Elliptical phrases do grammatical handstands and backflips.

But Jones's jumble of words can contain a point, something that became clear on March 11, 2011, when he told the league's top executives about the meeting between the owners, a federal mediator, and the NFL Players Association.

With the league's collective bargaining agreement set to expire that night, the director of the Federal Mediation and Conciliation Service, George Cohen, tried yet again to nudge the owners and players together. After months of halting negotiations, two extensions, and sixteen days of mediation, the sides remained far apart. The players were unwilling to give in to the owners' demand to cede an additional $1 billion, or 18 percent, of the league's revenue, and they wanted the owners to open their books to confirm they were as hard up as they claimed. The league's request for two additional regular-season games was a nonstarter. An eighteen-game season would bring in more money, but it would mean more wear and tear on the players, who wanted fewer contact practices and offseason workouts.

Without a deal, the owners vowed to lock out the players and trigger the first work stoppage in almost a quarter century. Since 1993, when a new labor deal reduced the threat of missed games, NFL revenue had doubled. Yet the owners and players were on the brink of derailing the money train. The regular season would not start for six months, but the NFL estimated that it would lose $350 million if no deal was reached by the start of the preseason in August.

When Goodell, Jones, and the other owners—Richardson of the Panthers, Hunt of the Chiefs, Mara of the Giants among them—left to meet the mediator and the players, the NFL staffers who stayed behind assumed they would be gone for hours. Instead, they returned in about thirty minutes. The owners did not take their seats, so the staff members stood up. Goodell asked Jones to explain to the group what happened.

Jones said that when he was a child, sometimes in the spring, things did not make sense. The wind would blow from a different direction, or a creek would change course. "You know, things would be crazy, things would be backwards," he said. "And the way we knew it was backwards was the owls would start fucking the chickens."

Eyes rolled, but Jones continued.

"Now if you know anything about an owl and a chicken," he said, "it's biologically impossible that they could fuck. But the owl was in there trying. And two days later, he wouldn't even look at the chicken."

Finally, someone asked Jones what the hell he was talking about.

"We offered them a deal we shouldn't have, and they rejected it," Jones said of the league's latest proposal. "We're the luckiest people in the world."

Jones wanted the league to be more aggressive at the table in part because he and others had to pay for the new stadiums they built. A lockout would hurt their bottom lines, so he went along with the league's last and best offer. But in his mind, if the players were too stubborn to accept the deal, then they would get a lockout, with the threat of missed paychecks.

DeMaurice Smith, the executive director of the Players Association, had been preparing the players for a lockout from the day he took the union's top job two years earlier. He told the owners if they wanted to extend labor talks yet again, they had to turn over ten years of audited financial records by 5 p.m.[1] The owners said the union already had access to clubs' audited financials. The league insisted they were prepared to keep talking. The union said the league was lying and bent on locking the players out.

With the two sides far apart, Smith, with the authority of the players, dissolved the union, a first step before suing the league.

Jeff Pash, the league's top lawyer, told reporters the union was intent on litigating, not negotiating. A few blocks away at the union's headquarters, Pash's counterpart, Jim Quinn, offered a rebuttal. "I hate to say this, but he has not told the truth to our players or our fans," Quinn said of Pash.[2] "He has, in a word, lied to them about what happened today and what's happened over the last two weeks and the last two years."

Before midnight, George Atallah, Smith's assistant, received an email from the league.

"I'll never forget, I was lying in bed thinking, 'I guess we're actually locked out now,'" Atallah recalled. "I was trying to figure out what it meant for tomorrow."

The next day, Tom Brady, Drew Brees, Peyton Manning, and seven other players filed a class action lawsuit in federal court in Minneapolis, which had oversight of the labor agreement forged in 1993.

A year before the lockout, the players accused the owners of cutting a side deal with the television networks to continue paying them—and not the players—if games were canceled. The union won that battle, ensuring the owners would start losing revenue at the end of the summer without a new labor deal.

Now, the Brady suit argued that the league could not lock them out because the players were no longer a union. The players used a version of this tactic in the late 1980s and it paved the way for free agency, a salary cap, and revenue sharing. But this time, the league was ready. In a statement, the NFL called the move a "sham" and said the lawsuit would "merely delay the process of reaching an agreement." The league knew that it was impossible to convince fans that billionaire owners were justified in demanding $1 billion from the players, so it appealed to their sense of loss. "We know that you want football," the league said in a statement.[3] "You will have football. This will be resolved."

The NFL turned out to be right, but not for another 136 days, the league's longest labor stoppage. For the first time in a generation, the players and the owners were at war. When their fight was over, they would agree on a new revenue sharing formula that would double the league's revenue in the following decade, to roughly $16 billion, and cement the NFL's dominance in the sports world.

Over the NFL's first century, several years stand out in the league's development as a business. In 1961, Congress passed the Sports Broadcasting Act, which let the owners jointly negotiate national television contracts. In 1966, the NFL and AFL agreed to merge and won an antitrust exemption that consolidated their monopoly on professional football. The players went on strike in 1982 and 1987 to fight for free agency, which was introduced in the 1993 labor deal.

The year 2011 is on that list, too. During the prior seventeen years, the NFL's economics exploded. Revenue soared to $8.7 billion in 2010, the year before the lockout. Middle-of-the-pack teams like the Ravens and Vikings sold for $600 million. In 2008, Steve Ross paid $1.1 billion for the Dolphins. Players finally got the paydays that athletes in other leagues were enjoying, and football's grip on American sports strengthened as lockouts and strikes plagued Major League Baseball, the NBA, and the NHL.

The seeds of the showdown in 2011 were planted in 2006 when Commissioner Paul Tagliabue and union chief Gene Upshaw negotiated their last labor deal. (Tagliabue retired soon after, and Upshaw died in 2008.) The owners gritted their teeth and signed off on the deal because they would have had to operate without a salary cap if the prior deal had expired. While labor peace was preserved, most owners felt the deal gave the players too big a share of revenue—about 60 percent before deductions—without addressing the owners' rising costs, particularly for stadiums. Jerry Jones called the six-year deal a "mean mother."[4]

Mike Brown of the Bengals and Ralph Wilson of the Bills voted against the deal. As soon as it was ratified, the owners began looking for ways to undo it. Jaguars owner Wayne Weaver called the deal the lesser of two evils, but "it turns out that Ralph was right, and he was far ahead of many of us."[5] As cochair of the owners' labor committee, Richardson vowed to claw back the $1 billion that the players won. In 2008, the owners voted to opt out of the deal at the end of the 2010 season, a year before it expired.

In theory, this gave both sides plenty of time to agree to a new deal. But Upshaw's death led to a six-month search for his successor. The players chose Smith, a former federal prosecutor with no experience in sports or unions. Smith had to get to know the two thousand players just as the threat of a lockout loomed.

Replacing Upshaw under any circumstances would have been hard. A Hall of Famer who led the union for a quarter century, Upshaw had the respect of the players and many owners. Smith renamed the union's headquarters "63 Upshaw Place" (Upshaw wore 63 during his career) and bronze plaques of Upshaw were installed in the lobby.

Smith spent his first nine months traveling to every NFL locker room to tell the players to prepare for a potential lockout, but as Atallah, his right-hand man, said, "He had an extra hurdle he had to overcome given that he never played before."

He tried to prepare the players even as he had dozens of meetings with the league. "Because it was important for me to make sure that the players understood that while I thought a lockout was inevitable, we had to be in a position to demonstrate that we did everything we could to avoid a lockout," Smith said.

Goodell was also negotiating his first labor deal. He had spent most of his career at the NFL helping owners manage problems like building new stadiums and relocating to other cities. Now the owners had an even bigger task for him: Wrest back league revenue from the players.

Goodell turned the league office into a war room and made sure every department focused not just on their daily assignments but also the looming labor strife. "They called it the 'walk-and-chew-gum' thing," one former executive said. "You're working in the officiating department, but you're chewing gum, too. What are you doing to help with the lockout? It was amazing to me how in the culture it was."

A deep recession added to the urgency. Ticket sales fell to a seven-year low in 2010, and spending on suites and club seats plummeted. The league office laid off 15 percent of its staff and froze salaries in 2009.[6] Goodell cut his $11 million compensation package (money that was repaid after a labor deal was finalized). The Giants borrowed heavily to pay for their share of the stadium they were building with the Jets, and interest on their variable-rate debt spiked.

The owners wanted to revise the formula for splitting revenue. The players' share of revenue—which paid for salaries and benefits—was based on a percentage of the league's revenue after certain costs were deducted. While the players' share of total revenue was about 60 percent, in actuality, they received closer to 52 percent after deductions that sometimes exceeded $1 billion a season. "Once the owners got wise to what the 2006 deal was, what do you think the trend was?" Atallah said. "They started putting more and more costs into the categories of expenses they could deduct," including stadium upgrades, the NFL Network, and expenses related to off-site preseason games.[7]

The exclusions, though, did not include new stadiums, which the owners wanted to build because they could keep the revenue from the club seats and suites in the new buildings. The owners tried to convince the players it was in their interest to share the costs of new stadiums because the buildings would generate more revenue that would be shared with them.

"Every owner was unhappy with the 2006 deal because of the revenue split and because of the fact that it was a disincentive to grow local revenues," said Mara, who was a labor lawyer before joining the Giants. "It was a disincentive to going out and trying to get new stadiums built. There had to be some credits for building them. Otherwise, it made less and less economic sense."

The owners wanted to opt out of the labor deal, but they were not unified in how far to push the players. Owners who inherited their team, like the Rooneys in Pittsburgh, or purchased their team decades earlier, like Wilson in Buffalo, knew there was enough money to go around. Everyone was getting richer; it was just a matter of degree.

The owners who paid nine or ten figures for their teams like Steve Ross in Miami had loans to repay and wanted to be more aggressive in negotiations.

"We have teams that won't be able to take risks to grow revenue because the margins are too small in this system," Kraft said in 2010.[8] "So why go out and do things when you're just going to lose money and trade dollars?"

Player safety, although not strictly an economic issue, was also a bargaining chip. The owners and union were criticized for not doing enough to help former players, some of whom were found to have the degenerative brain disease CTE. Hall of Fame tight end Mike Ditka publicly shamed the league and union for not doing more to help the players.

"Ain't no one going broke in football," he said.[9] "Greed is a great sin."

Then there was the clash between Goodell and Smith. Both wanted to prove their mettle to their constituents. Goodell was an NFL lifer who was chosen commissioner to make more money for the owners, who had tremendous leverage because losing even a few games would be proportionately more costly for the players, whose careers were short.

Goodell worked long hours, was punctual and organized, and he expected the same from his staff. Smith, by contrast, was a first-time labor leader and new to the NFL. He was not shy about ringing alarm bells and wanted to show that he and the union would not be pushed around.

"If Roger says, 'We're going to meet at 10 a.m. on Friday,' he's got a meeting on his calendar, he's talked to a bunch of people, he probably has notes, and he's ready to go," one former NFL executive said. "De's world is, 'Yeah, ten o'clock is good. But if I'm a few minutes late, it's no big deal. And I forgot what we're going to talk about, so

I'm going to riff.' It's not that he's unprepared or not smart or strategic, it's just a different mindset."

Atallah, one of Smith's first hires, said Smith did this deliberately. "De viewed Roger at that time with a certain level of contempt" because he was "driving the lockout train." Atallah said Smith considered Goodell as irrelevant because the real power brokers were the owners.

"He viewed Roger as somebody who was representing the interests of a group of people who wanted to stop our players from earning their money, taking care of their families, being protected on health and safety," Atallah said. "He either was driving that train or couldn't stop it. Either way, as a union leader, you have to treat him accordingly."

Both sides weaponized this friction. The players increasingly saw Goodell and the owners as aggressors. A few days after the owners locked out the players in March 2011, Smith did not mince words about the league's push to cut player pay by 20 percent, make them play two extra games, and freeze their pensions.

"The NFL publicly projected by 2027, they want to have revenue numbers of approximately $25 billion," Smith told radio host Mike Francesa.[10] "If we would have taken the *worst deal in the history of sports*, by the time they are making $25 billion off the backs, fingers, and legs of our players, our share of all revenue would be somewhere around 25 percent. My simple question to you as a fan of this sport for a long time: Does that sound fair?"

Richardson was among the owners who felt Smith was being belligerent. At an owners meeting in Orlando in 2010, a year after receiving a heart transplant, he tried to fire up his fellow owners. "We signed a [expletive] deal last time, and we're going to stick together and take back our league and [expletive] do something about it," one witness told Yahoo! Sports.[11]

Tall and imposing, Richardson had a temper. During a break in negotiations, Richardson pulled out his flip phone and left a voice mail for Raiders owner Al Davis. "Al, this is Jerry," Richardson said. "Call me back, but don't leave a message because I don't know how this fucking phone works."

He was a hard-ass at the negotiating table. A day before the Super Bowl in 2011, Sean Morey, a wide receiver on the union's bargaining committee, reeled off statistics about player safety and the average length of their careers. "You guys made so much [expletive] money," Richardson said.[12] "If you played three years in the NFL, you should own your own [expletive] team."

In the same meeting, Richardson gave a speech about team finances and turned to Peyton Manning. "Do I need to help you read a revenue chart, son?" he said, according to Jay Feely, a player present at the meeting.[13] "I need to help break that down for you because I don't know if you know how to read that."

Several owners said this was just Jerry being Jerry. The players and their lawyers saw it differently. "I give Jerry Jones the benefit of the doubt," said Jeffrey Kessler, the players' outside counsel. "I do *not* give Jerry Richardson the benefit of the doubt of whether he was being condescending or not, and I'm happy to go on the record with that."

Indianapolis Colts center Jeff Saturday, a lead negotiator for the players, was equally annoyed. "We used to say this all the time, the players make the league, right? But I feel like at times Jerry felt like the owners had created this thing as opposed to the other way around."

Jerry Jones was as eager as Richardson to get a good deal. But Jones believed he could charm anyone, and many participants said he used folksy phrases at key junctures to move the talks along. "Fellas, we're getting to the point where we're circumcising mosquitoes," Jones said when he thought everyone was getting lost in the details.

Jones claimed he could sell the players on an eighteen-game season. Mara told Jones there was no chance the players would accept it. "Jerry, if you go in there and sell them on 18 games, I will wear a Cowboys jersey in Times Square every day for the next week," Mara told him.[14] "We all go in there, as soon as he mentioned 18 games, 'No way. Absolutely not. We're not even discussing.'"

More conciliatory owners like Mara were viewed the same. "No matter how they treated us, when it came down to money and the decisions, it was big bank take little bank, and we had to be as strong as we possibly could," said Steelers safety Ryan Clark, who was on the negotiating team. "I think from a negotiating standpoint, the big-money guys, Jerry Jones, they're the loudest. But the Rooneys and the Maras, they still want the same things. They just approached you differently. It wasn't like any owner was on our side. It just meant some owners wouldn't disrespect us the way others would."

There were no games to cancel during the first weeks of the lockout. But free agency was delayed, and offseason workouts were canceled as the two sides went to court. District Court Judge Susan Nelson heard arguments about whether the owners could lock out the players. The two sides were also still in mediation, though neither side had an incentive to negotiate before Nelson ruled. "It would be hours and hours where we just sit in a room, hang out, BS, and our representative would come back and say, 'Oh, the NFL wants this, NFL wants this,'" said Ben Leber, the Minnesota Vikings player representative. "'And we're not going to budge. And by golly, they're trying to take advantage of us.' It was like the same sort of thing over and over again."[15]

The media was hungry for any news. Both sides huddled in their rooms at the federal courthouse. One day, Pete Abitante, Goodell's chief of staff, ordered sandwiches from Jimmy John's for the owners.

When the food arrived, Abitante tried to pay with a credit card. The deliveryman only took cash, so Richardson took out a wad of hundred-dollar bills and peeled off one, two, three, four, five and asked the deliveryman if that was enough. He nodded yes and pocketed a huge tip. Reporters interviewed the deliveryman as he left the building. What did they order? Lots of roast beef. What was their mood? Great. Did you get a tip? A huge tip. Reporters tweeted this out, and a few surmised the owners must be confident of winning if they were doling out fat tips.

On April 25, Nelson issued an injunction that ended the lockout. The NFL appealed, and the next day the Draft began at Radio City Music Hall, where Goodell was showered with boos and greeted by chants of "We want football!" from the fans.[16] "I hear you. So do I," he replied. Later, he wrote on Twitter: "I'm with you, I get it."

A few days later, the Court of Appeals for the Eighth Circuit in St. Louis reimposed the lockout while it considered the NFL's appeal. On July 8, a three-judge panel agreed that the NFL had the right to lock out the players.[17] The players had lost their leverage and returned to the table just weeks before the start of training camp to hammer out a deal.

"Everybody talks a big game, years out, months out, and then like, not all the people, but a lot of the guys who are all bravado and toughness, they often are the same guys who complain about the deal after it's done," said Domonique Foxworth, a negotiator for the players.[18] "Those are the guys who are calling and emailing stressed out when we're getting close to the deadline, and we might actually miss some paychecks, actually miss the season or actually miss the money."

The media scrutiny was intense, so the two sides met in secret locations. One spot was the retreat at Wye River in Maryland, where Bill Clinton, Benjamin Netanyahu, and Yasir Arafat signed a peace agreement in 1998. Richardson called the bucolic conference center near Chesapeake Bay a "hippie plantation."

Other locations were less secluded, like one hotel outside Chicago. After dinner, everyone said good night. Jerry Jones, though, got thirsty and went across the street to an Irish bar and bought rounds of drinks for the customers. "It's funny because we would try to meet in these locations and have it be secret," Mara said. "But Jerry would fly in with his Cowboys plane with the star on it and the media would find out."

To reduce the tension, the two sides excluded their lawyers and, in some sessions, Goodell and Smith. This let the owners and players speak to each other more directly and created an opening for Jeff Saturday and Robert Kraft to get the deal across the finish line. If Richardson was the heavy and Jones the salesman, Kraft was the closer. He was involved intermittently during the early part of the lockout because his wife, Myra, was dying of cancer. Frustrated by the posturing during negotiations, he would return to Boston to be with her.

"The people that I worked with during the lockout knew that I meant business, that I was serious, that I didn't want to fiddle around with foolishness and waste time," Kraft said.[19] "I didn't want to be there, to be honest, and left many times when I felt there was foolishness going on. Maybe in a small way that helped to set a tone of what was important."

The players noticed.

"You can't bullshit, like this man's taking time away from his dying wife," Foxworth said. "So I think it added some seriousness and urgency to it. And I do think that just his presence alone, aside from his intelligence, but like his decision to be there, like a man, meant a lot to a lot of people there."

Fans were frustrated, too.

Mara recalled walking with Jones to an attorney's office in Manhattan when they passed a Starbucks. Mara went in to get a coffee and Jones said he would wait outside. When he returned, Jones said, "God, finally. I'm glad you finally got here." Mara asked why.[20] "Because I don't know how much more I could have taken people walking by yelling 'fuck the Cowboys,'" Jones said.

The biggest hurdle was how to divide league revenue. The two sides agreed to base the percentage not on net revenue, as before, but on gross revenue before deductions. The players would get a smaller percentage of a far bigger pie. The headline number would decline from around 53 percent to about 47 percent, but the players wouldn't have to worry about the owners deducting a raft of expenses.

Joe Siclare, the NFL's financial officer, created a formula to split revenue into three baskets with different percentages. The league's media contracts had few costs associated with administering them, so the players would receive about 55 percent of that revenue. The league's national sponsorship and merchandise deals, which were smaller than the media deals, had more costs but also relied on the star players. The players would get about 45 percent of that revenue. The last basket was revenue from local sponsorships and stadiums, the costs of which fell heavily on the owners, who would receive about 60 percent of that revenue. When the baskets were blended, the players received roughly 47 percent of revenue, though the percentage fluctuated each year.

The breakthrough got the deal to the finish line.

"It wasn't like inventing cold fusion in the sink," Siclare joked.[21] "It's just common sense. For the owners, it recognizes the revenue areas that will require the additional investment to grow the game."

With the new revenue sharing formula settled, other items fell into place. One was the rookie wage scale, which both sides wanted. The owners had a track record of showering guaranteed money on top draft picks who turned out to be duds. The poster child was LSU quarterback JaMarcus Russell, the first overall pick in 2007, who received a six-year, $61 million contract from the Raiders.[22] Russell won just seven games in three seasons. The Raiders paid him $36 million and voided the second half of his contract.

The St. Louis Rams picked Oklahoma quarterback Sam Bradford first overall in 2010, and he signed a five-year, $65 million deal,[23] which at the time was more than what Tom Brady was paid. Bradford had a better debut than Russell—he was the offensive rookie of the year in 2010, passing for 3,500 yards—but the Rams had a losing record all four years he played in St. Louis.

"As a guy who has been in the league for 14 now going on 15 years and being around other veteran guys, for a young guy to get paid that kind of money and never steps foot on an NFL football field, it's a little disheartening to think of," said Kevin Mawae, the president of the Players Association during negotiations.

Goodell agreed, saying the rookie deals skewed the economics of team rosters. "And that money is not going to players that are performing," he said.[24] "It's going to a player that never makes it in the NFL. And I think that's ridiculous."

With a salary cap, money spent on rookies was money not spent on veterans. There was evidence that the big rookie contracts helped some veterans because they set a benchmark in their contract negotiations. But teams had only so much money to spend. The new rookie wage scale left more money for veterans but hurt the next generation of players, starting with Cam Newton, the first overall pick in 2011, whose contract was tens of millions of dollars less than what Russell and Bradford had gotten before him.

Another major feature of the deal was its length. The NFL labor deals were typically no longer than five years. No owner could recall who broached the idea of a ten-year contract in 2011, but it was clearly a priority because a decade-long contract would provide stability and give the owners leverage in negotiations with CBS, Fox, and other networks.

The networks would commit more money, but after accounting for inflation, the latter years of a ten-year deal would be relatively cheap.

Unions generally resist committing to longer deals because so much can change. In the NFL, where the average playing career is less than four years, a decade-long contract would give the next generation of players fewer chances to negotiate better terms. Yet the owners recalled facing little resistance. The players tried to add an opt-out after seven or eight years but were rebuffed.

"You want the contract to be long enough that you don't have to fight every year but short enough that you have the opportunity to address things that are unanticipated," said Doug Allen, Upshaw's longtime number two at the Players Association. "Four, five, six years in a situation where careers are only four or five years long is the outside edge."

But Atallah said that the ten-year contract worked out. The salary cap grew 65 percent over the life of the 2011 deal. The players also won a salary floor that forced every team to spend all its allotted money.

"The ten-year deal was rooted in the philosophy that owners have to drive revenue and players will thrive off that revenue growth," Atallah said. "The trade-off was, okay, maybe we're not going to get fifty-fifty here. But 47 percent of a much bigger pie is much better than their earlier proposals of 37 percent of a much smaller pie. And the 2011 deal established labor peace and important economic measures."

The new deal also provided a bump in pensions to players who retired before 1993. The union thwarted the effort to expand the regular season to eighteen games and won safety measures, including a reduction in the number of full-padded practices and offseason workouts. As the league and union rushed to finalize the deal in late July, Rich McKay, the president of the Falcons and head of the Competition Committee, was awoken in the middle of the night. Goodell,

Pash, and Peter Ruocco, who worked in labor relations, called from Goodell's office. The league had already agreed to cut the number of offseason workouts from fourteen to eleven. The trio wanted to know if the league could reduce that number to ten.

"Are you going to have a problem?" they asked. McKay had been wearing a mouthpiece and when he took it out, one of his teeth fell out, too, so he spoke with a whistling sound. "Jeff kept saying, 'What's wrong with your voice?' It was like a Lucy skit. I couldn't stop laughing. But that was kind of the final thing for me. We agreed that night that we could go to ten."

There were last-minute tweaks. The owners gathered in a room around 11 p.m. one night. Jones, an eternal optimist, opened a bottle of scotch, and after a round or two, the union returned with another request. A woozy Clark Hunt was dispatched to nail down the details.

Amid the frenzy, Kraft continued to shuttle back to Boston to be at his wife's side. She encouraged him to take part in negotiations because he could make a difference. But when she died on July 20, Kraft and his family began a seven-day mourning period. Kraft wavered on whether to attend the final round of meetings on July 25. After prayers at his home, Kraft asked his sons and friends, including Senator John Kerry, what to do. All of them said Myra would have wanted him at the meetings.

That led to the enduring image of the lockout: Kraft and Jeff Saturday hugging. The owners, NFL executives, Smith, and the players gathered on a sidewalk in Washington, DC, to announce they had a deal. Kraft, who was normally well-dressed, was wearing a black tie and had not shaved because he was in mourning.

"I believe you're going to see a very great NFL over the next decade," Kraft said. "And I hope we gave a little lesson to the people in Washington because the debt crisis is a lot easier to fix than this deal was."

Moments later, Saturday thanked everyone, including the wives of the participants. He gave a special shoutout to Myra Kraft for allowing her husband to participate.

"Without him, this deal does not get done," Saturday said before embracing Kraft.

A few days later, player representatives from every team except the Steelers voted for the deal. Teams scrambled to sign players and get their rookies up to speed, something that usually happened over several months. The only casualty was the Hall of Fame game between the Chicago Bears and St. Louis Rams in early August.

Many in the media said the owners had won, primarily because their share of league revenue grew to 53 percent. Smith and union officials tried for years to undo that perception, but explaining the subtleties of the deal, including gross versus net revenue, did not make for neat headlines or sound bites.

The perception that Goodell and the owners schooled Smith and the players continued into 2015, when Smith ran for reelection. Sean Gilbert, a defensive end in the 1990s and early 2000s, ran to unseat Smith.

"The owners not only drove a hard bargain, they sealed that bargain for a decade," Gilbert wrote in *The $29 Million "Tip": How Roger Goodell Earned His Big Payday.* "That was unprecedented, and it has to make you wonder one simple question: Why would the owners—the people who are experts in the money side of football—ever agree to such a long-term deal if they weren't completely sure that the deal was to their liking?"

Goodell insisted that no one at the league brag about the deal. He and Smith signed the new CBA on the steps of the Pro Football Hall of Fame in Canton, shaking hands and mugging for the cameras. Goodell wrote letters to many staffers who took part in the negotiations. At the first meeting of top executives after the deal was signed, Goodell thanked his team again and told them there would be some extra cash in their bank accounts. Then he told them he wanted to sew up negotiations with the NFL's broadcast partners in another month or so to prove to the players they had made a good choice agreeing to the new revenue sharing formula.

"The point of that was to secure as much advantage with the broadcasters as you could," one of the participants at the meeting said. "But it was also because that was the proof point of the win-win deal. We did not want people writing that De said in March that was the worst labor deal and then agreed to a deal that was much worse than that. We want, 'These guys were shrewd, here's how it's paying off.'"

11.

TWO FINE LEGACIES

The 2011 labor deal turned out to be the peak of Richardson's influence in league matters, and only a few owners showed up on a crisp day in March 2023 to send him off. Close to a thousand friends and former colleagues of the "Big Cat" filed into the Jerry Richardson Indoor Stadium on the Wofford College campus in Spartanburg, South Carolina, to commemorate his life as former NFL player, business titan, and founding owner of the Panthers.[1] Plenty of players, and a gaggle of reporters, were there, including Cam Newton and Greg Olsen. Roger Goodell was absent, but I saw the league's general counsel, Jeff Pash, and Paul Tagliabue chatting as a pianist played "Here I Am, Lord" and "You'll Never Walk Alone."

Richardson, who had died at eighty-six about three weeks earlier, lived a remarkable American life. He won a championship as a receiver on the Colts, used his bonus money to start the Hardee's hamburger chain, then bought an expansion team that brought NFL football to his native North Carolina. For many years, he was among the most powerful NFL owners.

Then in December 2017, he was accused of sexually harassing women staffers at the Panthers headquarters in Charlotte.[2] He asked women to wear jeans to the office on Fridays and got them to turn around and wiggle their backsides. He asked women employees to give him foot massages. Workers referred to him simply as "Mister." He wrote female employees notes that included cash and instructions to use the money on massages and clothing. The details, revealed in *Sports Illustrated*, turned him into a pariah.

Only Texans owner Bob McNair publicly mustered a defense.

"I hope that this thing turns out that he's innocent," McNair said.[3] "They allege. I don't know. But some of the comments that he might have made could have been made jokingly but misunderstood. That's entirely possible. I'm sure he didn't mean to offend anybody."

McNair was pilloried for trying to wave off the allegations.

Richardson had been making plans to sell the club for years, and soon after the allegations emerged, he put the team on the market. He spared his fellow owners the trouble of having to consider whether to force him to sell his team the way the NBA did with Los Angeles Clippers owner Donald Sterling, who was caught on tape using racist language.

By the time of the memorial, Richardson had been out of the NFL for five years. He was an uncomfortable footnote to the same owners he had worked hard to help. Only three of them traveled to Wofford College. It was a reminder that most owners owe their fame to the reflected glory of the NFL. Once they sell their teams, they become just another billionaire.

Even Jones and Kraft, two of the most successful owners, grapple with their legacies. Both in their eighties and their teams unable to return to the Super Bowl, they spent chunks of their time on documentaries and philanthropy.

Unlike the owners who inherited their wealth, Richardson was self-made. He grew up poor in North Carolina in the last years of the Depression, the only child of a barber. His family got its first car when he turned sixteen. Richardson was so skinny he was called "Stick," but through determination and skill, he won a partial scholarship to Wofford. He set school records as a receiver and was drafted by the Colts in 1958 but chose to finish his BA in psychology first.

After graduation in 1959, he reported to Colts camp. He and his wife, Rosalind, had only one car, and when she needed to go shopping, Richardson hitched rides to practice with quarterback Johnny Unitas. His rookie season, Richardson caught 7 passes for 81 yards, but he made them count: Three were for touchdowns and another was in the 1959 championship game against the Giants. Richardson was voted the Colts rookie of the year.

In 1960, Richardson caught another eight passes, but the Colts lost their last four games and finished 6-6. Coach Weeb Ewbank offered Richardson $9,750 to return for a third season. Richardson wanted a five-figure salary: $10,000. Ewbank refused, so Richardson moved back to Spartanburg and used some of his $4,000 championship bonus from the prior year to invest in the first Hardee's hamburger shop. Sportswriters thought Richardson was nuts to walk away over $250, but he called it "a matter of principle."

Richardson and his former college teammate, Charlie Bradshaw, bought more Hardee's restaurants as America's car and youth culture exploded. Richardson was fastidious and hard-driving, a Marine who never served. On visits to stores, he picked up trash in the parking lots, mopped the floors, and flipped burgers with the staff.

The "Ray Kroc of the South" was so successful his company was listed on the New York Stock Exchange in the 1970s. The company added Denny's and Quincy's Steakhouses. After Richardson's company took on too much debt in the 1980s, Kohlberg Kravis Roberts, the takeover specialists, bailed out the company but left him in charge.

In 1987, Richardson set out to achieve his lifelong dream of bringing pro football to the Carolinas. He approached Hugh McColl, who later ran Bank of America, about acquiring an NFL franchise. Together, they lobbied the NFL, assembled an investment group, and explored how to build a stadium in Charlotte.

McColl's bank helped Richardson purchase the Panthers for $140 million and then loaned him more than $190 million to build a stadium. The NFL owners unanimously approved Richardson, and the Panthers became the league's twenty-ninth team on October 26, 1993.[4]

To help pay for the stadium, Richardson sold personal seat licenses, which fans had to buy before they could purchase season tickets. Richardson received 41,632 orders for PSLs the first day they went on sale, raising $54 million.[5] Other owners soon copied him.

Richardson pulled back from his corporate work after his company, Flagstar, was hit with several discrimination suits, including one filed by six Black Secret Service agents who claimed they were denied service at a Denny's in Annapolis, Maryland. Another suit alleged that just eight out of the one thousand or so Denny's franchises nationwide were owned by Blacks. His company paid roughly $1 billion to settle the cases.

Richardson already had his franchise, so the other owners could only bite their tongues. Anyway, Richardson was exactly the kind of owner they needed: a former NFL player, a successful businessman, and a hero in the fast-growing Carolinas.

The Panthers were a quick success, making the playoffs in their second season. But they never put together back-to-back winning seasons during Richardson's twenty-three-year tenure. They made it to two Super Bowls and lost both.

Richardson could be blustery. He rarely spoke to the media and was fierce at the bargaining table. He could be brutish toward his players even though he was a former player who understood the brutality of the game.

But Richardson was a league-first owner who put the league ahead of his team. The NFL shield was painted at the 50-yard line in his stadium, not the Panthers logo. He rarely sought special treatment and never sued the league to get his way like Al Davis or Jones. He helped owners get new stadiums and cochaired the search committee that selected Goodell as commissioner.

"He was very focused on retaining the character of the league," said former NFL lawyer Frank Hawkins. Richardson, he added, "wanted very much to keep the old ownership groups in and not have the turnover to Roger's hedge fund guys, the financialization guys," who he thought would put profits ahead of football.

One of those old groups was the Bidwill family, who had owned the Cardinals for nearly a century. Michael Bidwill flew from Arizona to attend the memorial because, he told me, Richardson helped him get a new stadium. Bidwill recalled how he invited Richardson to the team's previous home in Tempe, Arizona, to show him how hot it was in the stands. At one mid-October game, he made Richardson march to the top deck on the sun side of the stadium. After a few minutes, Richardson, dressed in a suit and tie, said he had seen enough and asked to leave.

"We weren't going to wait the full fifteen minutes because he was already dripping wet, and I was dripping wet," Bidwill said.

As chair of the league's stadium committee, Richardson lobbied local politicians for public support for his fellow owners. When the Bidwills' new home outside of Phoenix opened in 2006, the stadium and site improvements cost $455 million; the Cardinals paid for about a third of it, and taxpayers and government agencies covered the rest.

Richardson's role as the stadium czar ended when the owners approved the LA stadium proposed by Rams owner Stan Kroenke over the one that he preferred, a joint bid by the Chargers and Raiders. After the defeat, Richardson stopped attending league meetings. His longtime allies were either dead (Ralph Wilson of the Bills) or no longer loyal.

"All my friends are gone," Richardson lamented to a friend.

Whatever misgivings Richardson had about financial wizards owning NFL teams dissolved in May 2018, when Richardson sold the club for a record $2.25 billion to hedge fund billionaire David Tepper. The league fined Richardson $2.75 million on his way out the door.[6] In 2020, Tepper removed a giant statue of Richardson in front of the stadium.[7] To make sure no one missed it, the Panthers published a slideshow on their website of workers removing the statue. It was like Richardson was being erased from the history books.

Jerry Richardson was, in NFL terms, no longer relevant.

The fear of becoming irrelevant must have weighed on Dan Snyder's mind in the waning days of his twenty-four-year reign of terror as owner of the Washington Commanders. For Snyder, leaving the powerful perch as an NFL owner was probably even harder than it was for Richardson because he was younger. From the moment he bought the club in 1999, he was petty and contemptuous, and he seemed to want to piss off as many owners as possible. Snyder proved that for all their money, the owners could be terrible judges of character.

Snyder first teamed up with Howard Milstein to buy the team, which was being sold by the estate of Jack Kent Cooke. But most of Milstein's money was tied up in real estate, not the cash needed to buy an NFL team. Milstein also co-owned the New York Islanders, which were losing piles of money. Then there was his reputation.

At an owners meeting in Atlanta, Colts owner Jim Irsay said the quiet part out loud. "I heard rumors that you're basically a litigious asshole," Irsay said, according to an NFL executive at the meeting. "I don't want to let someone like that in as a partner. So, are you prepared to commit today that you won't sue the league?"

Milstein stammered through a nonanswer. Snyder raised his hand and said, "I'm prepared to commit that I won't." Milstein and Snyder's bid fell apart, so Snyder formed a new group with Mort Zuckerman and Fred Drasner, co-owners of the New York *Daily News*. Their bid was approved in part, the league executive said, because of Snyder's pledge.

At the meeting to approve Snyder's new group, John Mara from the Giants was sitting next to Jets president Steve Gutman. After more than twenty years at the league, Gutman had seen his share of rapscallions. As they listened to Snyder and his group describe why they should be accepted, Gutman said to Mara, "The next guy's always worse."

It was a joke, but it turned out to be prescient. From the start, Snyder angered fans, politicians, the media, coaches, and league executives. Raiders president Amy Trask remembered being told by one of Snyder's assistants to avoid making eye contact with him. She took that as an invitation to look Snyder in the eye every chance she got.

Despite being in his thirties, Snyder insisted on being called "Mr. Snyder." When Steve Bisciotti was accepted as majority owner of the Ravens in 2004, word spread through the meeting about a brief interaction he had with Snyder, who was five years younger.

"Hi Dan," Bisciotti said. "It's Mr. Snyder," Snyder shot back. "Fuck you, Dan," Bisciotti said before walking away.

Snyder's quirks might have been tolerated if he wasn't steering his club into a ditch. Snyder borrowed $350 million to buy the team and, eager to repay his debts, looked for money wherever he could find it. He charged visiting teams to park their buses at FedEx Field and was the first owner to charge fans to attend training camp. (Other owners eventually copied him.)

He fired nine coaches, including Norv Turner, whom he once berated in front of his players. He hired coaching legends like Joe Gibbs and Mike Shanahan, but their second acts were worse. Snyder also paid assistant coaches what head coaches had been receiving, raising the bar for other owners, who were not pleased.

Snyder blew about $100 million on over-the-hill superstars in 2000 alone. Deion Sanders, who signed a seven-year, $56 million contract, played just one season. Jeff George, a former first overall pick, signed an $18.25 million four-year deal to play backup quarterback, but went 1-6 in two seasons as a starter. Bruce Smith, an aging defensive lineman, signed a five-year deal worth $23 million and lasted three seasons.

"I don't play for the money, although the money is fine, God bless you, Mr. Snyder," Sanders said at his introductory news conference, referring to his $8 million signing bonus.[8]

Over 24 seasons, Snyder's teams won just two playoff games and never made it to the conference championship, let alone the Super Bowl. Once the top-drawing team in the league, the Commanders were last at the turnstiles in 2021.

Snyder went to war with the media. He sued a newspaper for defamation and resisted calls to change the team's name, which some Native Americans considered a slur. "We'll never change the name," Snyder said in 2013, when the team and league were fighting with the U.S. Patent Office over the team's trademarks.[9] "It's that simple. NEVER—you can use caps."

The bad karma reached a boiling point in 2020 when Snyder fought with three limited partners who owned 40 percent of the club. They believed Snyder mishandled the team's finances and stiffed them on dividends. A messy boardroom fight spilled into state and federal court after *The Washington Post* published reports about dozens of former team employees who said they were sexually harassed.

The owners feared that if they tried to push out Snyder, they would set a precedent that could be used against them. So rather than force Snyder to sell his team, the owners let him borrow an additional $450 million to buy out his partners.[10] The league fined Snyder $10 million and banned him from the club after an investigation found that Snyder had overseen a toxic workplace.

Goodell buried the 135-page written investigation, which prompted cries of a cover-up, a congressional inquiry, and investigations by attorneys general in Virginia, Maryland, and the District of Columbia. Sponsors walked away from the club, and what little political support there was for helping Snyder build a new stadium vanished. In October 2022, at an owners meeting in New York, Irsay once again said what many owners would only express privately.

"I believe that there is merit to remove him as owner of the Redskins," Irsay said, using the team's old name.[11] "I think it's something that we have to review. We have to look at all of the evidence and we have to be thorough going forward, but I think it's something that has to be given serious consideration."

Snyder fought back, issuing a statement bad-mouthing Irsay and telling others to buzz off. Two weeks later, he capitulated. In a statement, he said that he had hired Bank of America to explore a potential sale of part or all of the club.

On paper, Snyder should have been the kind of owner the NFL needed. He was a young, successful businessman who loved his hometown team and was willing to spend oodles of money on the franchise. Rarely have the owners been so wrong.

When Snyder joined the league and was told about how the owners tried to leave some money on the table in negotiations with the television networks, his response was: Why not charge them triple?

Growing up in Maryland, Snyder didn't come from money. His father, Gerry, was a freelance writer. Dan's first job, at fourteen, was working at a B. Dalton bookstore.[12] In high school he mopped floors at the National Institutes of Health in Bethesda. He had an entrepreneurial bug. In college, he and a friend leased planes to fly college students to Florida and the Caribbean for spring break. Snyder said they made about $1 million. He dropped out of the University of Maryland at twenty.

Snyder persuaded Zuckerman to invest $3 million in his new venture, *Campus USA*, a magazine for college students. The publication collapsed after three years because of a lack of ads. In 1989, Snyder borrowed money from his father and, with his sister, Michele, who maxed out her credit cards, started Snyder Communications, a direct marketing company. The venture took off, which gave Snyder the means to buy several other businesses. By 1996, Snyder took the company public and became, at thirty-two, the youngest CEO to list a company on the New York Stock Exchange. Four years later, he sold the company for more than $2 billion.[13]

By then, Snyder had already bought the Washington franchise for a then-record $800 million. The purchase included a two-year-old stadium in Landover, Maryland, which had the most luxury suites and club seats in the NFL.

In addition to the $350 million Snyder borrowed to pay for the team, he assumed $155 million in debt on the stadium. He sold the naming rights to the stadium to FedEx for more than $200 million. Snyder's spending on marquee free agents shook the old boys' club. "He's making Jerry Jones look like Art Rooney," the genteel Steelers owner, the joke went.[14] "Yes, we've met," Giants owner Wellington Mara said. "I wouldn't use the word 'charming' with him, but he's been fine."

Snyder even angered Dan Rooney, one of the friendliest owners. In 2003, Hawkins gave a presentation to the owners on team debt levels that included a chart with a vertical bar for each team's amount. The chart looked like a bell curve with Snyder's team, which had the most debt, represented by the highest bar, which happened to be in the middle of the chart.

Rooney was fond of doodling during meetings. Afterward, he went to Hawkins and gave him the sketch he had drawn. Then he whispered: "Thanks for giving Snyder the middle finger."

Snyder was unapologetic. "I'm aggressive, I'm entrepreneurial, I want to win," he said in 2000.[15] "I want to win fast and now. All of this is true, absolutely.

"But I've run a lot of businesses and I've been very rational," he added. "And I've been in a lot of competitive environments, and this is just another competitive environment where if you want to win you really need to be aggressive. If you're not, you won't win."

The NFL, of course, was not "just another competitive environment." There was a salary cap that required savvy to navigate. The NFL operates largely like a socialist collective where roughly two-thirds of every team's revenue is shared.

Few owners wanted to rock that boat, but Snyder couldn't help himself. He chewed out coaches and micromanaged front-office decisions. Snyder fired about two dozen employees, including longtime secretaries, and terrorized his employees.

Snyder's closest ally was Jones, though some suspected that he liked Snyder because the Cowboys could benefit if Washington—a division rival—was dysfunctional. But Jerry and Dan had a lot in common. Through the early 2000s, their clubs were the top earners in the league. Snyder expanded the number of club seats and suites and raised ticket prices.

He advertised in the Baltimore region despite an agreement between owners not to compete in one another's markets. The team was fined $25,000 for using their public address system to blare noise when visiting teams were on offense. Snyder sued the *Washington City Paper* for defamation, seeking $1 million and damages for a story called "The Cranky Redskins Fan's Guide to Dan Snyder," which included an illustration that he considered anti-Semitic.[16]

Then there was the team's name. Native American activists sued to remove the team's patent protections for its name and logos, citing a U.S. Patent and Trademark Office provision that prohibits offensive titles and names.

Once again, it was left to Goodell to shield the owners from controversy. Goodell told reporters in 2013 that "there are different views" of the team's name and the club had a "proud tradition."

"By no means, growing up in Washington and being a Redskins fan, have I ever considered it derogatory as a fan," Goodell said. "I think that's how the Redskins fans look at it. The Redskins have always presented it as part of their tradition, their history. 'Hail to the Redskins' is part of that proud tradition. But whenever you have a situation like this, you have to listen and recognize that some other people may have different perspectives. And clearly there are cases where that's true here. That's what I suggested, and I've been open about it that we need to listen and carefully listen and make sure that we're doing what's right."

Snyder lost several rulings in 2014 and 2015 but refused to budge, which added to the perception that the NFL was callous. In 2014, Snyder set up an organization, the Washington Redskins Original Americans Foundation, which Snyder said in a letter to season ticket holders would "address the urgent challenges plaguing Indian country."[17] The foundation turned out largely designed to make Snyder look empathetic. Some Native Americans considered the grants a form of bribery. The foundation all but stopped providing assistance by 2018.[18]

The team's name *was* a complicated issue. Some Native American activists, like Suzan Shown Harjo, viewed it as racist. She remembered being taunted by fans at Washington home games.

"You're not just dealing with the Washington franchise, but the whole of the N.F.L.," Harjo told me.[19] "It's one moonlight after another laden with money and the power it represents."

But the Native American community is not monolithic. In 2014, while driving from the Grand Canyon to Phoenix, I stopped at a dusty roadside lean-to where two locals were selling handmade silver jewelry. At the end of the table, a man wore a Redskins cap. I asked why he rooted for a team located thousands of miles away. His father had worked at a naval base in Norfolk, Virginia, he said, and passed along his love of the team to his son.

"You think because I'm Navajo I shouldn't root for them?" he added.

Well, it had crossed my mind, I replied.

He said the term "redskin" was what white people called Native Americans who rubbed red clay on their faces as sunblock. Then he pointed to the woman at the end of the table.

"Look at my aunt, she roots for the Cowboys!"

She was indeed wearing a Cowboys cap.

Snyder ditched the team's name on July 3, 2020, but only because his biggest sponsors, including FedEx, threatened to walk away from the team.[20] FedEx was led by Fred Smith, who was trying to sell his 10 percent stake in the team. After Snyder refused to buy it, Smith joined with Robert Rothman and Dwight Schar, who owned another 30 percent, in pushing for the entire team to be sold. Soon after, *The*

Washington Post published stories that included accusations of a toxic workplace and sexual harassment.[21]

Snyder hired Beth Wilkinson, the DC-based lawyer who had worked at times for the league, to investigate the allegations. The NFL took over the investigation soon after to remove any appearance of tampering. When the league penalized Snyder on July 1, 2021, Goodell released only an executive summary, leading critics to ask if the commissioner was burying damning details.

Within a few weeks, the House Oversight Committee began hearings where new revelations were unearthed.[22] This forced Goodell to start a second investigation as calls grew for Snyder to sell the team.

Except for Irsay, no one called for Snyder to sell lest he sue them and the league. But Jones said no one would blame Snyder if he took a giant offer for his team.[23] Falcons owner Arthur Blank bid Dan Snyder and his wife, Tanya, adieu.

"I think their family has moved to London, I believe," he said, confirming that Snyder was already half gone. "We'll see what will happen. He's a young man, his children are young, his wife's young, and they have a whole life ahead of them. I certainly wish them well."

It was Blank's way of telling Snyder he ought to get used to life on the outside. Sure, you won't be relevant anymore, but you turned an $800 million investment into $6 billion and you have a nice family.

Since Snyder sold the team in July 2023, he could only watch as the Commanders won two playoff games in 2024, reaching the NFC Championship Game. New owner Josh Harris needed two seasons to achieve what Snyder had failed to do during his twenty-four-year reign.

For an alpha male billionaire, having nothing to control can be misery. Not yet sixty years old, Snyder has a couple decades of being miserable ahead of him.

12.
UNDER ATTACK

On the morning of October 17, 2017, inside league headquarters on Park Avenue in Manhattan, Roger Goodell confronted the most complex issue of his eleven-year tenure as commissioner. He was facing unprecedented pressure from fans, sponsors, and, most of all, his bosses—the league's thirty-two owners—to end the protests by players who were kneeling during the playing of the national anthem to draw attention to social inequality and police brutality. The protests, which San Francisco 49ers quarterback Colin Kaepernick started in the preseason a year earlier, had already pitted fans against fans, and fans against the league.

The protests grew to include a handful of other players, then faded from the headlines because the 49ers were awful and rarely on national television. In the offseason, though, Kaepernick became a free agent and went unsigned, raising questions about whether teams blacklisted him because of his political views.[1]

As the 2017 season got underway, the players' protests returned, renewing a national conversation about race, the police, and the limits of free speech. Then, three weeks into the season, President Trump made an already toxic situation worse when he called the players unpatriotic. During a speech on a Friday night in late September, Trump told an audience in Alabama: "Wouldn't you love to see one of these NFL owners, when somebody disrespects our flag, to say, 'Get that son of a bitch off the field right now, out, he's fired.'"

Suddenly, the NFL's controversy leapt into the realm of national politics and stoked the passions of fans and the fears of the league's advertising and broadcasting partners. Some prominent owners, including Jerry Jones of the Cowboys and Bob McNair of the Texans, agreed with Trump. They were among the nine owners who had each donated more than $1 million to the president's inauguration that year.[2] But they knew that banning the protests could trigger a backlash from the players—about 70 percent of whom were men of color—and alienate fans who supported the players' right to express themselves peacefully.

The president's broadside caught the league by surprise. The morning after Trump's attack, Goodell and his top lieutenants, including general counsel Jeff Pash and chief spokesman Joe Lockhart, began calling every owner to see how they wanted to respond. The stakes were enormous: Some players were so angry they were considering not playing that weekend.

Goodell handled one of the most critical calls, to Jaguars owner Shad Khan, who was in London, where his team was scheduled to play the weekend's first game. Khan came to the United States at sixteen, became an engineer, and later took over Flex N Gate, a car bumper maker. He also was one of the few owners of color. Though he donated to Trump's inauguration, he said he did so because he supported the president's economic policies. Soon after, he came out against the president's ban on visitors from predominantly Muslim countries.[3]

Less than a day before kickoff in London, Khan sensed from his conversations with Goodell that the league did not have a clear path forward.

"The last time I talked to Roger, I think Roger was under a lot of pressure to figure something out," Khan recalled. "But the thing which I really will never forget is the last conversation I had with him" that night. "He said, 'Oh, Shad, you guys are the first game up tomorrow for the NFL, so you're going to be setting the stage. So good luck.'"

The next day, Khan gathered his team leaders, both players and coaches, in Wembley Stadium. They decided to link arms together during the playing of the anthem. Khan stood between two of his team captains at the fifty-yard line, and the handful of players who knelt did so at the end of the line.

Some executives in the league office thought this was a stroke of genius because the players and owners stood together, and the protesters were largely out of view of the television cameras. Khan also thought the team presented a fair and unified solution. He has a framed photo of him locking arms with the players.

But after the game, Khan heard from other owners who "frankly, were very uncomfortable" because now *they* would be expected to do something similar. And unlike Khan, they weren't playing in London; they were playing in front of American fans, and they were already feeling the heat from sponsors and season ticket holders.

The crisis exposed how, for all their money and savvy, the owners tended to move cautiously. This approach usually paid off when it came to business decisions. But scandals are different. The owners often tried to wait out crises rather than make a misstep. Often, it worked because once the season started, fans cared more about the games than off-field controversies.

When the problems are too large to ignore, such as after Ravens running back Ray Rice was shown on video knocking out his fiancée in an elevator, the owners threw money at a nonprofit group or a television campaign to try to quell the outrage.

For many owners, particularly Jones, the kneeling protests that Kaepernick started were bad for business. Television ratings had started to slip, which worried sponsors who paid hundreds of millions of dollars to attach their brands to the NFL. John Schnatter, the CEO of Papa John's, "the official pizza of the NFL," said the protests were hurting sales. Jones owned many Papa Johns franchises in Texas and was friends with Schnatter. Jones and Dan Snyder urged Schnatter to bash the NFL for not doing more to end the protests.

"Goodell is a coward, and he is incompetent and he's just lucky," Schnatter told talk show host Jason Whitlock.[4]

Other sponsors, including Pepsi and Verizon, quietly voiced their concerns. Some others wanted Goodell to intervene.

So on that sunny October day in 2017, Goodell hosted some of the most powerful people in the country's most powerful sport—owners, players, union officials, league executives—to hash out a compromise as quickly as possible. The meeting was a rare moment when players, owners, and league and union officials representing a cross section of political and economic interests worked together to try to find a single solution.

To outsiders, the owners can look like a group of uncaring plutocrats. But they had varied political opinions. At the table that day, Arthur Blank of the Falcons, Stephen Ross of the Miami Dolphins, and Jeffrey Lurie of the Philadelphia Eagles were in the liberal wing. They had all donated to progressive causes, though Ross also hosted a fundraiser for Trump.[5]

McNair of the Texans and Terry Pegula of the Buffalo Bills were among the most conservative owners. Both made their money in the oil and gas business and were against the player protests.

Then there was Art Rooney II of the Steelers, John Mara of the Giants, and Michael Bidwill of the Cardinals, third-generation owners whose wealth came from their teams. These old guard owners considered the league an institution to be preserved, and they were generally sympathetic to the players but wanted order to be restored.

In the middle was Kraft, a social chameleon and political operator whose influence on league business was so strong that he was known as the "shadow commissioner." He walked a fine line between the three camps of owners. His large circle of friends—left, right, and center—allowed him to cross lines between the conservative and liberal wings of the league in a way Goodell could not.

Kraft was also friendly with DeMaurice Smith, the head of the players union, who was also in attendance. In 2011, Kraft won over Smith when he helped end a contentious lockout and secure a new ten-year labor agreement.

Kraft also had relationships with several players, including Malcolm Jenkins, one of the de facto leaders of the thirteen players at the meeting. An accomplished defensive back, Jenkins had pushed for issues like bail reform. Just a month before the meeting, Jenkins met Goodell in Philadelphia to help him understand the problem. Kraft had visited Philadelphia, too, and became deeply invested in social justice initiatives.

Jenkins, Anquan Boldin, Darius Butler, and Chris Long were among the centrist players at the meeting. They were eager to find a practical solution that would ratchet down the heat on the players while giving them resources to help address problems in communities of color. Two months before the summit in New York, Boldin warned Goodell about the brewing storm in NFL locker rooms and urged him to help the players find practical solutions.

Boldin was in training camp with the Bills. Before a preseason game, several players knelt during the playing of the national anthem. The next day, head coach Sean McDermott told the team that while he didn't mind if players knelt, he wanted them to tell him in advance next time. Boldin was offended. He felt players didn't need to ask to speak their minds. Back in his hotel room, Boldin called Troy Vincent, the former cornerback in charge of NFL football operations, and asked to speak to Goodell.

"I told him that players weren't looking for permission from the league" to kneel, Boldin said. Goodell asked him what the players wanted. Boldin said they needed the league to join the players' grassroots efforts and lobby for legislative change. "If an owner or the commissioner goes into a meeting with me, the conversation changes from a photo op to talking about true issues," Boldin said.

Goodell and some of his executives began meeting the players to hash out ways to help.

But just as the owners had their opinions, so did the players. Eric Reid, Michael Thomas, and Russell Okung were among those who felt that any compromise with the owners had to include recognition of Kaepernick. They believed the league was trying to bury his contribution and the owners wouldn't sign him. They pointed to less talented quarterbacks who had filled roster spots across the league.

Everyone in the room had worked under pressure before, but the tension was particularly thick that day. For the first time in its long history, the NFL had been attacked by a sitting president.

Trump's attack changed everything, because the NFL was at the center of a national shouting match that had leapt out of its control. Conservatives considered the players unpatriotic and skewered the league, while liberals tended to view the league, and the owners in particular, as intolerant.

The debate highlighted long-simmering racial fissures. Roughly 70 percent of the NFL players were Black or Hispanic, and about 70 percent of NFL fans were white. Kaepernick was a hero to some fans, while many other fans vowed to turn their back on the league; thousands canceled their season ticket plans.

Goodell began the session with a plea: secrecy. "Most important, really truly listen," he said. "We learn and we understand, and I think that's really critical for us to reach any kind of agreement," he continued. "It's time to regain that message that I think has been lost, in large part, by people hijacking our own message." He didn't say who the hijackers were.

Then, in keeping with his cautious personality, Goodell asked everyone at the table not to speak to the media.

"The last thing I would say before we get going is confidentiality," Goodell said. Unbeknownst to him, the meeting was secretly recorded, and I would obtain a copy as part of my reporting for *The New York Times*.[6]

The recording of the nearly three-hour meeting provided a rare, unvarnished look at the inner workings of a league in turmoil. Most owners flit from city to city in private jets and summer on mammoth yachts, speaking infrequently to reporters or in carefully curated settings. Rarely are they heard talking unscripted among themselves.

The central tension between the players and owners during the meeting boiled down to most of the owners trying to persuade the players to end their protests and the players asking the owners to understand *why* they were protesting.

Goodell nodded to the players and asked them to speak first.

Jenkins began. He told the owners that the players were working in their communities to address racial inequality and lobby lawmakers for legislative change. Then he voiced his frustration.

"Quite frankly, we are kind of disappointed as players because with all that we do in the work, and as closely as you guys as owners work with us and see what we do, we've been allowed to be painted as unpatriotic, anti-police, and as a nuisance," he said. "And not that you guys painted that, but that's where the narrative went and that's where we allowed it to go.

"So now there is a need because the uproar was so, so loud that now we want to change that solution."

Boldin followed. A wide receiver who had played with Kaepernick, Boldin had a cousin who was shot and killed by a plainclothes police officer in Palm Beach Gardens, Florida, two years earlier. He began campaigning for police reform, including on Capitol Hill, and joined the Players Coalition, a group of NFL players looking for solutions to problems Kaepernick was highlighting. He pushed the owners to back the players.

"Like I told Commissioner Goodell, support isn't coming out with a statement and saying, you know, it's okay for guys to kneel, it's okay for guys to protest during the anthem. To me, that looks like more permission than anything and guys don't need permission to take a stance for something that they really believe in."

Later in the meeting, Boldin was more direct. "It's 'players are being militant,' we're looked at as villains," he said. "If we can have owners come and say, nationally, that no, they aren't, they're Americans, they care about the cities they're in, they care about these issues, we care about these issues, we're behind them, we're gonna educate ourselves about these issues, and we're gonna, we're gonna push forward. That changes us as a nation."

Lurie, the Eagles owner, was sympathetic. Not only did he own a team, he had a PhD in sociology and had taught classes on income inequality.

"This is a very, very difficult series of issues because they're all correlatives of poverty," he said. Americans "have a method to manage poverty through incarceration."

"OK, so you got billionaires and millionaires in this room," he continued. "We've been used in a, in a historical and common fashion, which is divide those that have people's attention to avoid progress on the exact same—on the exact issues that they don't wanna see progress made, which is poverty."

Lurie urged the owners and players to ignore the divider in chief in the White House.

"Another fact that I just wanna throw out there is many of us had no interest in supporting President Trump," Lurie said, his voice rising with emotion. "Yes, there's some. There's some players that did, too. But this is not where you brandish certain people because they happen to own assets of a sport we love supporting, what many of us perceived as, you know, one fucking disastrous presidency."

Nervous laughter erupted. "So, don't quote me," Lurie added.

"You're quoted," someone blurted out.

Most of Lurie's fellow owners were less interested in the subtleties of race relations and more focused on their businesses. They were socially conservative and supported Trump because they thought he helped their bottom line. Now their support for the president was being tested. They listened to Jenkins, Boldin, and Lurie, but they wanted the kneeling to stop.

Pegula crystallized that view. He was new to the league, having bought the Bills in 2014 with the money he made in fracking. Rheumy-eyed and awkward, Pegula rarely spoke in public. He didn't hear Boldin's impassioned plea so much as see it. In his view, the NFL needed a pitchman, and Boldin was perfect for the job because he was Black and well-spoken.

"For years, we've watched the National Rifle Association use Charlton Heston as a figurehead," Pegula said. "Anquan, you walked away from the game. You walked away from my team last year. You had a personal tragedy.[7] You're obviously motivated. You're here. I think that everyone in this room—if we had a spokesman who could be our figurehead—and I think it should be an African-American former player. I see a legend written on the paper here. Is that something you might be willing to do on a national level?"

To Pegula, the league had a perception problem. Many Black Americans thought the owners had shunned Kaepernick for addressing uncomfortable issues of race and power. Many white Americans felt the league had strayed too far into politics—liberal politics, at least—and that was getting in the way of their entertainment.

Pegula's idea fell flat. Boldin shifted the focus back to the owners and asked *them* again to support the players publicly.

"I don't have a problem with, with telling my story," Boldin said. But "the thing I think that has happened is, for whatever reason, players have been pinned against owners. And, like, the way that I've heard owners speak about players today, I don't think anybody outside of this room has heard that message. The way that owners say that they support players."

Pegula wasn't the only owner with a harebrained idea. Ross brought up Martin Luther King Jr. and the march he led in Selma, Alabama, in 1965. He suggested that the players and owners organize their own march on Washington, DC, to raise awareness. "Nobody gathers publicity like the NFL," Ross said.

Growing impatient, McNair flat out told the players to stop protesting.

"So let's deal with solutions and get past this other business," McNair said in his North Carolina drawl. "And you fellas need to ask your compadres, 'Fellas, stop that other business.'"

McNair had been a team owner for fifteen years, so he knew how the league worked. But he either didn't know or didn't care that the thirteen players in the room had no power to tell the other two thousand players what to do. Like the owners, they were far from united.

Kraft, ever the consensus builder, tried to bring everyone around.

"I must tell you, I mean, I think these dialogues are great, but the elephant in the room now in my opinion is this kneeling, which every player has a right to do," he said about an hour into the meeting.

"The problem we have is, we have a president that will use that as fodder to do his mission.

"I just hope that one of the things that can come out of here is that we find a way to be unified and be able to carry through and follow through. I think most teams are doing this stuff already."

Some players didn't want to be bought off and would continue to protest.

Eric Reid, who knelt with Kaepernick in 2016 when they were teammates on the 49ers, was leery. Jenkins had been raising his right fist rather than kneeling, which looked like an attempt to have it both ways. He also appeared chummy with Goodell when they met in Philadelphia to discuss bail reform a few weeks earlier. Reid first wanted the owners to acknowledge Kaepernick's role in raising these issues before they discussed solutions.

"I feel like he was hung out to dry," said Reid, who wore a T-shirt with the words "#IMWITHKAP" on it. "Yes, we've been doing—everybody in this room has been doing stuff in the community before the protests started. But as a man that felt like something was happening in this country, so much so that he needed to protest the anthem to get a message out, nobody stepped up and said, 'We support Colin's right to do this.'"

Reid's pleas were largely ignored, and the meeting proceeded with a plan that the owners and Jenkins hoped would be a win-win. Goodell introduced Johanna Faries, a vice president of marketing, who outlined a new initiative.

The owners would donate up to $89 million over seven years to match donations from the players, who would suggest which grassroots community groups would receive the money.[8]

Many details of the program that would be named Inspire Change came together in the following weeks. But the outline was based on the My Cause My Cleats initiative that the league began in 2016.[9] For a few weeks each season, players wore custom-designed cleats that promoted important causes or heroes. This let the players express themselves, albeit in prescribed ways, while allowing them to use the league's platform to promote good works.

When Kaepernick began kneeling in 2016, players were already working on many initiatives that would burst into prominence after the quarterback's protests. A loosely aligned group that became the Players Coalition had been trying to get the league's attention.

"At the start, we didn't call it Inspire Change," said Anna Isaacson, the league's senior vice president of social responsibility. "It was called Let's Listen Together. The idea was we didn't know enough, so we needed to listen to experts and listen to players. We were working on what the campaign should be. We didn't have the entire framework, but we wanted to announce something."

The $89 million headline number looked impressive. Divided between thirty-two teams, each owner would pay up to $2.75 million over seven years. The league would use its broadcast and social media platforms to highlight the grassroots efforts, and players could write slogans like "End racism" on their cleats. Celebrities and influencers would be recruited for public service announcements. The teams would sell merchandise with messages in support of social justice initiatives.

The campaign was consistent with the NFL's approach to other crises: Create a slogan that makes the league appear to be taking action to address a problem, then use the league's various media platforms to maximize exposure. Reid and a few other players saw this as the league's way to move past the protests.

But Boldin, Jenkins, and others in the Players Coalition backed the initiative. All that was needed was to craft a statement that would show how both sides were united in fighting police brutality, social inequity, and other issues. Goodell delegated this task to Smith, whom some players distrusted because they felt the Players Association had not done enough to support Kaepernick.

"I think it's good for us to say that we found that, that we have a lot more in common than we may have initially thought when we came in," Smith said to the players, sounding more like a mediator than a union leader. "And we have committed ourselves to a comprehensive and long-term plan to address those issues together."

The gambit worked. After the plan was announced a few weeks after the meeting, only Reid and a few other players continued to protest and take shots at the league.

"It's apparent the N.F.L. is trying to buy an end to the protests," Reid told me when he left the Players Coalition.[10]

Okung, an offensive lineman with the Chargers, also pulled out of the coalition. "The N.F.L. continues a disingenuous approach to player grievances, refusing to match the urgency of this moment," he said. "Their proposal is woefully inadequate."

Jenkins and most other players, though, stopped protesting, just as the owners hoped. As November rolled into December, the networks stopped discussing the protests, and fans were less up in arms, Trump no longer mentioned the topic publicly, and, as the playoffs neared, television ratings rebounded. Goodell had pushed the league past the crisis. It was back to business as usual, the business of making money.

Or so they thought. The protests during the 2017 season petered out, with only a dozen or so players kneeling by the end of the season. What caused it—the NFL's new grassroots campaign, protest fatigue, or something else—was unclear. Perhaps some players felt they had made their point or were injured or released and not on the sidelines before the game. This is, after all, the NFL.

But the owners couldn't leave well enough alone. When they met in May 2018, the most conservative owners pushed for an amendment to the Game Operations Manual to *require* players to stand during the playing of the national anthem or face potential financial penalties. Players could also stay in their locker room if they preferred.

"The membership also strongly believes that: 1. All team and league personnel on the field shall stand and show respect for the flag and the Anthem," the amendment to the manual read. The owners added four references to "stand and show respect for the flag and the Anthem."

Trump loved that the NFL caved. But being Trump, he went further. "Maybe you shouldn't be in the country," he said on *Fox & Friends* about players who did not stand for the anthem.[11]

By kowtowing to the president, the owners irked the players again. A spokesman for the players union said the revised policy was "not a compromise," and union officials "were not consulted or included."[12] The union threatened to file a grievance, which would have reignited the controversy, so the owners quietly did not enforce the policy.

The owners' heavy-handed move did not go unnoticed. In the fall, reports surfaced that Rihanna declined to perform at the Super Bowl halftime show because she supported Kaepernick. Normally, the NFL announced the halftime act during the regular season, but this time it waited until January, a sign it had difficulty finding A-list talent. The league chose Maroon 5 with a guest appearance by Travis Scott, a rapper from Houston.

Maroon 5's performance in February 2019 was panned. Jon Caramanica, a music critic at *The New York Times*, called the group "a quasi-soul, quasi-rock, utterly funkless band" and "likely the third or eighth or maybe 14th choice for a headliner.[13]

"In a year in which the Super Bowl halftime show has become a referendum on political mindfulness, in which the N.F.L. has become a staging ground for conversations about racial justice in America, Maroon 5 was a cynically apt choice," he added. "It is neutral, inoffensive, sleek without promising too much. For nearly two decades, it has been wildly popular without leaving much of a musical mark, as easy to forget as mild weather."

Maroon 5, he added, "might have lost some moral authority if it had any moral authority to lose."

The reviews didn't go unnoticed by the owners. The Super Bowl was a grand finale to the long season, and now artists were turning down the chance to perform on the NFL's exalted stage.

Less than two weeks after the Patriots beat the Rams, 13–3, in a listless Super Bowl, the league reached a settlement with Kaepernick and Reid, who had accused the owners of colluding to blackball them because of their political views.[14] The league paid the players less than $10 million; after legal fees, the players each received less than $2 million. It was a pittance to the NFL, which did not acknowledge any responsibility. But Kaepernick and Reid felt vindicated.[15]

The issue of how to woo top musicians back to the Super Bowl remained. Kraft knew the league alienated many African-American fans. Weeks before the big game, in January 2019—the same month he was twice spotted by police visiting a day spa in Jupiter, Florida—Kraft flew with Goodell to Los Angeles to meet Jay-Z, the impresario who wore a Kaepernick jersey on *Saturday Night Live* in 2017.[16] Kraft and Jay-Z were part of the Reform Alliance, a foundation focused on criminal justice reform, and Kraft thought the league and Jay-Z could work together.[17]

Over the next few months, the three men talked. Goodell rose to power by listening to the owners' concerns and helping solve their problems. He rarely charged ahead on controversial topics until he had heard from them. This time, perhaps sensing that owners might recoil at the idea of working with a rap star whose lyrics were not always family friendly, and one who publicly supported Kaepernick, Goodell did not solicit many owners' opinions.

A few weeks before the start of the season, the league and Jay-Z unveiled a plan to kill two birds with one stone:[18] Roc Nation, Jay-Z's entertainment and sports company, would take over production of the Super Bowl halftime show, including booking the best music acts. Roc Nation would also work with the league's social justice campaign, Inspire Change, to find recipients for millions of dollars in donations.

The NFL had convinced one of its most prominent critics to produce a show that he claimed he would never perform in. One blindsided owner called me to ask why Goodell formed this alliance. I called several other owners to see if they were concerned. They either did not know or care about Jay-Z's music, but they were pleased Roc Nation would bring buzz back to the Super Bowl halftime show.

When Goodell and Jay-Z met the media at Roc Nation's headquarters after their partnership was announced, reporters peppered Jay-Z with questions about why he cut a deal with a league accused of blackballing Kaepernick.

"I think we have moved past kneeling," he said. "I think it's time to go into actionable items."

The NFL would continue to be hammered for how it treated Kaepernick, including when Goodell arranged a tryout for the quarterback that backfired when Kaepernick pulled out and set up his own private workout.[19] But in partnering with Jay-Z, the NFL and Kraft had once again found a way to solve a crisis by throwing its money and marketing muscle around, and turning the attention back on the players and games, the lifeblood of the league.

13.

SLAVE AUCTIONS AND BRO HUGS

At 10 p.m. on a blustery Thursday in March 2023, the party was just getting going at Prime 47, one of Indianapolis's top steak houses. Agents, scouts, trainers, and reporters were three deep at the bar shouting and backslapping. The dinner tables reserved long in advance represented small islands of power. Stephen Jones, the son of Jerry Jones, flanked by assistants, held court at one of them.

Another table was taken by David Canter, the outspoken agent who represented three dozen NFL players, including DeMarcus Lawrence of the Cowboys and Keanu Neal of the Steelers. Analysts and scouts sat and stood around Canter's table with a handful of reporters, including Peter King, the dean of football writers. Canter made room for new arrivals. Each new guest made the rounds, complete with bro hugs and fist bumps. The noise and the crowds made it impossible to have a deep conversation, but nights at the Combine were meant for gossiping and drinking, not heart-to-hearts.

Everyone already knew King, a celebrity reporter who began covering the NFL before some people at the table were born. As many at the table nibbled on communal plates of pasta, King ordered a steak with mashed potatoes and sides. As bottles of wine flowed, Canter shared his unvarnished opinions but insisted they be off the record so he could "speak freely." Then the tequila arrived.

Canter and a few buddies started Cierto, a tequila brand. With Canter in the middle, they posed for photos. Another long night at the Combine was underway.

Indianapolis doesn't have much of a reputation as a party town. The city is probably best known as the headquarters for national sports organizations, including the NCAA. But every February, it becomes the center of the football universe. The Combine is the quintessential NFL event: a highly regimented coming-out party for college prospects trying to impress teams before the Draft in April. Many of the three hundred or so invited players drop out of college to train for the forty-yard dash, bench-press, and agility drills.

They also prep for interviews with coaches and front office staff who try to determine their mental makeup. Then there are medical evaluations to inspect knees, backs, and elbows. Any hint of a lingering injury can devalue a player's "draft stock." Teams sometimes leak this information to discourage other teams from drafting the player. Agents whisper their own counternarratives. These single-sourced nuggets are gold to sportswriters eager to fill their social media feeds, even if there's little way to vet the information.

The rumor mill can have financial consequences. The tweets and the chatter on NFL radio and television talk shows, where many "analysts" recycle football ephemera, can change where a player is drafted and thus how much he will earn. Caleb Williams, the USC quarterback taken first overall in 2024 by the Chicago Bears, signed a four-year, $39 million contract, which included a $25.5 million signing bonus. Jaylen Key, the last pick in the Draft, known as Mr. Irrelevant, bounced between the Jets and Bengals and earned $221,000 his rookie year.

Most Americans would love to be paid like Mr. Irrelevant. But athletes spend their school years trying to make it to the NFL and can lose it all to injury in a single play. For all but a few elite players, NFL teams have more leverage, and they assert their advantage unequivocally at the Combine. Team personnel analyze players in skintight outfits as they are paraded in front of television cameras, the league's way of bringing football to the fans. Commentators objectify the players by discussing their body type the way trainers talk about horses. Troy Vincent, who is Black, told owners that the Combine has the characteristics of a "slave market."[1]

The media who churn out content for hardcore football fans seem less concerned. NFL Network commentator Mike Mayock went viral at the Combine in 2015 when he gushed that Andrus Peat, an offensive tackle from Stanford University, had a pronounced "bubble butt."

"That lower body is unbelievable," Mayock said as Peat finished a sprinting exercise and the camera focused on his behind.[2] "Look at the body, look at that bubble butt...that's power." The objectification continues in interviews, where team personnel have been known to ask invasive and often irrelevant questions. In 2010, Dolphins general manager Jeff Ireland apologized for asking wide receiver Dez Bryant whether his mother was a prostitute.[3] Ireland admitted he used "poor judgment."

The Combine is part of an elaborate system of rules, customs, and events that help control the owners' biggest expense: player payroll. The salary cap protects the owners from the impulse to sign players to expensive contracts. Yet teams must figure out how to allocate their money efficiently by avoiding players with balky shoulders or an inability to read defenses and finding rookies with potential.

Cracks in this system have emerged. College players have become more aware of their rights, and a handful of prominent prospects have skipped the Combine, confident that their draft position will not be affected.

DeMaurice Smith argued that the Combine was so exploitive it should be scrapped. The players, he said, would be better served working out for NFL scouts at their universities or in private sessions, not live on ESPN or NFL Network.

"I mean, think about it," Smith said in 2023, the year he left the NFL Players Association. "The NCAA and the NFL structure a Combine during what should be every football player's what, last semester in college? Who decided that it was a good idea to take your son and have him exclusively try out for the NFL's exclusive way of getting into the league? As soon as you show up, you have to waive all of your medical rights. And you not only have to sit there and endure embarrassing questions, and I think that's horrible, and I don't want to poopoo any of that. But would you want your son to spend hours inside of an MRI and then be evaluated by thirty-two separate team doctors who, by the way, are only doing it for one reason. What's the reason? To decrease your draft value. So instead of trying to think about whether we enhance a Combine process, what would you want for our sons?"

Technology has made the Combine largely irrelevant, Smith said. "We're now in an era where we know exactly how fast these guys can run, how much they can lift, how far they can jump, do all of those things. Why do we insist on them showing up in Indianapolis? It's not for anything physical, right? It's for the teams to be able to engage in intrusive employment actions that don't exist anywhere else. Can you imagine a group of law school students who are the best in the country? And instead of picking your law firm, you all go to Indianapolis, and you try out and do legal puzzles for five days, and then they go, 'Hey, you've done great on the legal puzzle. Right after this, you're going to go into the back room and we're going to take a DNA sample and we're going to put you through an MRI because we're trying to figure out how to cut our costs for insurance premiums.' Is there anybody in the room that would do that if you were a lawyer?"

Smith's paean to workers' rights may be morally and even economically sound, but the NFL Players Association doesn't yet represent these players because they are not under contract.

Unsurprisingly, owners like Jerry Jones waved off Smith's calls. Jones said that teams should refrain from asking "dehumanizing" questions. "I think we can make it just exactly like you would if you were interviewing for a major company or something like that and ask those kinds of questions," he said.

For Jones and other owners, the Combine should be tweaked, not scrapped.[4] The owners know the college players are eager to impress future employers and will endure injustices, real or imagined. Even their agents, who should be their biggest advocates, understand the utility of the Combine.

Joby Branion, the founder of the Vanguard Sports Group, which represents Von Miller among others, has a firsthand understanding of the Combine. A defensive back at Duke, Branion attended the Combine in 1985 when the event was far smaller. He signed as a free agent with Washington but never made the club. He became an agent in the 1990s. The Combine, he said, could certainly be revised, particularly the interview process. But Branion likes it because players can also answer unresolved questions that teams might have.

"To me, the experience with the medicals almost always cuts both ways," Branion said at the Combine. "There are some people who are exposed. But people come in and say, 'We know he had this injury, but we have no idea.' And our doctor says, 'Hey, you know what? He's really good now.' So, the player just went from being a fourth rounder to a second rounder. It happens both ways."

Branion said Smith had an "overly cynical view" of the Combine. Teams will assess college players one way or another. Why not meet the teams halfway? "Clearly, not everybody is being squashed by definition," he said. "That can't be true."

But the NFL keeps expanding the Combine because it provides cheap programming for NFL Network and ESPN. Between the Super Bowl and the start of free agency in mid-March, talk shows are filled with analysts ranking the best college players. NFL Network had six days of live coverage of the event, and viewership rose 27 percent in some programming windows in 2023. A record 1,625 media members covered the Combine in 2023, more than double the number in 2010.[5]

The league sells sponsorships, too. In 2023, Nobull became the official sneaker of the Combine. In the Omni Severin Hotel, the company had a display in the lobby where players and their agents elbowed each other to get free shoes. "There's nothing better than crack cocaine and free shoes," one agent quipped.

The shoes were such a hit, some prospects wore them on the field for the vertical jump event. When they were told by the league the shoes were not allowed because Nike was the official shoe sponsor, some players skipped the event. Others had their agents run to a nearby shopping mall to buy Nike shoes.

The Combine has become so lucrative that other cities are angling to host the event. Jones wants to bring the Combine to Dallas. Others want to move it to Los Angeles. Both cities have big airports, plenty of training fields, hotels, and top hospitals for player exams. But Indianapolis is more compact; the entire event takes place within a roughly ten-square-block area. Walkways and tunnels connect hotels to the convention center, Lucas Oil Stadium, and restaurants. Scouts, agents, trainers, and other NFL personnel consider the Combine the highlight of the long slog from the college playoffs to the Senior Bowl and Super Bowl, then pro days and private workouts.

Brad Blank, a longtime agent, remembered his first Combine in 1988, a year after the event moved to Indianapolis after stops in Tampa, New Orleans, and Arizona. He stayed in the Holiday Inn with the players. The train station was the center of activity. "We all stayed at the same hotel because there wasn't the demand back then," he said. About a dozen journalists—Peter King, John Clayton—met at a pancake house and chatted with agents and prospects. Players didn't drop out of college to train for the Combine, and the workouts were top secret. "There was no media coverage, nobody cared. It wasn't on television," Blank said.

Now, players and agents dream of getting seats at St. Elmo, the steak house known for its mammoth shrimp cocktails and basement dining areas accessed through a private elevator.

If the Combine is the final exam for college football players, the Draft is graduation. After all the hard work perfecting their craft, the country's top prospects get to march across a stage to raucous applause (unless they're chosen by the Jets, whose fans routinely boo their team's picks), a nationally televised coming out party.

Each newly minted millionaire wears the specially fitted New Era cap instead of a mortar board and tassels and carries his new team's jersey with his name on the back instead of wearing a robe. The presentation is scripted down to the second. Teams call in their draft picks a minute or two before they are announced on television. This provides time for workers behind the stage, who have thirty-two versions of every cap in every player's head size, to grab the proper hat for the draft pick. The player's last name is quickly affixed to the back of the jersey.

The Draft is the best example of how the NFL fills its offseason. For weeks before the Draft, the nation's best college players are relentlessly analyzed and marketed yet are paid nothing in return. When they show up at the Draft, they are paraded and feted even though showing up has no influence on when they are selected.

The NFL Network and ESPN sell millions of dollars in ads during their Draft programming and glorify, and sometimes exploit, the players by focusing on those left waiting to be picked. In 2023, Kentucky quarterback Will Levis was shown fidgeting with his phone and staring into space as player after player was chosen ahead of him. He left the first night of the Draft without an employer and skipped the second night, when his name was eventually called. The networks have toned down their coverage of these players since 2005, when Aaron Rodgers was endlessly shown sitting around waiting to be chosen.

"It was good TV, not that we rooted for anyone to fall," said Seth Markman, who runs ESPN's Draft coverage. "But as TV providers, this is going to get an audience. We did recognize this ultimate reality TV moment. But over the years, you learn, you grow, and show a little more sensitivity, and maybe what we were doing wasn't the right thing and was unfair to the players."

The players' reputations can take a hit. In almost any other sport, being chosen in the second round would be an achievement. But for the players deemed top picks by analysts, those who "fall" to the second round can be seen as failures. This potential embarrassment is why Blank, who represented D'Brickashaw Ferguson and Chris Canty, told his top prospects to skip the Draft.

"My advice to anybody is: 'Don't go. Stay at home, no pressure,'" he said.

Some players ignored Blank's advice because they viewed the Draft, including the chance to hug Goodell on national TV, as a rite of passage. This, Blank conceded, is the genius of the NFL. The league created an event so appealing that the main characters, who aren't paid, are happy to be used as props. The mother of one top prospect lambasted Blank.

"She said, 'This is our moment. We're going and we're going to hug the commissioner.'"

There was a far simpler time, like during the early Obama years, when players walked onstage and simply shook hands with the commissioner. Then came the "Goodell Bro Hug" in 2010 when the Tampa Bay Buccaneers picked Gerald McCoy and he hugged Goodell for a few seconds. Nearly every player since has followed suit. Just as end zone celebrations have become more elaborate, so have the hugs. In 2012, Melvin Ingram shared a special handshake with Goodell that the two men rehearsed. In 2014, receiver Sammy Watkins was the first player to take a selfie with the commissioner. The next year, Danny Shelton became the first player to lift Goodell off his feet. Then Garett Bolles brought his newborn son, Kingston, onstage.[6]

The Goodell Bro Hug may appear benign, a random element of a highly orchestrated event. But Goodell, despite appearances, is *not* the players' friend. He is the embodiment of management, a highly paid workhorse for the thirty-two owners. The moment players sign their first contract, Goodell becomes their boss. He sits in judgment and fines players who violate the league's Personal Conduct Policy, and he does everything in his power to win more money for the owners at the bargaining table.

"The players want to go to the draft because it's a once-in-a-lifetime event and they want to be seen on TV," said Alan Herman, who represents about fifty NFL players. "But the irony of hugging Roger Goodell is, he's going to screw you in contract talks and injury protections."

Branion also tells his players to rethink giving Goodell any love. "I'm like, 'Dude, he never represents your interests,'" Branion said.

"They should be going across the stage and hugging the director of the NFLPA. That's the union that represents you and your brethren's interests against the guy you want to hug. That goes to show how uneducated many of the kids are coming into the league. You have to give kudos to the NFL for making it that way."

The league has expanded the Draft in ways that seem to defy economic sense. In 2015, the NFL moved the event out of New York because Radio City Music Hall, where the event was held for nine seasons, was booked on the NFL's preferred weekend. Rather than delay the Draft a week, which would give teams one less week to build their rosters and get their rookies up to speed, the league moved the event to Chicago, which offered elaborate subsidies.

On television, the Draft looked familiar because it was held in the Auditorium Theatre, which had a similar feel to Radio City. But across the street in Grant Park, more than one hundred thousand fans from across the Midwest attended a three-day fanfest with games for kids, snacks and drinks, and the vibe of a football block party.

Peter O'Reilly, the league's chief of events, remembers thinking the event was a smash when he saw a fan in a Chiefs jersey who had driven from Iowa the day before the Draft so he could be first to enter the theater. Then he met a Broncos fan and a Cowboys fan doing the same thing. "A lot of these guys are now friends," O'Reilly said.

The crowds convinced the league to find other cities. Chicago hosted the event in 2016 so the league could learn more about the process. In the meantime, O'Reilly was besieged with applications from Green Bay, Kansas City, Nashville, and other cities offering to spend millions of dollars on traffic, police overtime, and other inducements to lure the NFL to town. In 2017, the Draft moved to Philadelphia, where the event was held at the Philadelphia Museum of Art, near the statue of Rocky Balboa. In 2018, Jerry Jones hosted the event in AT&T Stadium. In Nashville, the event blended with the city's music clubs. During the Covid-19 pandemic, Goodell read the Draft picks from the basement of his house in Bronxville, New York. In the years since, the Draft has traveled to Cleveland, Las Vegas, Kansas City, Detroit, and Green Bay and turned into a quintessentially American event with hundreds of thousands of fans standing around drinking beer in parking lots watching something they could easily see on television.

The Draft became a version of the Super Bowl for NFL cities that were unlikely to host a championship game. An hour before the Draft began in Kansas City, Goodell made the rounds with friendly media partners. He chatted with NFL Network host Rich Eisen and described what the Draft cards look like. Then he spoke with ESPN, where he was asked about negotiations to extend his contract for four more years.

"The good news is I love the job and I love what I'm doing," he said. "If that's possible, then great. If not, I've been really fortunate to be in this job."

His comments triggered a wave of posts and stories speculating about whether Goodell was hinting that he might walk away. The owners, though, love Goodell. They have their gripes. Every team gets dinged by him at some point. Just ask the Patriots and Saints. But he brings in the bucks—the Draft as an example—and the owners aren't complaining.

14.

THE GAME TO END ALL GAMES

In the years after he left the game, former tight end Rob Gronkowski became a walking billboard for the modern NFL: a player with immense skills, a gift for self-promotion, and a goofball charm advertisers love. After injuries pushed him to retire after the 2018 season, "Gronk," as he is universally known, signed with the WWE, participating in WrestleMania 36 and winning a championship belt.[1] His old teammate on the Patriots Tom Brady convinced him to play two more seasons in Tampa Bay, where he won his third Super Bowl ring. After retiring again following the 2021 season, Gronk continued to cash in on his stardom, raking in tens of millions of dollars working as an analyst on Fox, appearing on television and in movies, and endorsing video games, insurance, and breakfast cereals.

Unsurprisingly, Gronk remains a fixture at the Super Bowl, the ultimate platform for NFL stars to monetize their fame. In Miami in 2020, Gronk unveiled "Gronk Beach," a music festival that featured Flo Rida and the Chainsmokers, and got his former coach Bill Belichick to show up. Women in bikinis and shirts that read "Make America Gronk Again" cheered Gronk as he guzzled Nasty Beast Hard Tea, an alcoholic drink he sponsored.

The Super Bowl is the biggest show in sports not just because of the game but because of the events before it. Everyone connected with the NFL descends on the host city to network, hawk products, and party. Each year, prices for tickets, hotel rooms, and television ads set records as bars, restaurants, and clubs host a football convention on steroids.

The Super Bowl is the intersection of money, sports, entertainment, and, increasingly, gambling. The league's premier showcase reached its apex in February 2024, when Las Vegas hosted the game for the first time. Gronk seemed to embody the moment. On the Wednesday before the game, he weaved through the crowds in the vast media center at the Mandalay Bay Convention Center to promote another sponsor, FanDuel, the sports betting app. Gaming was no longer just a Vegas thing. Tens of millions of Americans bet legally on games in almost thirty states, drawn by hundreds of dollars in free credits and come-ons from Jamie Foxx, Eli Manning, and other celebrities.

Before the previous Super Bowl, FanDuel created the "Kick of Destiny," which involved Gronk attempting to kick a twenty-five-yard field goal that fans could bet on. Leading up to the kick, Gronk had a fake feud with John Cena, the wrestling megastar who led "Team Miss."[2] Gronk's kick hooked left, and many fans claimed the event was rigged. Gronk insisted otherwise, and their "dispute" fueled "Kick of Destiny 2" in Las Vegas. To juice the event, Gronk visited Kay Adams, a chirpy television personality on the FanDuel TV set. In front of a dozen video cameras, Gronk fielded questions that were a microcosm of the modern Super Bowl: manufactured news about a gimmick fueled by a celebrity trying to get fans to part with their money.

Adams started by tapping into Gronk's frat-boy persona. "Over/under in tangible terms: hours you slept last night, two and a half?" she asked.

"Over," he said. "I got about four and a half. But it was kind of like where you're squirming all over the place. I can't sleep in Vegas, like it's impossible. And I swear, I don't go to bed sober in Vegas because then you wake up feeling like you're hung over. So I go to bed wasted and then you wake up and you're fine. So that's just how Vegas is."

Las Vegas had to wait until 2024 to host a Super Bowl because the NFL had held Sin City at arm's length for decades. The casinos and legal sports wagering, the league believed, might tempt players to place bets (or take bribes from unsavory sorts) that might influence their decisions on the field. The NFL had its share of gambling scandals, including one involving stars Paul Hornung and Alex Karras, but those transgressions did not occur in Las Vegas. Yet the NFL considered the city so toxic that league employees could be penalized for even walking through a sportsbook. A decade before the Super Bowl reached Las Vegas, Verizon paid hundreds of millions of dollars to be an NFL sponsor. As part of the deal, Roger Goodell agreed to speak at a company event at the Consumer Electronics Show in Las Vegas. To avoid violating the league's rules, Goodell had to enter the convention center through a back door. The league was so allergic to Las Vegas that in 2003, Commissioner Paul Tagliabue blocked the city from running their "What happens in Vegas stays in Vegas" television ads during the Super Bowl. The city's mayor, Oscar Goodman, a pugnacious lawyer who represented mobsters, didn't take kindly to what he saw as the league's hypocrisy.[3]

Tagliabue "better get his house in order before he talks about us," Goodman said at the time.[4] "There'll probably be more betting in the stadium in San Diego than in all of Las Vegas."

Then in 2018, the Supreme Court overturned a federal law that had limited sports betting to Nevada.[5] Sportsbooks spread quickly, and the league's opposition melted faster than an ice cube on The Strip. After wagging its finger at Las Vegas and sports gambling, the NFL did what it always did: created a plan to make money off the new reality.

By 2024, the league had signed deals worth nearly $1 billion with sportsbooks at MGM and Caesars as well as FanDuel and DraftKings, newer companies that Jerry Jones and Robert Kraft had invested in years before the sports gambling law was repealed.[6] The sites were legal because they peddled "games of chance." But Jones and Kraft knew sports gaming would be legalized nationally, and FanDuel and DraftKings could convert their games into "games of skill," aka sports betting.

Once sports gambling was legalized, teams across the league signed sponsorship deals with casinos and sportsbooks. The Washington Commanders leased space to a sportsbook in its stadium that includes twenty-one self-service betting kiosks and free Commanders hats for anyone who bets $20 or more.[7] To his critics, Goodell said the NFL was just "changing with the times." By 2023, just five years after sports betting was legalized, Americans wagered $120 billion on sports, 28 percent more than the prior year.

With gambling everywhere else, Las Vegas was no longer the league's Kryptonite. The Raiders moved from Oakland to Las Vegas in 2020. The Pro Bowl arrived in February 2022. A few months later, the NFL Draft was held at Caesars Forum, a bandshell tucked between casino hotels. Then the NFL awarded Las Vegas the Super Bowl.

By then, casinos in town had NFL-themed slot machines that promised $1 million jackpots. Screens on the machines showed players charging up and down the field. The NFL and NFL Players Association earned licensing fees on what Hector Fernandez, the CEO of Aristocrat Gaming, called "game-changing machines."

The NFL's embrace of gaming also contributed to a spike in gambling addiction. At his news conference two days before Gronk shilled for FanDuel, Goodell was asked about a comment Anna Isaacson, his vice president of social responsibility, made to *The New York Times*.

"We're in this now—we're in this business," Isaacson said about sports gambling.[8] "What can we do to make sure that we're not causing undue additional harm?"

Goodell said he had not read the quote, which unnerved NFL executives who knew "the Commish" didn't like surprises. He said the league had to protect "the integrity of the game" so fans "know the action on the field is genuine." Protecting the game was priority "one, two, and three."

Then he addressed Isaacson's point. The NFL was running commercials on "responsible gambling" and working with its partners—including, presumably, sportsbooks like DraftKings—to "help educate us and our fans" to make sure "we're treating our fans properly."

Reporters let Goodell off the hook when they changed the topic, asking about Taylor Swift, the singer who goosed NFL ratings in 2023 by attending games to watch her boyfriend, Chiefs tight end Travis Kelce. The Chiefs were in Las Vegas to defend their Super Bowl title, and it was unclear whether Swift would return in time from her concerts in Tokyo. Goodell was asked three questions about whether the league helped the Chiefs make it to the Super Bowl so Taylor could attend and generate more interest.

"I don't think I'm that good a scripter, or anybody on our staff," Goodell said, adding that he and his family saw Swift in concert twice.

The Super Bowl became a de facto national holiday almost instantly. The inaugural AFL-NFL Championship Game, as it was called, was a centerpiece of the merger of the NFL and the upstart AFL announced in June 1966. The first showdown between the leagues in January 1967 was cobbled together in just weeks because many other parts of the deal, like the combined college draft, had to be completed first. As a result, just sixty-one thousand fans showed up to the Los Angeles Memorial Coliseum, about two-thirds of capacity. There were several goofs. An arm fell off the game clock and the Packers had to kick off twice to start the second half because NBC was not back from commercial after the first kick. Yet a combined 50 million viewers watched the Packers trounce the Chiefs on CBS and NBC, which both showed the game because each had a deal with one of the leagues. Commissioner Pete Rozelle knew he had a winner but vowed that the Super Bowl—a term he hated—would never again fail to sell out. (The name caught on, so the league trademarked it in 1969.)

The week before the Super Bowl was also a hit. Title games had been played in the stadiums of the teams in the game, so the location was not known until a week before the game, which limited the entertainment and networking possibilities. Rozelle picked neutral sites in warm-weather cities so sponsors, broadcasters, and media could plan months in advance. With the location fixed, partners could invite their customers to Super Bowl Week no matter who played.

"At some point, the Super Bowl no longer became a game, but it became a show," Ron Wolf, the general manager of the Packers, told Michael MacCambridge in *America's Game*. "And from that, football no longer became a game, it became a business."

The first fifteen Super Bowls were played in Southern California, Miami, New Orleans, and Houston. Starting with the second

Super Bowl, the games sold out and television audiences grew. By the time the Super Bowl returned to the Coliseum in Los Angeles in 1973, more than ninety thousand fans watched the Miami Dolphins complete the NFL's only perfect season.[9] By Super Bowl XVI in 1982 (the NFL adopted Roman numerals to add gravitas), 49.1 percent of households watched the 49ers beat the Bengals, the fourth most-watched program in percentage terms, after episodes of *M*A*S*H*, *Dallas*, and *Roots*.[10]

The Super Bowl quickly became a national party. Americans eat more food on Super Bowl Sunday than any day except Thanksgiving.[11] For the Super Bowl in 2017, Americans were expected to consume 1.3 billion chicken wings[12] and 12.5 million pizza pies.[13]

Cities began lobbying to host the game to attract well-heeled fans and be showcased on television. The owners began awarding the game to cities that built new stadiums for their teams. In 1979, Michigan Governor William Milliken and Detroit Mayor Coleman Young offered the NFL free use of the Silverdome in Pontiac, Michigan, which the owners gladly accepted. The owners also wanted to reward General Motors and Ford, both league sponsors. The Super Bowl made its way to Minneapolis and Indianapolis, which had new domed stadiums, and MetLife Stadium in New Jersey, the only Super Bowl played outdoors in a cold-weather city.

To win a Super Bowl, cities needed to provide tens of thousands of hotel rooms and had to meet thresholds for security, convention space, and airport access. In the early years, league executives Don Weiss, Jim Kensil, and Joe Browne handled many of the preparations for the game. In 1979, the league hired Jim Steeg to run the Super Bowl and other events full-time. By today's standards, though, the Super Bowl was still a shoestring operation. In the 1980s, Thelma Elkjer, Rozelle's secretary, asked Nancy Behar in the broadcast department to take the Lombardi Trophy to that year's game.

Security teams normally took the trophy, but there was a snafu, so Elkjer bought Behar a first-class ticket. The crate holding the trophy was strapped into the cockpit. In Tampa, Behar couldn't leave the trophy unattended, so she took it everywhere, including on dates.

Other years, the trophy sat in a bathtub behind a shower curtain in the hotel room Steeg used as an office. Suitcases with hundreds of tickets were stashed under the bed.

These days, Goodell rides around Super Bowl cities in a limousine, often with police escort. But in the 1980s, he was one of several young league employees who drove Rozelle to parties and events during the week.

Super Bowl tickets were scalped not just by hustlers but by the seventh husband of Rams owner Georgia Frontiere. Teams in Super Bowl cities get an extra allotment of tickets for their season ticket holders and corporate partners. When Super Bowl XIV was in Pasadena in 1980, Dominic Frontiere, a well-known composer of scores for TV shows and movies, sold about 1,800 of the 27,500 tickets given to the Rams. Frontiere failed to report the income from the sale, was convicted of tax evasion, and was sentenced to a year and a day in prison.[14]

The week before the Super Bowl became a convention for sponsors, network executives, and advertisers, and a pit stop for scouts, analysts, and other player personnel who travel from the Senior Bowl in Mobile, Alabama, to the Super Bowl to Indianapolis for the Combine. It is also the end of the season for many football writers and television reporters who ping-pong across the country starting in training camp in July. Hundreds of them work in vast media workrooms and on Radio Row, a mosh pit for radio and television reporters.

In the early years of the Super Bowl, most radio reporters were affiliated with the teams in the game. But in 1992, Mike Francesa and

Chris Russo, aka Mike and the Mad Dog, took their popular New York sports talk radio show to Minneapolis, site of Super Bowl XXVI. They wanted to broadcast from the lobby of the Hyatt, the main media hotel, but were asked to pay $40,000 to rent the space, so the pair moved to a nearby Holiday Inn. Steeg recognized talk radio was the future, so he provided a meeting room for radio stations the following year.

"It caught on because the stations realized they'd have dedicated space," he said.

Radio Row grew in the early 2000s when the NFL Network built an indoor set, and CBS, Fox, and other networks followed. Hundreds of current and retired players, including Joe Montana and Antonio Brown, began visiting Radio Row to hawk products and highlight causes. Randy Grimes, a center with the Tampa Bay Buccaneers for ten seasons, discussed his work helping players battle addiction to painkillers.[15] Representatives from the league's Player Care Foundation and Gridiron Greats, a nonprofit group started by former Bears coach Mike Ditka, make the rounds, too.

As the week rolls on, somber talk about battered players is replaced by lighter topics like the halftime show. For the first twenty-five or so Super Bowls, the musical acts were often college marching bands and Up with People, a youth-oriented singing entourage. But in 1992, Fox drew viewers away from the Super Bowl by running its popular comedy *In Living Color* during halftime of that year's game.

The owners were spooked. So league president Neil Austrian hired producers from Radio City Music Hall to revamp the halftime show, and in October 1992, the owners approved Michael Jackson as the next halftime act. To that point, shows rarely cost more than $1 million. Jackson's show was going to cost far more, so the league signed Frito-Lay as the sponsor to defray the cost. Jackson said little at his pregame press conference, but his appearance created buzz and the impression that the NFL hired top-shelf talent.

Jackson didn't disappoint. Onstage, he stood motionless for more than a minute as the crowd roared. He sped through abbreviated versions of his hits, then the crowd held colored signs that together showed drawings of children as "We Are the World" played. Hundreds of children ran onstage. The show was such a success it "led to, 'Who do you bring in next year to make it even bigger?'" Austrian said.

Eleven years after her brother performed, Janet Jackson had her infamous "wardrobe malfunction" courtesy of Justin Timberlake, who exposed her breast, which had been covered by a nipple shield, to fans in Houston and tens of millions of television viewers. Conservative politicians held a hearing on "indecency on television" in Congress. Tagliabue, Dan Rooney of the Steelers, and Jerry Richardson of the Panthers testified. Tagliabue blamed Les Moonves, the chief executive of CBS, which broadcast the game, because he had asked the league to pick MTV, a sister company, to produce the halftime show.

Tagliabue said the league "flatly rejected" several performers MTV suggested, but it signed off on Jackson and Timberlake as the headliners, with P. Diddy and Kid Rock making cameos. Tagliabue said that MTV resisted disclosing details of the show, so the league was unaware of what was going to transpire.

"Inexplicably, we gave the keys to the car to someone else for them to drive without assuring ourselves that they knew how to drive safely—and the car crashed," Tagliabue said.

The NFL swore off MTV and for several years picked "safer" artists like Paul McCartney, the Rolling Stones, and Bruce Springsteen.

The Super Bowl is by far the league's biggest moneymaker and helps cover some of the costs of running the league, including Roger Goodell's eight-figure compensation package. The NFL sets the prices for Super Bowl tickets, which have grown far faster than inflation. The most expensive ticket to the first Super Bowl was $12, or about $110 in 2024 dollars. That might cover the cost of parking at the Super Bowl in Las Vegas, where the cheapest tickets went for more than $2,000. The league gets a slice of concessions and merchandise.

A sea of underpaid and free labor is hired by subcontractors and the host cities. Take the halftime show. The league hires production companies that hire smaller companies to handle sound systems, lighting, and so on. These contractors pay stagehands, electricians, set designers, and other specialists as little as $12 an hour with no overtime. The workers accept because they want to add the NFL to their résumés. Many of these workers pay their own way and sleep six to a room in cheap hotels.

"A large percentage of the community that work at stadium shows are gypsies," said Mark Kiracofe, an international representative at the International Alliance of Theatrical Stage Employees, which represents entertainment workers. "They're living event to event, and want to get called the next time, so they don't want to make waves."

Though the Super Bowl is an NFL event, the league is not responsible for most of these workers. But the league does get blamed. After the Super Bowl in Atlanta in 2019, the city council president, Felicia Moore, sent a letter to Goodell complaining that a local staffing company authorized by the NFL had not paid more than two hundred people who worked the event.[16]

"These people worked 70-plus hours, standing on their feet 14 hours a day...," another city councilman said.[17] "They are seniors...students. People are literally trying to pay their light bills with this money."

The owners have a different focus: who to sit with at the game. In October 2003, they decided who would share luxury boxes at the

Super Bowl the following February in Houston, where Janet Jackson exposed her breast. The owners of the Bengals and Colts chose to share a suite, according to meeting notes. Lamar Hunt of the Chiefs and Bud Adams of the Titans—two AFL founders—shared another box. Georgia Frontiere sat with Bill Bidwill, who had moved the Cardinals from St. Louis to Arizona fifteen years earlier. The owners of the Jets and Giants shared a box, and Jerry Jones and Al Davis of the Raiders, two maverick owners, sat together.

Jones loved to surround himself with A-listers. At the Super Bowl in 2011, played in Jones's AT&T Stadium, his guest list included George W. Bush and Ross Perot; Catherine Zeta-Jones and her husband, Michael Douglas; and Harrison Ford, Jamie Foxx, and John Travolta. Billionaires Warren Buffett and Carlos Slim sat with former Cowboys running back Emmitt Smith and Evander Holyfield, the former heavyweight champion.[18]

As Jones mingled with luminaries, his reputation took a hit. Jones wanted to set a Super Bowl attendance record, so he added more than 1,200 bleacher seats. But they didn't pass code, and many of the ticket holders who had paid as much as $900 were forced to sit elsewhere or were invited to watch the game on televisions inside a club and promised refunds. Those who never made it inside were offered tickets to the next year's Super Bowl in Indianapolis.[19]

Jones lived for the biggest stage, yet the Cowboys haven't won a Super Bowl since 1996. Since then, he watched the Patriots and Robert Kraft play in nine Super Bowls. Kraft made news, too, in 2015 when he denied accusations the Patriots deliberately deflated game balls in the AFC Championship Game.[20]

In 2008, Kraft walked on the field before the Super Bowl with Ed Goren from Fox Sports, which was showing the game. Goren told Kraft that the Patriots were eleven-point favorites to beat the Giants and jokingly asked Kraft to keep the game close for three quarters.

Kraft knew his history and said that every time the Patriots played in a Super Bowl shown on Fox, "it seems to go down to the wire, so don't worry." The Giants upset the Patriots, 17–14.

The Patriots also staged the biggest comeback in Super Bowl history when they overcame a 28–3 deficit to beat the Falcons in Super Bowl LI. In the fourth quarter, the Falcons were on their way to their first Super Bowl title. Win, lose, or draw, Blank had for years watched the ends of games on the sideline. This time, he took his general manager, Thomas Dimitroff, and stood about fifteen yards from the Falcons bench. The Patriots scored nineteen unanswered points in the fourth quarter, forcing the Super Bowl's first overtime.

"When I saw that coin go up—I still see it—if that comes down wrong, we're done, because Brady's just so good at finishing," Dimitroff said.

The Patriots won the coin toss and scored, and Blank's Super Bowl dreams vanished.

"We were down there sitting or standing on the sideline through that whole debacle," Dimitroff said. "It was really, really bad."

Months later, Blank and Kraft were walking to dinner in Manhattan. Kraft gave his players Super Bowl rings with 283 diamonds to commemorate the deficit they overcame. The men were friends, but Blank was not amused. "I said to Robert, 'You didn't have to do the 28–3 in the ring,'" Blank told Mark Leibovich.[21] "It kind of pissed me off."

The Super Bowl has had plenty of snafus. Not enough hotel rooms in Jacksonville. Ice storms in Atlanta and Dallas. Brady's jersey was stolen from his locker in Houston. The lights went out at the Superdome in New Orleans.

But year after year, the NFL turns its biggest stage into a bigger stage. Paul McCartney once said about the Beatles and the 1960s:

"The Beatles weren't the leaders of the generation, but the spokesmen." In some ways, the NFL is the same. The league is not a leader of American culture, but a reflection of it. At the Super Bowl in the 1960s, Apollo astronauts read the Pledge of Allegiance. Michael Jackson, Whitney Houston, U2, and Lady Gaga have performed at the peak of their careers. The Super Bowl became a patriotic rally during Operation Desert Storm and after the attacks on September 11, 2001.

The NFL has tried to burnish its image by bathing itself in the reflective glow of the cities that host the Super Bowl. In 2019, Goodell, Blank, and other NFL heavyweights went to Martin Luther King Jr.'s childhood home and listened to Bernice King, the reverend's daughter, talk about her father.[22] They walked to Ebenezer Baptist Church, where Dr. King was a pastor.[23] Paul Tagliabue was among the VIPs and talked about how star players Mel Blount, John Mackey, and Gene Upshaw followed King's message and became leaders who fought for better contracts that players benefit from today.

But that glow could be selective. As the NFL honored King, Jay-Z and other musicians said that they would not perform at the Super Bowl if asked, out of sympathy with Colin Kaepernick, who accused the league owners of banning him because of his political views.

By 2024, the league had moved past the controversy. Goodell and the owners were focused on expanding the regular season to eighteen games, which would push the Super Bowl into Presidents' Day weekend in late February. It would overlap with "sweeps week," the seven-day period when the Nielsen Company compiles data on viewership and advertising. The Super Bowl would be the most viewed show that week, which could help networks raise their ad rates. Until then, Goodell, Jones, Kraft, and the rest of the NFL could crow about reaching the mountaintop in Las Vegas, where football, glitz, and gambling mingled seamlessly.

15.

"IF IT AIN'T BROKE, FIX IT ANYWAY."

In October 1994, Ann Kirschner, an NFL marketing and strategy consultant, met with the league's president, Neil Austrian, and Ron Bernard, who ran NFL Enterprises, to show them the next hot thing: an internet browser made by Mosaic. Kirschner had used email and other text-based communications, but Mosaic was a game changer because it produced colorful graphic websites. She knew the next generation of fans would get their news this way.

"I said some version of 'I've seen the future, and the reason this is important is because this is how young fans are going to experience the NFL,'" Kirschner said. "And they said yeah, yeah, yeah. They had absolutely no idea what I was talking about. They were guys who had their assistants doing their email for them."

Austrian and Bernard, though, were smart enough to know what they didn't know, so they hired Kirschner full-time to develop the league's first website. She assembled a small staff that rushed to launch one in time for the Draft six months later.

One key task was to acquire the NFL.com domain name. Unfortunately, it was owned by a podiatrist in Chicago who bought the name because it matched his marketing slogan, "No Foot Loss." The league bought www.nflhome.com as a placeholder, but to Kirschner's surprise, the doctor was willing to sell the domain name for a few thousand dollars and Bears season tickets for a year. The Bears finished 9-7 in 1995 and missed the playoffs.

The league's site went live less than two weeks before the Draft and included information from former Cowboys executive Gil Brandt on the top college prospects. On the first night of the Draft, Commissioner Paul Tagliabue, Roger Goodell, Brandt, and others huddled around a computer at the Paramount Theater in Madison Square Garden. With the roar of the fans in the background, Kirschner's team opened an online chat so fans could put questions to Tagliabue and several players. The first question was an eternal one: "Hey Commish, why do the Jets suck?"

Greg Aiello, a league spokesman, suggested they move on.

During the 1995 season, Kirschner started another chat room, which IBM sponsored, so fans could ask Troy Aikman and other quarterbacks questions. But Kirschner had to pull the plug because fans started using filthy language. "That was the end of the live chat because they were going after the players and then the commentator and it quickly went downhill," she said.

The NFL's entry to the internet age was emblematic of how the league functions as a business. The league wasn't the first big sports property to start a website; the Seattle Mariners and Portland Trail Blazers got there in 1994. But over time, it found its footing.

By NFL standards, setting up a site in six months was warp speed. The league quickly found ways to use the technology. Kirschner visited a stadium press box during a game and saw two men sitting side by side, one with binoculars calling out plays he saw on the field and his partner typing the information into a computer. The data was uploaded to a digital archive in the league's head office. She suggested using the data to also create more detailed online box scores for fantasy football players. The league did not have the resources, so Kirschner found an outside company.

"I wanted to do it all in-house, but it was very antithetical to the league, which did not think of itself as a tech company, or even a production company," she said.

They discovered there was hunger for NFL news. Visitors on the league's website more than doubled to 160,000 in 1997, from 70,000 the year before. Advertising revenue grew to $1.7 million, from $1.2 million, over the same period. Fans spent an average of three hours a week on the site. By 1998, the league had found enough new advertisers that the site broke even. Kirschner's group had freedom to dream up new ideas because even if the owners didn't understand the technology, they knew the website was attracting fans.

Austrian "had no interest in making money, but he wanted to explore and find out," said Jaan Janes, whom Kirschner hired to develop the website. "What he said to me was, 'If we did nothing else and made no money on the web but found a way to drive our ratings up by one-tenth of one point, then we'd be minting money.' The value of the league was really in the media rights, and the web was a mechanism to generate interest."

Clubs used the technology unevenly. The Cardinals posted the audio stream of *The Buddy Ryan Show* on their site, while Dan Kraft—Robert's second son—said the internet was a "priority" for the Patriots in 1996. According to the NFL's Interactive Committee, the

Chargers were "only interested in the Web if they think they can get a good R.O.I."

Kirschner discovered that if Tagliabue was new to the internet, the owners were further behind. Robert Tisch, the half owner of the Giants, asked Kirschner for a personal lesson on how to use a computer. She visited his office and showed him how to move the mouse. "He had absolutely no idea of what this stuff was about," she said. But when the number of visitors to NFL.com and online sponsorships grew, the owners "had dollar signs in their eyes, and then it was kind of like, 'Well, what are you doing actually?'"

Jones was one of those owners. Kirschner's group began putting play-by-play data on the web. During a Cowboys game at Texas Stadium, the league's computer in the press box that was uploading the data was unplugged. She never discovered who did it—Jones himself, one of his assistants, or perhaps someone tripped over a wire. But it shut down the feed. Jones made clear he was unhappy that the league was giving away what he considered *his* team's data.

Kirschner, Bernard, and Tola Murphy-Baran, who helped create Sunday Ticket, flew to Dallas to meet Jones. Sitting in his office, they explained that the feed worked only if every team cooperated. Jones, who kept confusing the word "streaming" with "streaking," thought the teams should handle their own feeds and charge for them. This would have created chaos, and he backed down.

As the league's internet operations grew, so did the restraints on Kirschner. "That was when I realized that my days as a swashbuckling entrepreneur at the NFL were over," she said. She left in 1999.

Building a presence on the internet was just one way the NFL became the undisputed king of sports and entertainment. Like a shark, the league must keep moving to justify its sky-high valuations. This hunger for growth became more pronounced under Goodell. In 2024, he received an email from a friend who sent him a story that said ninety-three of the top one hundred television broadcasts in 2023 were NFL games. Goodell's response? "We have a couple of more slots to fill!"

Seen another way, the league was a mature business—albeit a very healthy one—that must work harder to continue growing as quickly. Brian Rolapp, the league's chief media and business officer, called this the "tyranny of big numbers."

"It's a cliché, but I'll say it: Complacency is an enemy," he said. "Paul Tagliabue had a line I remember. He said, 'If it ain't broke, fix it anyway.' I think there's a healthy paranoia here about how do you keep it going, how do you keep it growing, how do you keep it fresh."

This paranoia has manifested itself, for example, in showing games on Black Friday and Christmas, and in the addition of extra playoff games. As Falcons owner Arthur Blank put it: "There's this notion that whether you're the gazelle or the lion, you get up in the morning, and you have to be running. You're going to be eaten or you're going to starve to death, one or the other. I think the league gets up every morning and is running. I think they're trying to grow."

Like most owners, Blank was aware of the challenges facing the league, the largest being the fracturing media landscape. For decades, the league dealt with a handful of networks—ABC/ESPN, CBS, Fox, NBC, and occasionally Turner. The introduction of Apple's iPhone in 2007 and other smartphones, though, let fans check scores, game highlights, and their fantasy teams without going to their computers or waiting for an announcer to read the results. Smartphones also included messaging apps, cameras, and video games that consumed a growing share of people's free time. To many younger fans, paying for a cable connection to watch games or *SportsCenter* was unthinkable. Families began ditching their cable subscriptions to save money, a trend that accelerated during the Covid-19 pandemic.

The percentage of homes with subscriptions peaked in 2009 and fell 34 percent, to 69 million, by 2024.[1] Analysts expect subscriptions to plummet another 28 percent, to 50 million, by 2029. The league still draws the most viewers, but the pool of them watching traditional television networks has declined, and those who are tuning in are getting older. In 2015, 51 percent of viewers of NFL games were fifty or above. That percentage ballooned to 73 percent by 2022.[2] This concerns the networks and their advertisers, as well as the league's sponsors, who want to reach younger consumers with more disposable income.

The decline in cable subscriptions is a more pressing problem for the NBA, Major League Baseball, and other leagues that show the bulk of their games on cable networks. The NFL by contrast puts about 90 percent of its games on network television. Before the 2024 season, David Berson, the president of CBS Sports, called the NFL "a rocket ship that is going to continue to drive interest." He added: "While there's a lot of success on other platforms, broadcast TV is still the best place to drive the biggest audience for the biggest events." He could not envision a day when CBS did *not* show NFL games.

CBS and other networks, though, have promoted their streaming services like Paramount and Peacock to reach fans without cable subscriptions. The revenue from streaming has not offset the declines in the networks' traditional businesses, which could find it harder to pay the NFL's broadcast rights fees.

"Nothing else is like the NFL," said Michael Nathanson, a sports media analyst. "It's a perfect sport for television. The timing is great, it's a short season. Gambling and fantasy football make it better and the viewership has been really, really strong in a world when more and more content" is moving away from network television.

But, Nathanson said, as the number of television viewers plummets further, "it's going to be hard for the networks to justify paying what they pay the league now."

The NFL also must decide what to do with its own cable channel, the NFL Network, which it created in 2003 to give the league leverage in negotiations with broadcasters, and to provide a home for a lot of its content. The network has not been immune from the troubles in the cable television market. The media group was profitable, and the network is a platform to promote the league.[3] Still, NFL Network had several rounds of layoffs "due to economic and industry-wide shifts."[4]

No one should weep for the NFL, because the league has courted technology companies with more cash than the networks. YouTube, which is owned by Google, paid more than $2 billion a year for the rights to the Sunday Ticket and RedZone streaming services.[5] Amazon paid the NFL about $1 billion a year to stream Thursday night games, and another $100 million to broadcast a game on Black Friday.[6] Netflix shelled out $150 million to show two games on Christmas Day in 2024.[7]

The league has helped its network partners by giving them desirable games to show exclusively on their streaming services.[8] The league promotes alternative broadcasts like ESPN's *ManningCast*, which features Peyton and Eli Manning discussing Monday night games while they are being played on ESPN's main channel.

"I think the way we measure it is, is it bringing more people in to the game who ordinarily wouldn't be there or is it keeping people around longer who ordinarily might not do that?" Rolapp said.

The NFL has its skeptics. In 2014, former Dallas Mavericks owner Mark Cuban predicted—incorrectly, as it turned out—that the NFL would dilute its power by playing games beyond Sundays and Mondays.

The league expanded its schedule to include occasional games on Wednesdays and Fridays. But the supply of games has remained largely the same. In 2020, the NFL added a seventeenth game that pushed the total number of regular-season games to 272, up from 256, where it was for nearly two decades.

"What's really interesting about the NFL is that the entire world around them changed and they stayed basically the same," said Mike Mulvihill, the president of insights and analytics at Fox. "And by staying the same, they took on a greater share of the market, a greater share of the highest rated shows. It's a really fascinating case study in the value of not changing too quickly or not evolving too much. It's essentially the same thing now that it was thirty years ago, with *Thursday Night* being the outlier. All they had to do was just keep doing the same thing."

Following the NFL, though, has become more expensive because games on Netflix, Amazon, and other streaming services require subscriptions. To watch every NFL game in 2024, a fan would have had to spend more than $1,000 to subscribe to streaming services and a cable connection.[9]

The cost could get greater if the owners expand the regular season to eighteen games and reduce the number of preseason games to two. In addition to bringing in more money in rights fees, it would allow the NFL to own more of the television calendar.

Some owners oppose a longer season. Fewer preseason games means teams would have less time to prepare for the start of the season. A longer regular season means larger rosters. There are questions whether fans crave two more weeks of football.

"If there's one word from the founders of the NFL, from George Halas to Tim Mara to Lamar Hunt, it's 'Don't forget to take care of the game,'" Colts owner Jim Irsay said. "The game, that's everything. That's the golden goose. You let anything damage the game, you're screwed. And don't try to squeeze every penny out of the game. Eighteen games is too many games. Seventeen is barely okay. And it's stupid because that's not where the money is anyway. The money is in Hollywood producing these new shows. The money is in gaming. The money is in Europe."

The league wants to expand the season in part so it can play more games overseas. In 2024, Goodell said that he expected sixteen games a season to be played overseas, with the league creating an international television package,[10] which could generate another $1 billion a year. In 2025, the league planned to play regular-season games in Berlin, Dublin, and Madrid for the first time, but the players would have to agree to a longer season, and they will no doubt ask for a greater share of revenue, larger rosters, and other accommodations.

The NFL started playing overseas in the 1980s with preseason games in London, Tokyo, and other cities. In the 1990s, the NFL created developmental leagues in Europe with mixed success. Starting in 2005, the NFL began playing regular-season games overseas, including games annually in London. The games lost millions of dollars, but sold out quickly and generated sponsorships and television deals with Sky Sports. Starting in 2013, the NFL began playing up to four games a year in London and added games elsewhere.

"It's an investment, but it's one the ownership supports tremendously," Goodell said.

Seemingly each fall, Goodell is asked when a team, or even a division of teams, will be based overseas. Goodell leaves open the possibility, but the odds are slim. The team or teams would have to deal with different tax codes, legal systems, housing, travel, and security. Free agents might be reluctant to sign with a club overseas, especially if the players have school-age children. Draft picks could decline to sign with teams overseas. Clubs would have to find replacement players many time zones away.

"I think for it to happen, you probably need supersonic travel, which we haven't had in a while," one owner told me.

Moving a team to Europe would obligate a handful of teams to make a transatlantic trip every year, because division rivals play each other at home and away.

Creating a division of new teams overseas is more remote because those teams would need to generate as much if not more revenue than the thirty-two teams would lose by expanding. In 2023, each club received about $400 million in national revenue per club. "If you put four new teams over there, you would need to at least have $1.6 billion in new, found media to avoid a dilution issue," the owner said.

For now, teams are finding their own fans and sponsors overseas.[11] The Global Markets Program started in 2022 was a recognition that fans root for players and their teams, not the league, and having teams marketing themselves was more effective. "Nobody roots for the shield," Kansas City Chiefs president Mark Donovan said, referring to the NFL's logo. "The seismic shift," he added, was the league realizing that it had "smart organizations that know their branding better than we do."

The Chiefs started using social media and other digital tools to reach fans in Mexico and Germany. Donovan recalled seeing a chart that showed only 20 percent of fans who root for Premier League teams are based in the United Kingdom. About 85 percent of NFL fans, by contrast, are based in the United States. "If we're going to continue growing, we have to get global."

Donovan said in 2024 that the Chiefs had invested more than $3.5 million in Germany and generated about $1.1 million in sponsorships and other revenue. The team saw a big jump in interest and revenue after the Chiefs played in Frankfurt in 2023. More international games would justify further investments, which is why the league needs to expand to an eighteen-game regular season, he said. "They're all tied together."

While the owners chase more dollars overseas, they are charging their fans back home more. League-wide attendance hit a record 18.9 million fans in 2024, but teams have focused more on "premium options." When Mercedes-Benz Stadium in Atlanta opened in 2017, it had four levels of suites. Stadiums that opened since then, like SoFi Stadium in Inglewood, California, have ten or more levels of clubs and suites. So, the Falcons added a field-level club behind each team's bench; they routinely sell out and quickly paid for themselves.

"It's the champagne kind of service crowd down there," Falcons president Greg Beadles said.

The Falcons added living-room-type suites on the second deck that were sponsored by AT&T and opened a two-tier club that costs $15,000 a season. In Las Vegas, the Raiders opened the 11,000-square-foot Wynn Field Club at Allegiant Stadium that includes 29 VIP tables and four bars.[12]

These amenities are one reason the average cost of attending a game surged 44 percent between 2015 and 2024,[13] faster than inflation. "The trend right now is premium, premium, premium," said the Chiefs' Donovan, who is a member of the league's Fan Engagement & Major Events Committee. "People hear 'premium' and they think suites. But it's the experience from leaving your driveway to returning to your driveway. Special entrances, seating options, food and beverage, access to pre- and postgame events."

With new stadiums opening in Buffalo and Nashville in 2026 and 2027, the average cost will rise further. Fans are being priced out of new stadiums because they can't afford to pay tens of thousands of dollars for nonrefundable personal seat licenses that are needed to buy season tickets, which will also be more expensive. Longtime season ticket holders in Buffalo were struggling.

Karl-Eric Reif, who went to his first Bills game in 1967 and bought his first season tickets in 1971, worried that on top of many thousands of dollars for seat licenses, his pair of tickets, which cost about $1,000 each, would skyrocket. "I find PSLs morally offensive," said Reif, a retired writer. "The idea seems so fan unfriendly. Everyone should be able to get in at an affordable price. I don't resent the wealthier fans. But it would be a sad split if the best decision for us was to give our tickets up."

Thomas DeLaus, a mailman and father of two young children from Rochester, faced paying $6,000 for licenses for each of his four seats, as well as nearly $10,000 a season for the tickets in the Bills' new stadium, twice as much as he was paying in the old stadium. The PSLs had little resale value and the tickets could keep going up in price, stretching his already tight budget.

"At the end of the day, I'm perfectly fine sitting on my couch. It's already expensive now; I can't imagine what it'll be like in ten years," DeLaus said.

Rich Luker, a sociologist who has tracked sports fans since the 1990s, said loyalty to players, teams, and cities has frayed for a generation. Younger fans are less likely to follow the team their parents or grandparents did and are more likely to latch on to football because they played Madden video games and fantasy football. For them, social media tops cable television shows, podcasts are more compelling than sports talk radio, and blogs have pushed aside traditional newspaper stories. With rare exceptions, influencers are more popular than sports writers. Ticket resellers like StubHub have made it easier to go to games without committing to season tickets.

The pace of change accelerated with the introduction of smartphones. "You've got a million options about what to do with your free time, and all sports and other forms of leisure were losing time,"[14] Luker said. "The people who run the sports are business people. They love their sports. But they are looking at what's going on and see people developing new technologies that surpassed things in their own sports, so the logical temptation is instead of trying to beat them to join them." Luker feared that the NFL and other leagues "crossed the transom from being a sports industry to being a media industry. They are focusing more on the technology and the media than the sport itself."

Fans are increasingly treated as customers, props for television broadcasts, and easy marks for sportsbooks. The league doesn't take a cut of every bet on NFL games—that money is split between the sportsbooks and state governments—but it licenses its data, and its logos and marks, to the sportsbooks. The more people gamble, the more valuable their data and intellectual property become.

People who play fantasy football and bet on games are more engaged. This is one reason the league partnered with Genius Sports, whose technology, BetVision, lets viewers customize their game broadcasts to include, among other things, gambling data. In time, artificial intelligence software will learn a viewer's preferences.

"We can talk about betting and gambling and that's not insignificant," said Steve Bornstein, the president of Genius Sports in North America, who previously ran the league's media group. "But betting and gambling has been around since the invention of the NFL. We haven't invented gambling, we just shined a light on it. And what I've seen today is the fact that we're actually able to manipulate it to make the consumption much more engaging."

The owners are exploring how else they can profit from gambling, including putting betting parlors in stadiums and displaying more gambling-related data on scoreboards. They also know sports gambling is highly addictive. In 2021, the league gave the National Council on Problem Gambling a three-year, $6.2 million grant to upgrade its telephone helplines,[15] a pittance for a $23 billion-a-year business. Goodell appointed John Mara to the league's Legalized Sports Betting Committee, which includes Jonathan Kraft from the Patriots and Charlotte Jones from the Cowboys. Mara is one of the few owners openly against gambling, ironic since his grandfather, Tim Mara, was a bookmaker. The commissioner told Mara he wanted him to act as a counterweight to the other owners.

"It makes me nervous," Mara said. "I just see young people gambling on games and you just worry about whether it's going to lead to more addictive behavior going forward. I acknowledge the fact that it's out there. It's going to happen anyway. Do you try to regulate it as much as possible? That's the argument that's always been given to us. So I pay attention to it, but I do with a great deal of caution."

Mara might be cautious about gambling, but he is optimistic about the future of the NFL. And why not? The league is as popular as ever. Owners have been selling more than 98 percent of their tickets. Television ratings fell only slightly during the 2024 season, which overlapped with a general election. Each NFL team received $402 million in national revenue in the 2023 season, 123 percent more than the $180 million they received in 2012. Team valuations skyrocketed. Terry and Kim Pegula paid $1.4 billion for the

Buffalo Bills in 2014. Less than a decade later, Josh Harris led a group that paid $6 billion for the Washington Commanders. Owners can sell up to 10 percent of their teams to private equity funds without ceding control.

To Mark Patricof, these are signs of a bubble in the making. A rare bear in a room full of sports bulls, he believes in the power and profitability of sports. After years working in the media and finance industries, Patricof started a private equity firm that pools investments from athletes and buys stakes in companies. But he believes the valuations of NFL teams have exceeded the future earning power of the league and made it harder for owners whose franchises are their primary assets—the Bears, for instance—to continue holding them. To him, courting private equity was a necessity, not a luxury.

Private equity firms promise their investors they will double or triple their money in only a few years. Yet the firms that invested in NFL teams have no way to influence the operation of the teams. Patricof said it's wishful thinking for the private equity firms to expect to resell their stakes for two or three times what they paid for them.

"I think it's going to be inevitable that they're going to want to exit at a premium, but who's going to pay?" he said. "Sure, no one thought that clubs would be worth $7 billion five years ago. But they've sucked every penny out of the networks. They've sucked every penny out of the fans. At some point, people get pissed off."

He added: "Are the investors going to double their money? It's a Band-Aid and everyone likes it because they think the league is so much more valuable than what these teams are now worth. At some point that balloon will pop."

The league's relationship with the Players Association will change, too. In 2023, the players chose Lloyd Howell, a longtime business consultant, as their union's new executive director because they wanted to maximize their value. Younger NFL players have come of age as college and even high school athletes are being paid for the use of their names, images, and likenesses (NIL). In time, they may fight for a better rookie wage scale, something the owners have used to suppress costs. Star players who signed six- and seven-figure NIL deals may stay in college rather than sign a less valuable rookie contract. Some of them may insist on being paid to attend the Combine or Draft.

"You're going to get older and more experienced players, but they're going to want more money," said Charles Grantham, a longtime executive at the NBA players union who directs the Center for Sport Management at Seton Hall. "They're going to come in more informed."

This tension won't dissuade a billionaire looking to buy an NFL team. Franchises only come on the market every few years, and anyone wealthy enough to spend billions of dollars for a team will view a rising salary cap as the cost of doing business. Besides, the tax breaks are advantageous.

This feeding frenzy has helped make Jones and Kraft fabulously rich. Neither could have imagined teams selling for $6 billion when they went deeply into debt to pay record prices for their money-losing teams. The NFL was already the country's most popular league, but its business engines were just starting to accelerate. For more than three decades, both men had a strong hand in supersizing the NFL.

"I have the largest, most really value-oriented idea about what the NFL is as anybody you can ever talk to," Jones told reporters. "I never dreamed it would be in the world and flying this high with the values that we are relative to our stature as content. I couldn't have imagined that in a million years. And I will say this, I'm more optimistic about how it grows from here than I was when I first came into the NFL in 1989 and any period in between."

But by 2024, they were well into their eighties and spending more time burnishing their images. Kraft was one of the main characters in the ten-part *Dynasty* documentary on Apple, and Jones was the centerpiece of a ten-part documentary that would appear on Netflix. While they remain fixtures and influential voices inside the league, Jones and Kraft may not play their same outsized roles in labor and media negotiations in the coming years as Clark Hunt, Greg Penner of the Broncos, and others grow in stature.

But as the saying goes, it takes only three generations to lose a fortune. In many businesses, the children of the founders lack their parents' passion and instinct. The NFL is no exception. Some handoffs have been successful. Dan Rooney succeeded his father, Art, and made the Steelers and the league stronger. The passing of the baton at other clubs—the Raiders and the Texans, for example—has been less impressive. In time, Jones's and Kraft's sons and daughters, who have worked with their fathers for decades, will take over their clubs.

"You know, as far as succession, succession is here," Kraft said in March 2025 when asked whether he will step back from running the club. "I have my eldest son, Jonathan, [who] has been part of every key decision I've made for the last thirty-odd years and is a full partner in everything."

Kraft acknowledged that Jonathan stays out of the limelight. None of his or Jones's children have the public stature of their dads. But it almost doesn't matter. The NFL is so wealthy that every team is almost guaranteed to turn a profit, no matter who is in charge.

"We need to be successful on the edges and be excellent because, I mean, Gomer Pyle could go run the thing and be successful," Colts owner Jim Irsay said, referring to the goofy mechanic played by Jim Nabors on *The Andy Griffith Show*. "It's like flying a 747. Just let autopilot fly it, please. Just sit here and take a nap and we'll be fine."

Goodell, fifteen years younger than Jones and Kraft, shows few signs of slowing. The league was on track to meet his (once unfathomable) target of reaching $25 billion in revenue by 2027—which is also when his latest contract expires. He turned sixty-five in 2024 but still travels widely for NFL games, to Capitol Hill to lobby Congress, and to events like the fanfest Fanatics held in New York. A Comic Con for sports, the event included games and exhibits, memorabilia shops, a trading card show, and autograph signings with players like Peyton Manning and Michael Strahan. Walking through the Jacob Javits Convention Center, Goodell posed for photos with Tom Brady and Rob Gronkowski dressed in Patriots uniforms. Fans took pictures. Smiling ear to ear, Goodell did not look like someone tired of his job.

In conversations with friends, Goodell sometimes ponders retirement. His friends say it's a front. Yes, he tires of some things, and of course, he has plenty of money. But they say he would quickly get bored. "He tries to lie to himself" that he wants to retire, one confidant said. "He should do this as long as they let him."

ACKNOWLEDGMENTS

In the summer of 2013, I hit a crossroad. For four years, I covered the business of sports for *The New York Times*, writing about every major sport and major topic. I covered the Olympics, the World Series, the Super Bowl, and more. I loved the beat, but I was whipsawed week to week.

Then Jason Stallman, the *Times*' sports editor, asked me to cover the NFL full-time. I groaned. I didn't want to travel from training camp to practices to stadiums from July to February. Fortunately, he had other ideas.

"Let's cover it as a really, really big business," he wrote. "I don't care if you're not at whatever folks consider to be the 'big game' of the week." Give readers "something entirely different: a probing look at the league."

There was no template for the beat, which appealed to my omnivorous curiosity, unfulfilled wanderlust, and preference for carving my own path. There were huge stories involving players like Ray Rice, Junior Seau, and Colin Kaepernick, and lawsuits, scientific debates, and social and economic issues. I visited NFL cities and Marshall, Texas, to write about youth football. I went to Amsterdam, Australia, and beyond to see how head trauma was treated overseas.

The hundreds of stories I wrote over a dozen years led me to this book. My agent, Ethan Bassoff, deftly helped me turn my writing and experiences into a fully formed proposal. Amar Deol was all-in from the moment we first spoke, and his enthusiasm never flagged. His advice, ideas, and humor were the glue that made the process seamless and, dare I say, fun.

Writing a book while holding down a day job was tough. Thankfully, Joe Drape, Jeff Duncan, Peter Goodman, Mark Leibovich, Josh Mills, Michael Powell, Motoko Rich, Katie Rosman, Rich Sandomir, and Bob Whiting shared book-writing advice, read passages, and listened to me think out loud.

In the years before I covered the NFL full-time, I sat next to Alan Schwarz, who broke many stories on long-term brain disease in former NFL players. Alan was generous with his help when I expanded on his work after he left our Sports section.

Thanks to my editors, Randy Archibold, Elena Bergeron, Connor Ennis, Matt Futterman, Melissa Hoppert, Tom Jolly, Steve Reddicliffe, Jay Schreiber, and Mike Wilson.

Thanks to my many friends from the now-departed Sports Section: Harvey Araton, Greg Bishop, Alan Blinder, John Branch, Kevin Draper, Ben Hoffman, Jere Longman, Juliet Macur, Emmanuel Morgan, Bill Pennington, Bill Rhoden, Ben Shpigel, Jenny Vrentas, Billy Witz, and many more.

Many editors brought my copy to life: Andy Das, Jeff Furticella, Bob Goetz, Wayne Kamidoi, the late Gwen Knapp, Becky Lebowitz, Sam Manchester, Victor Mather, Naila Jean Meyers, Carl Nelson, Bedel Saget, Brad Smith, Elijah Walker, and Joe Ward. Fern Turkowitz and Terri Ann Glynn made it all possible.

My time on the beat overlapped with Dean Baquet's tenure as executive editor of the *Times*. Dean loves football, especially the New Orleans Saints. He found time to join story calls, suggest ideas, and send encouraging notes. His enthusiasm made me work harder.

I've been lucky to team up with many great reporters across the *Times*, including Kassie Bracken, Ben Carey, Serge Kovaleski, Robin Stein, and Hiroko Tabuchi, to name a few.

I wrote the proposal and first few chapters while on our union's bargaining committee, which provided real-world lessons in contract negotiations that informed my writing. Shout-outs to Bill Baker, Stacy Cowley, Dan Lenos, Jim Luttrell, Jenny Vrentas, and the rest of the B.C.

Football is a game of action, but covering the NFL includes standing in lobbies, courthouses, and offices with other reporters waiting for owners, league officials, and players. Judy Battista, Jarrett Bell, Tom Curran, Sam Farmer, Ben Fischer, Bob Glauber, Jonathan Jones, Mike Jones, Dan Kaplan, Mark Maske, Ryan O'Halloran, Ben Volin, Seth Wickersham, Jabari Young, and many others made it bearable.

The list of people who helped me understand the business of the NFL is long. Special thanks to Jodi Balsam, Upton Bell, Bob Boland, Andrew Brandt, Joby Branion, David Canter, Nellie Drew, Marc Ganis, Fred Gaudelli, Charlie Grantham, Bob LaMonte, Michael LeRoy, Ann McKee, Mike Mulvihill, Michael Nathanson, Liz Nicholson, Chris Nowinski, Neal Pilson, Brad Sohn, and Bob Stern.

To write about the league today, I spoke to many people formerly involved with the league. My lunches with Frank Hawkins were graduate-level classes. Thanks also to Greg Aiello, Doug Allen, George Atallah, Neil Austrian, Jim Barlow, Steve Bornstein, Beth Bowlen, Joel Bussert, Ray DeLorenzi, Thomas Dimitroff, Ed Goren, Steve Gutman, David Hill, Jeffrey Kessler, Ann Kirschner, Denny Lewin, Rich McKay, the late Mike Ornstein, Mark Patricof, Scott Pioli, Bill Polian, Carmen Policy, Chris Seeger, Jim Steeg, Leigh

Steinberg, Paul Tagliabue, Amy Trask, and Steve Underwood. Jon Kendle opened the archives at the Pro Football Hall of Fame for me.

Over the years, I visited nearly every NFL team, some more inviting than others. Thanks to David Bassity, Tad Carper, Ted Crews, Mark Dalton, Jeff Garza, Pat Hanlon, Joanna Hunter, Stacey James, Brett Jewkes, Bob Lange, Burt Lauten, Dave Pearson, Ryan Petkoff, Aaron Popkey, Josh Rupprecht, Pete Ward, and Jim Woodcock.

Many players, past and present, helped me understand their relationship with the league. Ricardo Allen, John Moffitt, Russell Okung, Richmond Webb, and Eric Winston were particularly helpful. Aaron Gibson, Randy Grimes, and Eric Hipple shared their stories of addiction and pain unabashedly.

For a dozen years, executives at the NFL have fielded my many calls and requests. Thanks to Paul Hicks, Katie Hill, Anna Isaacson, Brian McCarthy, Jeff Miller, Mike North, Peter O'Reilly, Alex Riethmiller, Brian Rolapp, Hans Schroeder, Joe Siclaire, Mike Signora, and Dr. Allen Sills.

Special thanks to my mentors: Rhoda Lipton, Josh Mills, Ruth Padawer, and Michael Shapiro; Mark McQuillan and Mike Flagg; Kevin Krolicki and Reed Stevenson; Brian Bremner and the late Irene Kunii; Susan Chira, Jim Cobb, Bruce Headlam, Pat Lyons, Lorne Manly, Norm Mayersohn, Kevin McKenna, Nori Onishi, Tom Redburn, Jodi Rudoren, Carolyn Ryan, and Terry Tang.

The countless hours spent reporting and writing this book took me away from my family, time I can't repay. I appreciate your patience and support, especially my mom, who kept tabs on me, and my wife, who made this entire project possible.

NOTES

Introduction: The Best Acrobats

1. Ken Belson, "How Roger Goodell Became the N.F.L.'s $20 Billion Man," *The New York Times*, October 12, 2024, https://www.nytimes.com/2024/10/12/business/roger-goodell-nfl.html.

2. Ben Volin (@BenVolin), "Raiders owner Mark Davis on what he plans to do with the proceeds from selling 15 percent of his $7 billion team: 'I'm going to In N Out Burger,'" X (Twitter), December 11, 2024, https://x.com/BenVolin/status/1866944454260822374.

3. NFL Concussion Settlement (website), https://www.nflconcussionsettlement.com/.

4. Tammy LaGorce, "For Some Couples, Marrying on Super Bowl Weekend Is a Win," *The New York Times*, February 10, 2024, https://www.nytimes.com/2024/02/10/style/super-bowl-weddings.html.

5. Brett Knight and Justin Teitelbaum, "The World's 50 Most Valuable Sports Teams 2024," *Forbes*, December 21, 2024, updated January 21, 2025, https://www.forbes.com/sites/brettknight/2024/12/12/the-worlds-50-most-valuable-sports-teams-2024/.

6. Joshua Robinson, "Steelers Shared Resources with 2 Teams During World War II," *The New York Times*, January 14, 2009, https://www.nytimes.com/2009/01/15/sports/football/15steagles.html.

7. Michael MacCambridge, *America's Game: The Epic Story of How Pro Football Captured a Nation* (Random House, 2004), 438.

8. "Goodell-Bot," video clip from the episode "Go Fund Yourself," *South Park*, season 18, episode 1, September 24, 2014, *South Park* (website), https://southpark.cc.com/video-clips/nd2sxp/south-park-goodell-bot.

9. Chris Cwik, "Ed Hochuli Says There Were Multiple Times Per Game He Thought a Player Died on the Field," Yahoo! Sports, December 13, 2018, https://sports.yahoo.com/ed-hochuli-says-multiple-times-per-game-thought-player-died-field-232521215.html.

10. Bob Hohler, "Darkness on the Edge of the Patriots Dynasty," *The Boston Globe*, December 8, 2022, https://www.bostonglobe.com/2022/12/08/sports/patriots-2001-team/.

11. Brandon Contes, "Aaron Rodgers Rips ESPN Transforming into a Bounty of 'Unfounded or Asinine' Takes, While on ESPN," Awful Announcing, December 10, 2024, https://awfulannouncing.com/nfl/aaron-rodgers-espn-unfounded-asinine-takes.html.

12. Brandon Contes, "Mina Kimes Notes Blatant Hypocrisy in Aaron Rodgers' ESPN Criticism," Awful Announcing, December 12, 2024, https://awfulannouncing.com/espn/mina-kimes-hypocrisy-aaron-rodgers-criticism.html.

13. Channel Seven, "Steelers vs Ravens, Who Runs the AFC North?, Best/Worst Christmas Songs, and More! Ep. 64," YouTube, December 23, 2024, video, 22:20, https://www.youtube.com/watch?v=7aLDfC17FzA.

1. "Do you want a yarmulke or a helmet?"

1. Barry Wilner, "Tagliabue Memoir a Strong Look into the NFL's Inner Workings," Associated Press, August 30, 2021, https://apnews.com/article/sports-entertainment-nfl-new-orleans-saints-football-b6dd3e56197829fcad7ce2e754415bb9.

2. Gerald Eskanazi, "Pro Football; N.F.L. Labor Accord Is Reached, Allowing Free Agency for Players," *The New York Times*, January 7, 1993, https://www.nytimes.com/1993/01/07/us/pro-football-nfl-labor-accord-is-reached-allowing-free-agency-for-players.html.

3. Hess Toy Truck (website), https://hesstoytruck.com/.

4. Mark Long, "Billionaire Owner Shad Khan Has the Jaguars Reaching New Heights After Some Dreadful Lows," Associated Press, October 4, 2023, https://apnews.com/article/jacksonville-jaguars-shad-khan-9ac03e30bc358b51a2a279c4a5c23436.

5. Justin Teitelbaum, "The NFL's Most Valuable Teams 2024," *Forbes*, August 29, 2024, updated January 21, 2025, https://www.forbes.com/sites/justinteitelbaum/2024/08/29/the-nfls-most-valuable-teams-2024/.

6. Dallas Robinson, "NFL Salary Cap History Throughout the Years," Pro Football & Sports Network, March 13, 2023, https://www.profootballnetwork.com/nfl-salary-cap-history/.

7. Dom Cosentino, "The 1987 NFL Players Strike Created the Modern NFL," Deadspin, January 25, 2018, https://deadspin.com/the-1987-nfl-players-strike-created-the-modern-nfl-181915218.

2. "Rupert, you don't have to do this!"

1. James K. Sebenius, "Rupert Murdoch, the NFL, and the Negotiation That Remade TV," *Harvard Business Review*, April 10, 2019, https://hbr.org/2019/04/rupert-murdoch-the-nfl-and-the-negotiation-that-remade-tv.

2. Bryan Curtis, "The Great NFL Heist: How Fox Paid for and Changed Football Forever," The Ringer, December 13, 2018, https://www.theringer.com/nfl/2018/12/13/18137938/nfl-fox-deal-rupert-murdoch-1993-john-madden-terry-bradshaw-howie-long-jimmy-johnson-cbs-nbc.

3. Leonard Shapiro, "And the Fourth Shall Be First: How Fox Stalked the NFL and Bagged TV Deal," *The Washington Post*, December 26, 1993, https://www.washingtonpost.com/archive/sports/1993/12/26/and-the-fourth-shall-be-first-how-fox-stalked-the-nfl-and-bagged-tv-deal/f848a209-8ffd-44f6-a09b-99b28d75d203/.

4. Richard Sandomir, "Fox Network's Bid Beats CBS for Rights to N.F.C. Football," *The New York Times*, December 18, 1993, https://timesmachine.nytimes.com/timesmachine/1993/12/18/290693.html.

5. Richard Sandomir, "Barry Frank Dies at 87; Sports Agent, Negotiator and Programmer," *The New York Times*, November 1, 2019, https://www.nytimes.com/2019/11/01/sports/barry-frank-dead.html.

6. Richard Sandomir, "Television; Summerall's Struggle with Alcohol," *The New York Times*, June 27, 1992, https://www.nytimes.com/1992/06/27/sports/television-summerall-s-struggle-with-alcohol.html.

7. Theme Park Music, "Batman The Ride: Six Flags Great America," YouTube, November 12, 2021, video, https://www.youtube.com/watch?v=-QZLPVqop1M.

8. John Koblin, "Batman on Steroids: How the NFL on Fox Theme Song Was Born," Deadspin, January 31, 2014, https://deadspin.com/batman-on-steroids-how-the-nfl-on-fox-theme-song-was-b-1481367234.

9. Sports Today, "FLASHBACK Terry Bradshaw Introduces the First Ever Fox NFL Sunday Dec 12, 2018," YouTube, December 12, 2018, video, https://www.youtube.com/watch?v=KAJWOA2Agg0.

3. "I like to smear that Cowboys peanut butter on everything."

1. Abbie VanSickle and Steve Eder, "Where Clarence Thomas Entered an Elite Circle and Opened a Door to the Court," *The New York Times*, July 9, 2023, updated July 12, 2023, https://www.nytimes.com/2023/07/09/us/clarence-thomas-horatio-alger-association.html.

2. Kalyn Kahler, "Are Jerry Jones' Fan Tours a Hurdle to a Cowboys Super Bowl?" ESPN, October 23, 2024, https://www.espn.com/nfl/story/_/id/41926378/dallas-cowboys-fan-tours-fishbowl-jerry-jones-2024-season.

3. Frank Litsky, "Leonard Tose, 88, Is Dead; Owned Philadelphia Eagles," *The New York Times*, April 16, 2003, https://www.nytimes.com/2003/04/16/sports/leonard-tose-88-is-dead-owned-philadelphia-eagles.html.

4. Jon Machota (@jonmachota), "Dak Prescott: 'I stopped, honestly, listening to things (JerryJones) says to the media a long time ago. It doesn't really hold weight with me,'" X (Twitter), August 29, 2024, https://x.com/jonmachota/status/1829252806085374005?s=43&t=pijou4aAILuwk7_rnFNzEg.

5. Trendy Tee Hub, "Jerry Makes Me Drink Shirt," Dribbble, archived September 7, 2024, at https://web.archive.org/web/20240907203735/dribbble.com/shots/24822002-Jerry-Makes-Me-Drink-Shirt.

6. Frank Caliendo (@FrankCaliendo), "Jerry Jones Wants to Change a Very Important Rule," X (Twitter), April 11, 2020, https://x.com/FrankCaliendo/status/1249138861957091328.

7. Paul Attner, "The Ring Master," *Sporting News*, March 13, 1995.

8. Sam Farmer, "For Cowboys Owner Jerry Jones, Southern California Has Always Been a Second Home," *Los Angeles Times*, September 19, 2021, https://www.latimes.com/sports/chargers/story/2021-09-19/cowboys-owner-jerry-jones-southern-california-second-home.

9. David Moore, "Arminta Jones, Mother of Cowboys Owner Jerry Jones, Dies at 90," *The Dallas Morning News*, October 23, 2012, https://www.dallasnews.com/sports/cowboys/2012/10/24/arminta-jones-mother-of-cowboys-owner-jerry-jones-dies-at-90/.

10 David Maraniss and Sally Jenkins, "Jerry Jones Helped Transform the NFL, Except When It Comes to Race," *The Washington Post*, November 23, 2022, https://www.washingtonpost.com/sports/interactive/2022/jerry-jones-black-coaches-nfl/.

11. Tom Ley, "Jerry Jones Calls Photos with Strippers a Misrepresentation," Deadspin, August 11, 2014, https://deadspin.com/jerry-jones-calls-photos-with-strippers-a-misrepresenta-1619324520/.

12. SportsDay Staff, "Jerry Jones Recalls Training Camp Memories, Including Making His First Trip to California After Saying Troy Aikman 'Looks Good in the Shower,'" *The Dallas Morning News*, August 13, 2016, https://www.dallasnews.com/sports/cowboys/2016/08/13/jerry-jones-recalls-training-camp-memories-including-making-his-first-trip-to-california-after-saying-troy-aikman-looks-good-in-the-shower/.

13. Monte Burke, "When Jerry Jones Nearly Bought the Chargers and Learned About Business the Hard Way," *Forbes*, May 2, 2012, https://www.forbes.com/sites/monteburke/2012/05/02/when-jerry-jones-nearly-bought-the-chargers-and-learned-about-business-the-hard-way/.

14. University of Arkansas, Fulbright College of Arts & Sciences, Pryor Center for Arkansas Oral and Visual History, interview with Jerry Jones, https://pryorcenter.uark.edu/interview.php?thisProject=Arkansas%20Memories&thisProfileURL=JONES-Jerry&displayName=&thisInterviewee=471#:~:text=He%20graduated%20in%201965%20with,and%20gas%20venture%20in%201971.

15. David Moore, "An Ever-Growing Snowball: The Inside Story of Jerry Jones Taking the Game, People He Loves for Wild Ride to Hall of Fame," *The Dallas Morning News*, July 27, 2017, https://www.dallasnews.com/sports/cowboys/2017/07/27/an-ever-growing-snowball-the-inside-story-of-jerry-jones-taking-the-game-people-he-loves-for-wild-ride-to-hall-of-fame/.

16. John Breech, "Jerry Jones Asked Hoffa's Teamsters for a Loan to Buy the Chargers in 1966," CBS Sports, September 22, 2015, https://www.cbssports.com/nfl/news/jerry-jones-asked-hoffas-teamsters-for-a-loan-to-buy-the-chargers-in-1966/.

17. Steve Pokin, "Pokin Around: Maybe Jerry Jones, Owner of Cowboys, Could Help YMCA Buy a New Sign," *Springfield (MO) News-Leader*, November 28, 2017, https://www.news-leader.com/story/news/local/ozarks/2017/11/27/pokin-around-maybe-jerry-jones-owner-cowboys-could-help-ymca-buy-new-sign/898890001/.

18. "Topics of The Times; Cowboy Takeover," editorial, *The New York Times*, February 28, 1989, https://www.nytimes.com/1989/02/28/opinion/topics-of-the-times-cowboy-takeover.html.

19. "Buss Expected to Join List of Dallas Cowboys Bidders," *Los Angeles Times*, February 16, 1989, https://www.latimes.com/archives/la-xpm-1989-02-16-sp-3935-story.html.

20. Jeff Sullivan, "30 Years Ago, Jerry Jones Made His Biggest Deal," Dallas Cowboys, February 25, 2019, https://www.dallascowboys.com/news/30-years-ago-jerry-jones-made-his-biggest-deal.

21. Gary Myers, "The Selling of the Cowboys: How Jones Bought the Cowboys and Johnson Replaced Landry," *The Dallas Morning News*, March 3, 1989.

22. SportsDay Staff, "Flashback: The Story Behind Jerry Jones and Jimmy Johnson's Meeting at Mia's," *The Dallas Morning News*, February 25, 2014, https://www.dallasnews.com/sports/cowboys/2014/02/25/flashback-photographer-at-mia-s-told-i-think-that-s-enough-after-5-clicks-feb-25-2004/.

23. Thomas C. Hayes, "Cowboys: America's Team to Wonder About; New Owner His Own Man," *The New York Times*, July 23, 1989, https://www.nytimes.com/1989/07/23/sports/cowboys-america-s-team-to-wonder-about-new-owner-his-own-man.html.

24. Paul Domowitch, "Owners Derail Jones' Attempt to Pull Fast One," *The Oklahoman*, April 10, 1993, https://www.oklahoman.com/storynews/1993/04/10/owners-derail-jones-attempt-to-pull-fast-one/62462688007/.

25. Associated Press, "Tagliabue Assails Cowboys Owner Jones," *Deserert News*, January 29, 1996, https://www.deseret.com/1996/1/29/19221928tagliabue-assails-cowboys-owner-jones/.

26. Todd Archer, "Jerry Jones' Maverick Ways Changed NFL's Business Model," ESPN, February 1, 2017, https://www.espn.com/blog/dallas/cowboys/post/_/id/4758043/jerry-jones-maverick-ways-changed-nfls-business-model.

27. Richard Hoffer, "Cowboys for Sale the NFL Is Not Amused by Maverick Owner Jerry Jones," *Sports Illustrated*, September 18, 1995, https://vault.si.com/vault/1995/09/18/cowboys-for-sale-the-nfl-is-not-amused-by-maverick-owner-jerry-jones.

28. Associated Press, "Tagliabue Assails Cowboys Owner Jones."

29. Thomas Heath, "NFL, Cowboys Settle Suits," *The Washington Post*, December 13, 1996, https://www.washingtonpost.com/archive/sports/1996/12/14/nfl-cowboys-settle-suits/615d4564-c1d0-437d-bad6-d47a9ba4eea5/.

30. Bill King, "The Lone Star: Jerry Jones," *Sports Business Journal*, May 21, 2017, https://www.sportsbusinessjournal.com/Journal/Issues/2017/05/22/People-and-Pop-Culture/Jerry-Jones-Lifetime-Achievement.aspx.

31. Attner, "The Ring Master."

32. Darren Rovell (@darrenrovell), "How many NFL owners would walk down Bourbon Street on a Saturday night. I'll go with...just one," X (Twitter), September 29, 2019, video, https://x.com/darrenrovell/status/1178314409724317696.

33. Tobias Bass and Saad Yousuf, "Cowboys Owner Jerry Jones Snaps Back at Critics over Sunday's Blowout Loss," The Athletic, *The New York Times*, October 14, 2024, updated October 27, 2024, https://www.nytimes.com/athletic/5844999/2024/10/15/jerry-jones-the-fan-critics-cowboys/.

34. Justin Teitelbaum, "The NFL's Most Valuable Teams 2024," *Forbes*, August 29, 2024, updated January 21, 2025, https://www.forbes.com/sites/justinteitelbaum/2024/08/29/the-nfls-most-valuable-teams-2024/.

35. Ken Belson, "In Jerry Jones, Dallas Cowboys Have a Lightning Rod Made of Mettle," *The New York Times*, January 10, 2015, https://www.nytimes.com/2015/01/11/sports/football/in-jerry-jones-dallas-cowboys-have-a-lightning-rod-made-of-mettle.html.

36. Ken Belson, "Cowboys' Star on the Rise in a Dallas Suburb," *The New York Times*, January 3, 2016, https://www.nytimes.com/2016/01/04/sports/football/cowboys-star-is-on-the-rise-in-dallas-suburb.html.

4. The Ultimate Middleman

1. Ken Belson and Ben Shpigel, "New England Patriots' Owner, Still Sore at N.F.L., Has Payback in Sight," *The New York Times*, January 19, 2017, https://www.nytimes.com/2017/01/19/sports/football/patriots-robert-kraft-nfl-roger-goodell.html.

2. Matthew Rozsa, "Donald Trump's Mar-a-Lago Club Has a New Feature: Watch the President Discuss Top Secret Security Issues!," *Salon*, February 13, 2017, https://www.salon.com/2017/02/13/donald-trumps-mar-a-lago-club-has-a-new-feature-watch-the-president-discuss-top-secret-security-issues/.

3. Tonya Alanez, "Patriots Owner Robert Kraft's Wife, Dana Blumberg, Among Kennedy Center's New Board Members," *The Boston Globe*, February 13, 2025, https://www.bostonglobe.com/2025/02/13/metro/trump-kennedy-center-robert-kraft-josh-dana-blumberg/.

4. Allison Stewart, "In His Image: Bob Kraft's Vision for Columbia Football," *The Eye*, November 20, 2018, https://www.columbiaspectator.com/the-eye/2018/11/20/in-his-image-bob-krafts-vision-for-columbia-football/.

5. Jeff Howe, "The Inside Story of How, 25 Years Ago, Robert Kraft Improbably Bought the Patriots," The Athletic, *The New York Times*, January 18, 2019, https://www.nytimes.com/athletic/772125/2019/01/18/the-inside-story-of-how-25-years-ago-robert-kraft-improbably-bought-the-patriots/.

6. Howe, "The Inside Story of How, 25 Years Ago, Robert Kraft Improbably Bought the Patriots."

7. "Timeline: The Life of Robert Kraft," *Sports Business Journal*, May 9, 2022, https://www.sportsbusinessjournal.com/Journal/Issues/2022/05/09/Portfolio/Timeline/.

8. Will McDonough, "For Kraft, It Was One Hard Fight," *The Boston Globe*, February 28, 1994.

9. Jane Weingarten, "Power and Wealth Haven't Spoiled Robert Kraft," *The Jewish Advocate*, October 3, 1991.

10. Joseph P. Kahn, "Myra Kraft; a Player off the Field; For the Wife of Patriots Owner Robert Kraft, Philanthropy Wins Out over Football," *The Boston Globe*, January 25, 1997.

11. "Give Parcells Picks, He Will Find Gold," *South Florida Sun Sentinel*, September 26, 2021, https://www.sun-sentinel.com/2007/12/30/give-parcells-picks-he-will-find-gold/.

12. "The Agreement That Brought Bill Belichick to New England 20 Years Ago," The Patriots Hall of Fame (website), https://www.patriotshalloffame.com/the-agreement-that-brought-bill-belichick-to-new-england-20-years-ago/.

13. Evin Demirel, "Jerry Jones," *Arkansas Democrat-Gazette*, January 3, 2012, https://www.arkansasonline.com/news/2012/jan/03/jerry-jones/.

14. Jeff Benedict, *The Dynasty* (Avid Reader Press, 2020).

15. David M. Halbfinger, "A Fan's Fan, but an Owner First; Decision on Patriots Put Economics Ahead of Emotions," *The New York Times*, November 29, 1998, https://www.nytimes.com/1998/11/29/nyregion/fan-s-fan-but-owner-first-decision-patriots-put-economics-ahead-emotions.html.

16. Nick Cafaro, "Kraft Denies R.I. Offering $10 Million Lure," *The Boston Globe*, September 10, 1997.

17. Gerry Fraley, "Is Jerry Jones Good for the NFL?" *Inside Sports*, July 1996.

18. David Purdum and Darren Rovell, "Patriots' Robert Kraft, Cowboys' Jerry Jones Retain DraftKings Stakes Amid Shift to Sportsbooks," ESPN, August 28, 2018, https://www.espn.com/chalk/story/_/id/24502023/nfl-owners-robert-kraft-jerry-jones-retain-investments-draftkings-amid-sportsbook-shift.

19. Brendan Coffey, "Robert Kraft, Billionaire Meckenzie Selling Millions of DraftKings Stock," Sportico, October 5, 2020, https://www.sportico.com/business/finance/2020/robert-kraft-billionaire-meckenzie-selling-draftkings-1234614267/.

20. Richard Sandomir, "Wooed by Many, N.F.L. Chooses Itself," *The New York Times*, January 31, 2006, https://www.nytimes.com/2006/01/31/sports/football/wooed-by-many-nfl-chooses-itself.html.

21. Benjamin Mullin, Ken Belson, and Nico Grant, "YouTube Reaches Deal for N.F.L. Sunday Ticket," *The New York Times*, December 22, 2022, https://www.nytimes.com/2022/12/22/business/youtube-nfl-sunday-ticket.html.

22. Eben Novy-Williams, "NFL Hires Goldman Sachs to Explore Minority Sale of Media Properties," Sportico, June 23, 2021, https://www.sportico.com/leagues/football/2021/nfl-goldman-sachs-media-1234632598/.

23. "Robert Kraft to Join Board of New Viacom," New England Patriots (website), November 22, 2005, https://www.patriots.com/news/robert-kraft-to-join-board-of-new-viacom-151711.

24. Ken Belson, "Adding Innovations, the Pro Bowl Is Trying to Be Relevant. Stop Laughing," *The New York Times*, January 24, 2015, https://www.nytimes.com/2015/01/25/sports/football/adding-innovations-the-pro-bowl-is-trying-to-be-relevant-stop-laughing.html.

25. Andy Bernstein, "Reebok, NFL Try Fresh Start," *Sports Business Journal*, May 27, 2001, https://www.sportsbusinessjournal.com/Journal/Issues/2001/05/28/This-Weeks-Issue/Reebok-NFL-Try-Fresh-Start.aspx.

26. "Most Valuable NFL Teams," *Forbes*, August 29, 2006, https://www.forbes.com/2006/08/29/06nfl_valuable_slide.html.

27. Judy Battista, "Sideline Spying: N.F.L. Punishes Patriots' Taping," *The New York Times*, September 14, 2007, https://www.nytimescom/2007/09/14/sports/football/14patriots.html.

28. Brent Schrotenboer, "Patriots Owner Robert Kraft: Love and Loss Marked Eccentric Life Before Spa Scandal," *USA Today*, March 15, 2019, https://www.usatoday.com/story/sports/nfl/2019/03/15/robert-kraft-love-and-loss-marked-eccentric-life-before-spa-scandal/3150945002/.

29. Robert Huber, "I'm Robert Kraft. Do You Know Who I Am?" *Boston*, September 29, 2015, https://www.bostonmagazine.com/news/2015/09/29/robert-kraft/2/.

30. "Video of Patriots Owner Robert Kraft Appearing in Audition Tape Goes Viral," *Sports Business Journal*, July 11, 2002, https://www.sportsbusinessjournal.com/Daily/Issues/2012/07/12/People-and-Pop-Culture/Kraft.aspx.

31. Mike Reiss, "Robert Kraft Visits Meek Mill in Prison: 'He Shouldn't Be Here,'" ESPN, April 10, 2018, https://www.espn.com/nfl/story/_/id/23107730/robert-kraft-new-england-patriots-visits-meek-mill-prison.

32. Daniel Flick, "Patriots' Robert Kraft Reveals 'Mayo Moment,'" *Sports Illustrated*, January 19, 2024, https://www.si.com/nfl/patriots/news/new-england-patriots-owner-robert-kraft-jerod-mayo-bill-belichick-hire-moment.

33. "New England Patriots Book Goes Inside Secretive and Controversial Franchise and Robert Kraft, Tom Brady and Bill Belichick," ESPN, September 29, 2021, https://www.espn

.com/nfl/story/_/id/32294122/new-england-patriots-book-goes-secretive-controversial-franchise-robert-kraft-tom-brady-bill-belichick.

34. Scott Olster, "Football's True Patriot," *Fortune*, November 3, 2010, https://fortune.com/2010/11/03/footballs-true-patriot/.

35. Don Van Natta Jr., "'Winners Write History': Inside Robert Kraft's 12-Year Hall of Fame Quest," ESPN, September 11, 2024, https://www.espn.com/nfl/story/_/id/41073940/the-secret-history-robert-kraft-hall-fame-quest.

5. "All's Well That Ends Well."

1. Barry Shuck, "Art Modell—10 Poisons He Inflicted on the Browns," Dawgs by Nature, SB Nation, March 26, 2020, https://www.dawgsbynature.com/2020/3/26/21193496/art-modell-10-poisons-he-inflicted-on-the-browns.

2. Tom Goldman, "ABC Broadcasts Final 'Monday Night Football,'" *Day to Day*, NPR, December 26, 2005, https://www.npr.org/2005/12/26/5069985/abc-broadcasts-final-monday-night-football.

3. Danny Spewak, "State Pays Off Debt on U.S. Bank Stadium 20 Years Earlier Than Expected," KARE 11, June 26, 2023, https://www.kare11.com/article/news/local/state-pays-off-debt-on-us-bank-stadium-20-years-earlier-than-expected-minnesota/89-f45dac18-79a8-4d44-8bc3-4c0f8be64b32#.

4. Austin Huguelet, Katie Kull, and Joel Currier, "'Under Cover of Darkness': The Inside Story of How the Rams Worked the NFL and Ditched St. Louis," *St. Louis Post-Dispatch*, May 16, 2022, https://www.stltoday.com/business/local/under-cover-of-darkness-the-inside-story-of-how-the-rams-worked-the-nfl-and/article_0df390b8-40d5-5ead-b78b-779cb5187f9e.html.

5. Huguelet et al., "'Under Cover of Darkness.'"

6. Ken Belson, "Wary of Losing Rams, St. Louis Is Set to Huddle on Stadium," *The New York Times*, November 4, 2014, https://www.nytimes.com/2014/11/05/sports/football/wary-of-losing-rams-st-louis-is-set-to-huddle-on-stadium.html.

7. Ken Belson, "Stadium Sponsor Unveiled in Move to Keep Rams in St. Louis," *The New York Times*, October 6, 2015, https://www.nytimes.com/2015/10/07/sports/football/stadium-sponsor-unveiled-in-move-to-keep-rams-in-st-louis.html.

8. Ken Belson, "N.F.L. Forms Committee to Oversee Any Potential Return to Los Angeles," *The New York Times*, February 10, 2015, https://www.nytimes.com/2015/02/11/sports/football/nfl-roundup.html.

9. Ken Belson, "Raiders and Chargers Are Willing to Share Stadium near Los Angeles," *The New York Times*, February 20, 2015, https://www.nytimes.com/2015/02/21/sports/football/raiders-and-chargers-willing-to-share-stadium-near-los-angeles.html.

10. Ken Belson, "With N.F.L. Relocation Fates in Owners' Hands, the Games Begin," *The New York Times*, January 12, 2016, https://www.nytimes.com/2016/01/13/sports/football/with-nfl-relocation-fates-in-owners-hands-the-games-begin.html.

11. Ken Belson, "San Diego Voters Reject Funding of New Chargers Stadium," *The New York Times*, November 9, 2016, https://www.nytimes.com/2016/11/10/sports/football/san-diego-rejects-chargers-stadium.html.

12. Ken Belson, "St. Louis Sues N.F.L. over Rams' Departure," *The New York Times*, April 12, 2017, https://www.nytimes.com/2017/04/12/sports/football/st-louis-nfl-lawsuit-rams-relocation.html.

13. Ken Belson, "N.F.L. to Settle Lawsuit Over Rams' Relocation for $790 Million," *The New York Times*, November 24, 2021, updated November 30, 2021, https://www.nytimes.com/2021/11/24/sports/football/nfl-st-louis-rams-relocation.html.

14. "Los Angeles Rams Franchise Value from 2002 to 2024," Statista, https://www.statista.com/statistics/194504/los-angeles-rams-franchise-value/.

15. Seth Wickersham, "Los Angeles Rams Owner Stan Kroenke Angers NFL Owners with Financial Pivot Related to Lawsuit on St. Louis Move, Sources Say," ESPN, October 27, 2021, https://www.espn.com/nfl/story/_/id/32486646/los-angeles-rams-owner-stan-kroenke-angers-nfl-owners-financial-pivot-related-lawsuit-st-louis-move-sources-say.

16. "Bolt Pride," Tailgating Hall of Fame.com, https://tailgatinghalloffame.com/BoltPride.htm.

6. The Senator's Son

1. "Roger Goodell," Washington & Jefferson College, https://www.washjeff.edu/education-lifetime/goodell-roger/.

2. Daniel Kaplan, "Goodell Sets Revenue Goal of $25B by 2027 for NFL," *Sports Business Journal*, April 4, 2010, https://www.sportsbusinessjournal.com/Journal/Issues/2010/04/05/This-Weeks-News/Goodell-Sets-Revenue-Goal-Of-$25B-By-2027-For-NFL.aspx.

3. "NFL Commissioner Roger Goodell: Super Bowl XLIX News Conference, Arizona, January 30, 2015," NFL Communications, News Archive, https://nflmediaarchive.nfl.net/ArchiveHTMLPDF/2015-01-31__nfl%20commissioner%20roger%20goodell%20-%20super%20bowl%20xlix%20news%20conference.html.

4. Ken Belson and Kevin Draper, "N.F.L. Signs Media Deals Worth over $100 Billion," *The New York Times*, March 18, 2021, updated May 26, 2021, https://www.nytimes.com/2021/03/18/sports/football/nfl-tv-contracts.html.

5. Ken Belson, "Roger Goodell's Pay for Two Years Reached Nearly $128 Million," *The New York Times*, October 28, 2021, https://www.nytimes.com/2021/10/28/sports/football/roger-goodell-salary-nfl.html.

6. Drew Magary, "Before the Super Bowl, Let's Remember Roger Goodell's 25 Dumbest Moments," *GQ*, January 31, 2017, https://www.gq.com/story/roger-goodell-nfl-25-dumbest-moments.

7. Michael Grant, "Recalling Bill Simmons Calling Roger Goodell a Liar," MSN, September 16, 2024, https://www.msn.com/en-us/sports/nfl/recalling-bill-simmons-calling-roger-goodell-a-liar/ar-AA1qEIt1.

8. Peter King, "The Man of the Hour," *Sports Illustrated*, February 7, 2011, https://vault.si.com/vault/2011/02/07/the-man-of-the-hour.

9. Mark Goshgarian, "Inside the Chautauqua Institution's Summer Assembly," Spectrum News 1, July 4, 2022, https://spectrumlocalnews.com/nys/jamestown/news/2022/07/04/inside-the-chautauqua-institution-s-summer-assembly.

10. Darren Rovell (@darrenrovell), "The moon landing, 55 years ago today, was mostly joyous...," X (Twitter), July 20, 2024, second photo, https://x.com/darrenrovell/status/1814710742873960575/photo/2.

11. "Miss Jorgensen Asks Agnew for an Apology," *The New York Times*, October 11, 1970, https://www.nytimes.com/1970/10/11/archives/miss-jorgensen-asks-agnew-for-an-apology.html.

12. Frank Lynn, "Charles E. Goodell, Former Senator, Is Dead at 60," *The New York Times*, January 22, 1987, https://www.nytimes.com/1987/01/22/obituaries/charles-e-goodell-former-senator-is-dead-at-60.html.

13. Sean Gregory, "Cover Story: How Far Will Roger Goodell Go, to Protect the Game He Loves?" *Keeping Score* (blog), *Time*, December 6, 2012, https://keepingscore.blogs.time.com/2012/12/06/cover-story-how-far-will-roger-goodell-go-to-protect-the-game-he-loves/.

14. Lawrence Delevingne, "Top Hedge Fund Exec Bill Goodell Switches Teams," CNBC, June 3, 2015, https://www.cnbc.com/2015/06/03/top-hedge-fund-exec-bill-goodell-switches-teams.html.

15. Eric Williamson, "Re-Energized," *UVA Lawyer*, Fall 2018, https://www.law.virginia.edu/uvalawyer/fall-2018/article/re-energized.

16. Tamarind Phinisee, "Saint Mary's Hall Making Changes to Pave Path for the Future," *San Antonio Business Journal*, August 19, 2011, https://www.bizjournals.com/sanantonio/print-edition/2011/08/19/saint-marys-hall-making-changes-to.html.

17. "Roger Goodell," Washington & Jefferson College.

18. Darren Rovell (@darrenrovell), "34 Years Ago Today: A 22-year-old Roger Goodell writes a letter to Pete Rozelle to try to get a job at the NFL," X (Twitter), July 2, 2015, photo, https://x.com/darrenrovell/status/616589652753936385/photo/1.

19. King, "The Man of the Hour."

20. "Why NFL Commissioner Goodell Turned Down Coaching Job with the New York Jets," Bloomberg, January 21, 2025, video, https://www.bloomberg.com/news/videos/2025-01-21/why-nfl-commissioner-goodell-turned-down-coaching-job-video.

21. Dave Goldberg, "Goodell the Favorite, but NFL Commissioner Job Still Up for Grabs," *Pocono Record*, August 5, 2006, https://www.poconorecord.com/story/sports/2006/08/05/goodell-favorite-but-nfl-commissioner/53067701007/.

22. "Jane Skinner Goodell," LA Times NFL Speaker Series, February 10, 2022, https://asaptext.com/asap_media/media/1073/1366/browse_file.php?browse_file_name=transcripts/116963.html.

23. T. J. Simers, "NFL Owners OK Rams' Move to St. Louis," *Los Angeles Times*, April 13, 1995, https://www.latimes.com/archives/la-xpm-1995-04-13-mn-54268-story.html.

24. "Tagliabue Eases Cleveland Council Concerns on Stadium Deal," *Sports Business Journal*, March 4, 1996, https://www.sportsbusinessjournal.com/Daily/Issues/1996/03/05/Leagues-Governing-Bodies/TAGLIABUE-EASES-CLEVELAND-COUNCIL-CONCERNS-ON-STADIUM-DEAL.aspx.

25. Judy Battista, "Goodell Gets Enough Votes to Lead N.F.L.," *The New York Times*, August 9, 2006, https://www.nytimes.com/2006/08/09/sports/football/09nfl.html.

26. "Roger Goodell," Washington & Jefferson College.

27. "NFL Owners Elect Goodell as New Commissioner," ESPN, August 8, 2006, https://www.espn.com/nfl/news/story?id=2543783.

28. Judy Battista, "Tagliabue Lifts Suspensions but Not Blame in Bounty Case," *The New York Times*, December 11, 2012, https://www.nytimes.com/2012/12/12/sports/football/tagliabue-vacates-saints-suspensions-in-bounty-case.html.

29. Ken Belson, "N.F.L. Domestic Violence Policy Toughened in Wake of Ray Rice Case," *The New York Times*, August 28, 2014, https://www.nytimes.com/2014/08/29/sports/football/roger-goodell-admits-he-was-wrong-and-alters-nfl-policy-on-domestic-violence.html.

30. Roger Goodell, letter to NFL owners, in Belson, "N.F.L. Domestic Violence Policy Toughened in Wake of Ray Rice Case," https://graphics8.nytimes.com/packages/pdf/sports/Roger_Goodell_NFL/Roger_Goodell_letter.pdf.

31. Ken Belson, "A Punch Is Seen, and a Player Is Out," *The New York Times*, September 8, 2014, https://www.nytimes.com/2014/09/09/sports/football/ray-rice-video-shows-punch-and-raises-new-questions-for-nfl.html.

32. Ken Belson, "N.F.L. Examines Its Record on Hiring of Women in Wake of Ray Rice Case," *The New York Times*, September 25, 2014, https://www.nytimes.com/2014/09/26/sports/football/nfl-examines-its-record-on-hiring-of-women-in-wake-of-ray-rice-case.html.

33. KPIX | CBS News Bay Area, "NFL Commissioner Breaks Silence on Ray Rice Video," YouTube, September 9, 2014, video, https://www.youtube.com/watch?v=66aVAvVkfvY.

34. Fox 5 Atlanta, "Roger Goodell NFL Press Conference," YouTube, September 19, 2014, video, https://www.youtube.com/watch?v=RxtJvcU9OEI.

35. Chris Burke, "Goodell Calls for Action, Sidesteps Details in Press Conference," *Sports Illustrated*, September 19, 2014, https://www.si.com/nfl/2014/09/19/roger-goodell-nfl-domestic-violence-press-conference-ray-rice-adrian-peterson.

36. Andrew Beaton, "Roger Goodell Has a Secret Defender on Twitter: His Wife," *The Wall Street Journal*, October 12, 2017, https://www.wsj.com/articles/roger-goodell-has-a-secret-defender-on-twitter-his-wife-1507839658.

37. "Mt. Rainier Climb for United Way," Seattle Seahawks (website), https://www.seahawks.com/photos/mt-rainier-climb-for-united-way-24326#ab3a3d25-2530-11e8-b0e8-005056b04871.

38. Mike Fisher, "Papa John's Ex CEO: Cowboys' Jerry Jones Wanted Me to Fire NFL's Roger Goodell," *Sports Illustrated*, May 7, 2022, https://www.si.com/nfl/cowboys/news/papa-johns-ceo-dallas-jerry-jones-fire-roger-goodell-daniel-snyder.

39. Ken Belson, "Jerry Jones Threatens to Sue N.F.L. to Block Roger Goodell's Contract," *The New York Times*, November 8, 2017, https://www.nytimes.com/2017/11/08/sports/jerry-jones-nfl-roger-goodell-david-boies.html.

40. Ken Belson, "In the N.F.L., Stability Comes with a $200 Million Price Tag," *The New York Times*, December 13, 2017, https://www.nytimes.com/2017/12/13/sports/goodell-says-this-contract-is-his-last-as-owners-pay-200-million.html.

41. Ken Belson, "Roger Goodell Forces Jerry Jones to Pay Millions," *The New York Times*, March 7, 2018, https://www.nytimes.com/2018/03/07/sports/jerry-jones-roger-goodell-payment.html.

42. Marissa Payne, "NFL Reporters Shocked After Roger Goodell Says He's Available to the Media 'Almost Every Day,'" *The Washington Post*, January 30, 2015, https://www.washingtonpost.com/news/early-lead/wp/2015/01/30/nfl-reporters-shocked-after-roger-goodell-says-hes-available-to-the-media-almost-every-day/.

43. Ken Belson, "N.F.L. Ordered to Pay Billions in Sunday Ticket Lawsuit," *The New York Times*, June 27, 2024, https://www.nytimes.com/2024/06/27/business/media/nfl-sunday-ticket-lawsuit-billions-damage.html.

44. James Boyd, "Colts Center on Roger Goodell's Wish for 18 Games: 'Put on a Helmet for 18 of Those Games, Then Come Talk to Me,'" The Athletic, *The New York Times*, June 5, 2024, https://www.nytimes.com/athletic/5544056/2024/06/05/nfl-schedule-18-games-roger-goodell-ryan-kelly/.

45. David Purdum and Ryan Rodenburg, "NFL's Evolving Stance on Sports Betting and Las Vegas," ESPN, May 14, 2018, https://www.espn.com/chalk/story/_/id/19015998/nfl-oral-history-nfl-changing-stance-gambling-las-vegas.

7. "One of those rare existential threats."

1. Ken Belson, "Brain Injuries Drew Millions from N.F.L., Report Says," *The New York Times*, November 16, 2012, https://www.nytimes.com/2012/11/17/sports/football/nfl-paid-millions-over-brain-injuries-article-says.html.

2. Alan Schwarz, "N.F.L. Scolded over Injuries to Its Players," *The New York Times*, October 28, 2009, https://www.nytimes.com/2009/10/29/sports/football/29hearing.html.

3. "Police Report: Junior Seau Used .357 Magnum to Kill Himself, Had No Pulse When Officers Arrived," CBS News, May 16, 2012, https://www.cbsnews.com/news/police-report-junior-seau-used-357-magnum-to-kill-himself-had-no-pulse-when-officers-arrived/.

4. Mary Pilon and Ken Belson, "Seau Suffered from Brain Disease," *The New York Times*, January 10, 2013, https://www.nytimes.com/2013/01/11/sports/football/junior-seau-suffered-from-brain-disease.html.

5. Ken Belson and Jon Hurdle, "Crowded Courtroom for N.F.L. Lawsuit," *The New York Times*, April 9, 2023, https://www.nytimes.com/2013/04/10/sports/football/judge-hears-nfl-arguments-to-dismiss-head-trauma-cases.html.

6. "NFL Concussion Case Takes Center Stage at Columbia Law Conference," Columbia Law School, March 21, 2018, https://www.law.columbia.edu/news/archive/nfl-concussion-case-takes-center-stage-columbia-law-conference.

7. Will Hobson, "The Concussion Files," *The Washington Post*, January 31, 2024, https://www.washingtonpost.com/sports/interactive/2024/nfl-concussion-settlement/.

8. Tim Rohan and Ken Belson, "Relief, but Disappointment, for Plaintiffs in N.F.L. Case," *The New York Times*, August 30, 2013, https://www.nytimes.com/2013/08/31/sports/football/relief-but-disappointment-for-plaintiffs-in-nfl-case.html.

9. Ken Belson, "Brain Trauma to Affect One in Three Players, N.F.L. Agrees," *The New York Times*, September 12, 2014, https://www.nytimes.com/2014/09/13/sports/football/actuarial-reports-in-nfl-concussion-deal-are-released.html.

10. Ken Belson and Alan Schwarz, "N.F.L. Shifts on Concussions, and Game May Never Be the Same," *The New York Times*, March 15, 2016, https://www.nytimes.com/2016/03/16/sports/nfl-concussions-cte-football-jeff-miller.html.

11. Ken Belson, "N.F.L. Makes Open-Ended Commitment to Retirees in Concussion Suit," *The New York Times*, June 25, 2014, https://www.nytimes.com/2014/06/26/sports/football/nfl-makes-open-ended-commitment-to-retirees-in-concussion-suit.html.

12. Ken Belson, "When Settlement Buys Time," *The New York Times*, July 18, 2014, https://www.nytimes.com/2014/07/19/sports/football/former-nfl-players-make-difficult-choice-in-opposing-concussion-settlement.html.

13. Ken Belson, "Kevin Turner, Ex-Player Who Fought N.F.L. on Concussions, Dies at 46," *The New York Times*, March 24, 2016, https://www.nytimes.com/2016/03/25/sports/football/kevin-turner-nfl-lawsuit-dies-at-46-als.html.

14. Ken Belson, "Debilitated Players Accuse N.F.L. of Stalling on Settlement Payments," *The New York Times*, November 13, 2017, https://www.nytimes.com/2017/11/13/sports/football/nfl-concussion-lawsuit.html.

15. NFL Concussion Settlement (website), https://www.nflconcussionsettlement.com/.

16. Ken Belson, "Black Former N.F.L. Players Say Racial Bias Skews Concussion Payouts," *The New York Times*, August 25, 2020, https://www.nytimes.com/2020/08/25/sport/football/nfl-concussion-racial-bias.html.

17. Alan Schwarz, "Congress Scolds N.F.L. and Union," *The New York Times*, June 27, 2007, https://www.nytimes.com/2007/06/27/sports/football/27nfl.html.

18. Ken Belson, "The N.F.L.'s Obesity Scourge," *The New York Times*, January 17, 2019, https://www.nytimes.com/2019/01/17/sports/football/the-nfls-obesity-scourge.html.

19. Ken Belson, "For N.F.L. Retirees, Opioids Bring More Pain," *The New York Times*, February 2, 2019, https://www.nytimes.com/2019/02/02/sports/nfl-opioids-.html.

20. Ken Belson, "To Allay Fears, N.F.L. Huddles with Mothers," *The New York Times*, January 28, 2015, https://www.nytimes.com/2015/01/29/sports/football/nfl-tries-to-reassure-mothers-as-polls-and-studies-rattle-them.html.

21. Sean Gregory, "Can Roger Goodell Save Football?" *Time*, December 17, 2012, https://content.time.com/time/subscriber/article/0,33009,2130975-7,00.html.

22. Ken Belson, "Goodell Speaks of Changes Needed in N.F.L. Culture," *The New York Times*, November 15, 2012, https://www.nytimes.com/2012/11/16/sports/football/roger-goodell-nfl-commissioner-speaks-on-concussions.html.

23. Ken Belson, "Roger Goodell Insists Football Is Safe: 'There's Risk in Life,'" *The New York Times*, February 5, 2016, https://www.nytimes.com/2016/02/06/sports/football/roger-goodell-insists-football-is-safe-theres-risk-in-life.html.

24. Ken Belson, "Junior Seau's Family Will Not Be Allowed to Speak at His Hall of Fame Induction," *The New York Times*, July 24, 2015, https://www.nytimes.com/2015/07/25

/sports/football/junior-seaus-family-will-not-be-allowed-to-speak-at-his-hall-of-fame-induction.html.

25. Daniel Kaplan, "Hall: No Plans to Include Issue of Concussions," *Sports Business Journal*, July 27, 2014, https://www.sportsbusinessjournal.com/Journal/Issues/2014/07/28/Events-and-Attractions/Pro-Football-Hall-of-Fame-Baker.aspx.

26. Ken Belson, "In Compromise, Pro Football Hall of Fame Offers to Let Junior Seau's Daughter Speak at Ceremony," *The New York Times*, August 1, 2015, https://www.nytimes.com/2015/08/02/sports/football/junior-seaus-daughter-will-speak-at-pro-football-hall-of-fame-ceremony.html.

27. Sydney Seau, "The Hall of Fame Speech Junior Seau's Daughter Couldn't Give," *The New York Times*, August 8, 2015, https://www.nytimes.com/2015/08/09/sports/football/junior-seau-hall-of-fame-sydney-seau-speech.html.

28. Steve Fainaru and Mark Fainaru-Wada, "NFL Backs Away from Funding BU Brain Study; NIH to Fund It Instead," ESPN, December 21, 2015, https://www.espn.com/espn/otl/story/_/id/14417386nfl-pulls-funding-boston-university-head-trauma-study-concerns-researcher.

29. Steve Fainaru and Mark Fainaru-Wada, "NFL-NIH Research Partnership Set to End with $16M Unspent," ESPN, July 27, 2017, https://www.espn.com/espn/otl/story/_/id/20175509/nfl-donation-brain-research-falls-apart-nih-appears-set-move-bulk-30-million-donation.

30. Ken Belson, "N.F.L. Doctor Who Discounted Dangers of Head Trauma Retires," *The New York Times*, July 20, 2018, https://www.nytimes.com/2016/07/21/sports/football/nfl-doctor-elliot-pellman-concussions-retires.html.

31. Steve Fainaru and Mark Fainaru-Wada, "Review Determines No Wrongdoing by Dr. Richard Ellenbogen," ESPN (website), September 16, 2016, https://www.espn.com/espn/otl/story/_/id/17565760/university-washington-panel-clears-dr-richard-ellenbogen-wrongdoing.

32. Art Stapleton, "Goodell Expected to Visit Giants Camp, Hold Town Hall for Season Ticket Holders at MetLife," northjersey.com, August 7, 2017, https://www.northjersey.com/story/sports/nfl/giants/2017/08/06/goodell-expected-visit-giants-camp-hold-town-hall-metlife/543914001/.

8. "The smartest guy in the room and hardly anyone knows him."

1. Peter King, "The Mystery Man Who Helped Modernize the NFL," *Sports Illustrated*, April 9, 2015, https://www.si.com/nfl/2015/04/09/nfl-joel-bussert.

2. "Why Was 'Shorty' Ray Considered an NFL Giant?" Sports History Network, September 12, 2022, https://sportshistorynetwork.com/football/hugh-shorty-ray/.

3. "Hugh Ray: Class of 1966," Pro Football Hall of Fame (website), https://www.profootballhof.com/players/hugh-shorty-ray/.

4. Associated Press, "Chiefs Rally Past Buffalo 42–36 in OT in Wild Playoff Game," ESPN, January 23, 2022, https://www.espn.com/nfl/recap/_/gameId/401326633.

5. Josh Sim, "NFL Accounts for 93 of Top 100 Most-Watched US Broadcasts in 2023," SportsPro, January 8, 2024, https://www.sportspromedia.com/news/nfl-us-tv-most-watched-broadcasts-top-100-2023-super-bowl-viewership/.

6. "1939 NFL Attendance Data," Pro Football Reference, https://www.pro-football-reference.com/years/1939/attendance.htm.

7. Judy Battista, "Hands Off for Patriots in Rematch with Colts," *The New York Times*, September 9, 2004, https://www.nytimes.com/2004/09/09/sports/football/hands-off-for-patriots-in-rematch-with-colts.html.

8. Tom E. Curran, "They Called It the 'Ty Law Rule'...and That Was OK with Him," NBC Sports Boston, August 3, 2019, https://www.nbcsportsboston.com/nfl/new-england-patriots/they-called-it-the-ty-law-rule-and-that-was-ok-with-him/393549/.

9. Jackson Michael, "Buffalo Bills No-Huddle Offense," *The Game Before the Money* (podcast), ep. 10, March 5, 2020, https://www.thegamebeforethemoney.com/buffalo-bills-no-huddle-offense/.

10. Cover, *Sports Illustrated*, December 6, 1993, *Sports Illustrated* Covers, https://sicovers.com/featured/can-the-nfl-be-saved-10-ways-to-save-a-boring-league-december-06-1993-sports-illustrated-cover.html.

11. "Fact or Fiction? A Team Has Gone from Last to First Every Season Since the 2002 Realignment," Pro Football Hall of Fame, November 26, 2013, https://www.profootballhof.com/news/2013/11/news-fact-or-fiction-a-team-has-gone-from-last-to-first-every-season-since-the-2002-realignment/.

12. Mike Baldwin, "Dallas' Jones Pushes for Salary Cap," *The Oklahoman*, July 30, 1995, https://www.oklahoman.com/story/news/1995/07/30/dallas-jones-pushes-for-salary-cap/62383585007/.

13. Abhimanyu Chaudhary, "Cowboys Legend Says Jerry Jones Is 'Screwed' as Dallas Pushes Against Salary Cap with Dak Prescott, CeeDee Lamb Deals Pending," Sportskeeda, July 16, 2024, https://www.sportskeeda.com/nfl/news-cowboys-legend-says-jerry-jones-screwed-dallas-pushes-salary-cap-dak-prescott-ceedee-lamb-deals-pending.

14. Daniel Parris, "What's the True Cost of NFL Injuries? A Statistical Analysis," Stat Significant, January 31, 2023, https://www.statsignificant.com/p/whats-the-true-cost-of-nfl-injuries.

15. "James Harrison," Fines & Suspensions, Spotrac, https://www.spotrac.com/nfl/player/fines/_/id/3564/james-harrison.

16. Joe Clark, "James Harrison: Roger Goodell Was 'King Dookie on Turd Island' During Meeting to Discuss Fines," Steelers Depot, May 16, 2024, https://steelersdepot.com/2024/05/james-harrison-roger-goodell-was-king-dookie-on-turd-island-during-meeting-to-discuss-fines/.

17. James Harrison (@jharrison9292), "@nflcommish ain't no fun when the rabbit got the gun huh?" X (Twitter), September 10, 2024, https://x.com/jharrison9292/status/509832809570377729.

18. Mark Dent and Rustin Dodd, *Kingdom Quarterback* (Dutton, 2023).

19. "Seattle Seahawks at New York Jets—December 6th, 1998," Pro Football Reference, https://www.pro-football-reference.com/boxscores/199812060nyj.htm.

20. Gerald Eskenazi, "Pro Football; Questionable Calls III: Officials Smile on the Jets," *The New York Times*, December 7, 1998, https://www.nytimes.com/1998/12/07/sports/pro-football-questionable-calls-iii-officials-smile-on-the-jets.html.

21. Richard Sandomir, "Pro Football; N.F.L. Wants to Restore Instant Replay for Playoffs," *The New York Times*, December 8, 1998, https://www.nytimes.com/1998/12/08/sports/pro-football-nfl-wants-to-restore-instant-replay-for-playoffs.html.

9. A High School Cafeteria for Billionaires

1. Barry Shuck, "When Al Davis Tried to Sabotage the NFL," Big Blue View, SB Nation, December 2, 2017, https://www.bigblueview.com/2017/12/2/16721994/when-al-davis-tried-to-sabotage-the-nfl.

2. Daniel Kaplan, "NFL Owners Meeting Includes Talk From N.Y. Times' David Brooks," *Sports Business Journal*, March 19, 2015, https://www.sportsbusinessjournal.com/Daily/Closing-Bell/2015/03/20/NFL-Owners.aspx.

3. Daniel Kaplan, "Reserved Seating, NFL Style," *Sports Business Journal*, March 16, 2014, https://www.sportsbusinessjournal.com/Journal/Issues/2014/03/17/Leagues-and-Governing-Bodies/NFL-seats.aspx.

4. Seth Wickersham, "Los Angeles Rams Owner Stan Kroenke Angers NFL Owners with Financial Pivot Related to Lawsuit on St. Louis Move, Sources Say," ESPN, October 27, 2021, https://www.espn.com/nfl/story/_/id/32486646/los-angeles-rams-owner-stan-kroenke-angers-nfl-owners-financial-pivot-related-lawsuit-st-louis-move-sources-say.

10. "Greed is a great sin."

1. "NFLPA Boss Smith Requests 10-Years of Financial Records from League to Accompany Extension," *Tampa Bay Times*, March 11, 2011, updated March 14, 2011, https://www.tampabay.com/archive/2011/03/11/nflpa-boss-smith-requests-10-years-of-financial-records-from-league-to-accompany-extension/.

2. Barry Wilner, Joseph White, and Amy Forliti, "With NFL Lockout Official, 2011 Season in Jeopardy," WBZ News, CBS News, March 12, 2011, https://www.cbsnews.com/boston/news/owners-confirm-nfl-lockout/.

3. "NFL Locks Out Players, Who File Suit," ESPN, March 11, 2011, https://www.espn.com/nfl/news/story?id=6205936.

4. "NFL Owners Approve Six-Year CBA Extension," ESPN, March 8, 2006, https://www.espn.com/nfl/news/story?id=2360258.

5. "Jaguars' Wayne Weaver Defends Ralph Wilson's CBA Stance," *Sports Business Journal*, May 2, 2006, https://www.sportsbusinessjournal.com/Daily/Issues/2006/05/03/Franchises/Jaguars-Wayne-Weaver-Defends-Ralph-Wilsons-CBA-Stance.aspx.

6. "Goodell Cuts Own Pay by 20 Percent," ESPN, February 25, 2009, https://www.espn.com.sg/nfl/news/story?id=3933228.

7. NFL Players Association, "NFL Collective Bargaining Agreement: 2006–2012," March 8, 2006, University of New Hampshire, Franklin Pierce School of Law, https://ipmall.law.unh.edu/sites/default/files/hosted_resources/SportsEntLaw_Institute/2006NFL_NFLPA_CBA.pdf.

8. "Robert Kraft Talks CBA, Says Current Deal Is 'Too One-Sided,'" *Sports Business Journal*, March 9, 2010, https://www.sportsbusinessjournal.com/Daily/Issues/2010/03/10/Leagues-Governing-Bodies/Robert-Kraft-Talks-CBA-Says-Current-Deal-Is-Too-One-Sided.aspx.

9. "Owners, Goodell Want New Labor Deal with Players Soon," NFL (website), October 12, 2010, https://www.nfl.com/news/owners-goodell-want-new-labor-deal-with-players-soon-09000d5d81b48898.

10. Gregg Rosenthal, "DeMaurice Smith Calls NFL Offer 'Worst Deal in the History of Sports,'" Pro Football Talk, NBC Sports, March 17, 2011, https://www.nbcsports.com/nfl/profootballtalk/rumor-mill/news/demaurice-smith-calls-nfl-offer-worst-deal-in-the-history-of-sports. (Emphasis in the original.)

11. Michael Silver, "Owner Rankings, Part 2: Split Decision at Top," Yahoo! Sports, September 3, 2010, https://sports.yahoo.com/ms-ownerrankingsparttwo090310.html. (Brackets in the original.)

12. Michael Silver, "Time to Bench Richardson from Bargaining Game," Yahoo! Sports, February 14, 2011, https://sports.yahoo.com/news/time-bench-richardson-bargaining-game-020700355--nfl.html. (Brackets in the original.)

13. Judy Battista, "N.F.L. Labor Dispute: Words but No Talks," *The New York Times*, February 15, 2011, https://www.nytimes.com/2011/02/16/sports/football/16labor.html.

14. Daniel Kaplan, "'We Were Miles Apart': Inside the Race to Prevent the NFL Lockout from Eating the Season 10 Years Ago," The Athletic, *The New York Times*, July 19, 2021, https://www.nytimes.com/athletic/2649487/2021/07/19/we-were-miles-apart-inside-race-to-prevent-nfl-lockout-from-eating-season-10-years-ago/.

15. Kaplan, "'We Were Miles Apart.'"

16. Dave Wilson, "Roger Goodell Booed by Fans," ESPN, April 28, 2011, https://www.espn.com/nfl/draft2011/news/story?id=6445458.

17. Tom Brady, et al. v. National Football League, et al., U.S. Court of Appeals, Eighth Circuit, No. 11-1898, July 8, 2011, corrected July 28, 2011, https://ecf.ca8.uscourts.gov/opndir/11/07/111898P.pdf.

18. Kaplan, "'We Were Miles Apart.'"

19. Shira Springer, "Robert Kraft Saves Football," *The Boston Globe*, January 1, 2012, https://www.bostonglobe.com/magazine/2012/01/01/robert-kraft-saves-football/CkyHbNQLivAfUSeRowC6nN/story.html.

20. Kaplan, "'We Were Miles Apart.'"

21. Peter King, "An Unsung Hero in the League Office," *Sports Illustrated*, August 1, 2011, https://vault.si.com/vault/2011/08/01/an-unsung-hero-in-the-league-office.

22. "JaMarcus Russell," Contract Details, Spotrac, https://www.spotrac.com/nfl/player/_/id/3913/jamarcus-russell.

23. "Sam Bradford," Career Earnings, Spotrac, https://www.spotrac.com/nfl/player/earnings/_/id/6510/sam-bradford.

24. JasonB, "Underqualified and Overpaid: Rookie Salaries in the NFL," Bleeding Green Nation, SB Nation, April 23, 2009, https://www.bleedinggreennation.com/2009/4/23/849271/underqualified-and-overpaid-rookie.

11. Two Fine Legacies

1. Memorial service for Jerry Richardson, March 18, 2023, Wofford College, Spartanburg, South Carolina.

2. L. Jon Wertheim and Viv Bernstein, "Sources: Jerry Richardson, Panthers Have Made Multiple Confidential Payouts for Workplace Misconduct, Including Sexual Harassment and Use of a Racial Slur," *Sports Illustrated*, December 17, 2017, https://www.si.com/nfl/2017/12/17/jerry-richardson-carolina-panthers-settlements-workplace-misconduct-sexual-harassment-racial-slur.

3. Mark Maske, "'Sometimes Things Get Misunderstood': Texans Owner Bob McNair Defends Panthers' Jerry Richardson," *The Washington Post*, March 25, 2018, https://www.washingtonpost.com/news/sports/wp/2018/03/25/sometimes-things-get-misunderstood-texans-owner-bob-mcnair-defends-panthers-jerry-richardson/.

4. Bryan Strickland, "October 26, 1993: Carolina Panthers Are Born," Carolina Panthers (website), October 26, 2017, https://www.panthers.com/news/october-26-1993-carolina-panthers-are-born-11633336.

5. Brandon McClung, "Jerry Richardson: Through the Years," *Sports Business Journal*, March 20, 2016, https://www.sportsbusinessjournal.com/Journal/Issues/2016/03/21/Champions/Richardson-timeline.aspx.

6. Victor Mather and Ken Belson, "Without Disclosing Details, N.F.L. Fines Jerry Richardson for Sexual Harassment and Racist Comments," *The New York Times*, June 28, 2018, https://www.nytimes.com/2018/06/28/sports/football/jerry-richardson-nfl-panthers.html.

7. Melissa Melvin-Rodriguez, "Moving of Jerry Richardson Statue from Bank of America Stadium," Carolina Panthers (website), June 10, 2020, https://www.panthers.com/photos/moving-of-jerry-richardson-statue-from-bank-of-america-stadium#8c0b6828-b1d5-4cf0-acfc-793d0d0a3ffa.

8. Associated Press, "Sanders Joins Redskins' Secondary," ESPN, June 7, 2000, https://www.espn.com/nfl/news/2000/0605/568178.html.

9. Erik Brady, "Daniel Snyder Says Redskins Will Never Change Name," *USA Today*, May 9, 2013, updated May 10, 2013, https://www.usatoday.com/story/sports/nfl/redskins/2013/05/09/washington-redskins-daniel-snyder/2148127/.

10. Ken Belson and Katherine Rosman, "N.F.L. Clears Way for End to Washington Football Team Turmoil," *The New York Times*, March 24, 2021, https://www.nytimes.com/2021/03/24/sports/football/dan-snyder-washington-harassment-feud.html.

11. Ken Belson and Jenny Vrentas, "Dan Snyder 'Needs to Be Removed,' Says One N.F.L. Owner," *The New York Times*, October 18, 2022, https://www.nytimes.com/2022/10/18/sports/football/dan-snyder-washington-commanders.html.

12. Harry Jaffe, "The Dan Snyder You Don't Know," *The Washingtonian*, September 1, 2006, https://www.washingtonian.com/2006/09/01/the-dan-snyder-you-dont-know/.

13. Greg Schneider and Peter Behr, "Snyder to Sell His Marketing Firm for $2 Billion," *The Washington Post*, February 21, 2000, https://www.washingtonpost.com/archive/business/2000/02/22/snyder-to-sell-his-marketing-firm-for-2-billion/deab34bd-2e3e-4ac6-84e3-52deff4364b9/.

14. Dave Anderson, "Sports of the Times; Redskins Get Thumbs Up from Snyder," *The New York Times*, September 25, 2000, https://www.nytimes.com/2000/09/25/sports/sports-of-the-times-redskins-get-thumbs-up-from-snyder.html.

15. Mike Freeman, "Redskins' Boss Makes Enemies and Super Bowl Plans," *The New York Times*, August 6, 2000, https://www.nytimes.com/2000/08/06/sports/pro-football-redskins-boss-makes-enemies-and-super-bowl-plans.html.

16. Dave McKenna, "The Cranky Redskins Fan's Guide to Dan Snyder," *Washington City Paper*, November 19, 2010, https://washingtoncitypaper.com/article/221900/the-cranky-redskins-fans-guide-to-dan-snyder/.

17. "Redskins' Dan Snyder Launches Original Americans Foundation," NFL (website), March 24, 2014, https://www.nfl.com/news/redskins-dan-snyder-launches-original-americans-foundation-0ap2000000336553.

18. Tom Schad, "As Redskins Review Name, Dan Snyder's Once-Touted Native American Foundation Has Gone Dark," *USA Today*, July 8, 2020, https://www.usatoday.com/story/sports/nfl/redskins/2020/07/08/redskins-dan-snyders-native-american-foundation-gave-0-2018/5384705002/.

19. Ken Belson, "Redskins' Name Change Remains Activist's Unfinished Business," *The New York Times*, October 9, 2013, https://www.nytimes.com/2013/10/10/sports/football/redskins-name-change-remains-her-unfinished-business.html.

20. Ken Belson and Kevin Draper, "FedEx Made a Demand Dan Snyder Couldn't Afford to Dismiss," *The New York Times*, July 10, 2020, https://www.nytimes.com/2020/07/10/sports/football/dan-snyder-washington-redskins-name-fedex.html.

21. Will Hobson and Liz Clarke, "From Dream Job to Nightmare," *The Washington Post*, July 16, 2020, https://www.washingtonpost.com/sports/2020/07/16/redskins-sexual-harassment-larry-michael-alex-santos/.

22. Ken Belson, "Congressional Leaders Ask N.F.L. for Documents from Washington Team Inquiry," *The New York Times*, October 21, 2021, updated October 26, 2021, https://www.nytimes.com/2021/10/21/sports/football/congress-nfl-investigation-emails-washington.html.

23. Jarrett Bell, "Cowboys Owner Jerry Jones on Dan Snyder: 'If He Decided to Move On, Who Could Possibly Blame Him?'" *USA Today*, via Yahoo! Sports, January 13, 2023, https://finance.yahoo.com/news/cowboys-owner-jerry-jones-dan-123228509.html.

12. Under Attack

1. Ken Belson, "Kaepernick's Protest Cascades into Protests over His Job Situation," *The New York Times*, August 23, 2017, https://www.nytimes.com/2017/08/23/sports/football/nfl-protest-colin-kaepernick.html.

2. Jacob Pramuk and Brian Schwartz, "Trump's Money Ties to NFL Owners Go Much Deeper Than Dolphins' Stephen Ross," CNBC, August 12, 2019, https://www.cnbc.com/2019/08/12/trump-ties-to-nfl-owners-go-deeper-than-stephen-ross-bob-kraft.html.

3. Ken Belson, "Jaguars Owner Shahid Khan Opposes Trump's Immigration Ban," *The New York Times*, February 4, 2017, https://www.nytimes.com/2017/02/04/sports/football/donald-trump-ban-shahid-khan-jaguars.html.

4. Mike Fisher, "Papa John's Ex CEO: Cowboys' Jerry Jones Wanted Me to Fire NFL's Roger Goodell," Dallas Cowboys on SI, May 7, 2022, https://www.si.com/nfl/cowboys/news/papa-johns-ceo-dallas-jerry-jones-fire-roger-goodell-daniel-snyder.

5. Maggie Severns, "Billionaire Stephen Ross Gets Backlash for Trump Fundraiser," *Politico*, August 7, 2019, https://www.politico.com/story/2019/08/07/billionaire-stephen-ross-trump-fundraiser-1452690.

6. Ken Belson and Mark Leibovich, "Inside the Confidential N.F.L. Meeting to Discuss National Anthem Protests," *The New York Times*, April 25, 2018, https://www.nytimes.com/2018/04/25/sports/nfl-owners-kaepernick.html.

7. Anquan Boldin, "Roadside Assistance Caught the Cop Who Killed My Cousin. Justice Shouldn't Be So Rare," *USA Today*, December 10, 2021, https://www.usatoday.com/story/opinion/voices/2021/12/10/nfl-anquan-boldin-police-killed-cousin/8652156002/.

8. Jim Trotter and Jason Reed, "Players Debating NFL's Proposed Donation to Social Justice Organizations," ESPN, November 29, 2017, https://africa.espn.com/nfl/story/_/id/21606390/nfl-offers-100-million-plan-social-justice-organizations-partnership-players.

9. "My Cause My Cleats," NFL (website), https://www.nfl.com/causes/my-cause-my-cleats/.

10. Ken Belson, "Players Criticize N.F.L. over Donation Proposal," *The New York Times*, November 29, 2017, https://www.nytimes.com/2017/11/29/sports/football/nfl-players-coalition.html.

11. Matthew Futterman and Victor Mather, "Trump Supports N.F.L.'s New National Anthem Policy," *The New York Times*, May 23, 2018, https://www.nytimes.com/2018/05/23/sports/nfl-anthem-kneeling.html.

12. Ken Belson, "N.F.L. Anthem Policy Bound to Please Only the N.F.L.," *The New York Times*, May 23, 2018, https://www.nytimes.com/2018/05/23/sports/national-anthem-nfl.html.

13. Jon Caramanica, "Maroon 5 Barely Leaves a Mark at the Super Bowl Halftime Show," *The New York Times*, February 3, 2019, https://www.nytimes.com/2019/02/03/arts/music/super-bowl-halftime-show.html.

14. Kevin Draper and Ken Belson, "Colin Kaepernick and the N.F.L. Settle Collusion Case," *The New York Times*, February 15, 2019, https://www.nytimes.com/2019/02/15/sports/nfl-colin-kaepernick.html.

15. Ken Belson, "N.F.L. Settlement with Kaepernick and Reid Is Said to Be Much Less Than $10 Million," *The New York Times*, March 21, 2019, https://www.nytimes.com/2019/03/21/sports/colin-kaepernick-nfl-settlement.html.

16. Jared Dubin, "Look: Jay-Z Rocks Custom Colin Kaepernick Jersey During 'SNL' Performance," CBS Sports, October 1, 2017, https://www.cbssports.com/nfl/news/look-jay-z-rocks-custom-colin-kaepernick-jersey-during-snl-performance/.

17. Lorenzo Reyes, "Robert Kraft Teams with Jay-Z, Meek Mill in Starting Criminal Justice Reform Organization," *USA Today*, January 23, 2019, https://www.usatoday.com/story/sports/nfl/2019/01/23/nfl-robert-kraft-jay-z-meek-mill-reform-alliance/2660470002/.

18. Ken Belson, "Questions About Kaepernick Hover over Jay-Z's Deal with the N.F.L.," *The New York Times*, August 14, 2019, https://www.nytimes.com/2019/08/14/sports/football/colin-kaepernick-jay-z.html.

19. Ken Belson, "Colin Kaepernick's Workout Derailed by Dispute with N.F.L.," *The New York Times*, November 16, 2019, https://www.nytimes.com/2019/11/16/sports/football/colin-kaepernick-nfl-workout.html.

13. Slave Auctions and Bro Hugs

1. Jonathan Jones, "NFL Owners Get Defensive After Scouting Combine Gets Compared to 'Slave Auction' by League Exec Troy Vincent," CBS Sports, December 15, 2022, https://www.cbssports.com/nfl/news/nfl-owners-get-defensive-after-scouting-combine-gets-compared-to-slave-auction-by-league-exec-troy-vincent/.

2. Matthew Tharrett, "NFL Commentator Praises College Football Player's Unbelievable 'Bubble Butt,'" LogoTV, February 26, 2015, archived at https://web.archive.org/web/20220811232926/www.logotv.com/news/3egec1impressive-bubble-butt-strikes-nfl-commentator-on-air.

3. Edgar Thompson, "Miami Dolphins' Jeff Ireland Apologizes to Dez Bryant; GM Asked Player If His Mother Had Been a Prostitute," *The Palm Beach Post*, April 28, 2010, updated March 31, 2012, https://www.palmbeachpost.com/story/sports/nfl/2010/04/28/miami-dolphins-jeff-ireland-apologizes/7579560007/.

4. Clarence E. Hill Jr., "Dallas Cowboys Owner Jerry Jones Doesn't See NFL Combine as Demeaning, Calls It Business," *Fort Worth Star-Telegram*, March 7, 2023, https://www.star-telegram.com/sports/nfl/dallas-cowboys/article272799135.html.

5. Rob Maaddi, "NFL Combine a TV Spectacle, Moneymaker; Value Under Scrutiny," Associated Press, March 6, 2023, https://apnews.com/article/nfl-combine-college-pro-days-55c1ef98fd21a1500bbaebb68598ce68.

6. "Evolution of the NFL Commissioner's Draft-Night Hugs," Carolina Panthers (website), video, https://www.panthers.com/video/evolution-of-the-nfl-commissioner-draft-night-hugs.

14. The Game to End All Games

1. Benjamin Hoffman and Ken Belson, "Patriots Suffer Big Loss: Gronkowski Will Retire," *The New York Times*, March 24, 2019, https://www.nytimes.com/2019/03/24/sports/rob-gronkowski-retires-patriots.html.

2. FanDuel, "Gronk Misses the FanDuel Kick of Destiny 2 Super Bowl LVIII Commercial," YouTube, February 11, 2024, video, https://www.youtube.com/watch?v=sZtdfuNZtIU.

3. Oscar B. Goodman, "The N.F.L.'s Gambling Problem," editorial, *The New York Times*, January 24, 2003, https://www.nytimes.com/2003/01/24/opinion/the-nfl-s-gambling-problem.html.

4. Christina Binkley, "Long Odds for Las Vegas Ads in Super Bowl, Thanks to NFL," *The Wall Street Journal*, January 14, 2003, https://www.wsj.com/articles/SB1042493323852372704.

5. Adam Liptak and Kevin Draper, "Supreme Court Ruling Favors Sports Betting," *The New York Times*, May 14, 2018, https://www.nytimes.com/2018/05/14/us/politics/supreme-court-sports-betting-new-jersey.html.

6. Jabari Young, "Tech, Gambling and Alcohol Helped the NFL Earn Almost $2 Billion in Sponsorships This Season," CNBC Sport, January 26, 2022, https://www.cnbc.com/2022/01/26/tech-gambling-alcohol-helped-nfl-earn-almost-2-billion-in-sponsorships.html.

7. Jenny Vrentas, "An N.F.L. Stadium Brings Sports Betting Inside," *The New York Times*, September 14, 2023, https://www.nytimes.com/2023/09/14/sports/football/nfl-sportsbook-washington-commanders.html.

8. Jenny Vrentas, "N.F.L.'s Rapid Embrace of Gambling Creates Mixed Signals," *The New York Times*, February 4, 2024, https://www.nytimes.com/2024/02/04/business/nfl-gambling-super-bowl.html.

9. "Super Bowl History," The Football Database, https://www.footballdb.com/seasons/super-bowls.html.

10. "Super Bowl Ratings History (1967–Present)," Sports Media Watch, https://www.sportsmediawatch.com/super-bowl-ratings-historical-viewership-chart-cbs-nbc-fox-abc/.

11. Jason Waggoner, "Don't Let Bacteria Score a Touchdown at Your Super Bowl Party," U.S. Department of Agriculture, January 29, 2015, https://www.usda.gov/media/blog/2015/01/29/dont-let-bacteria-score-touchdown-your-super-bowl-party.

12. National Chicken Council, "Americans to Eat 1.33 Billion Chicken Wings for Super Bowl," press release, PR Newswire, January 25, 2017, https://www.prnewswire.com/news-releases/americans-to-eat-133-billion-chicken-wings-for-super-bowl-300396743.html.

13. "An Estimated 12.5 Million Pizzas Will Be Ordered on Super Bowl Sunday," The American Pizza Community, archived at https://web.archive.org/web/20240905175716/www.americanpizzacommunity.com/an-estimated-12.5-million-pizzas-will-be-ordered-on-super-bowl-sunday.html.

14. Michael Janofsky, "N.F.L. to Review 1980 Ticket Scalping," *The New York Times*, December 10, 1986, https://www.nytimes.com/1986/12/10/sports/nfl-to-review-1980-ticket-scalping.html.

15. Ken Belson, "For N.F.L. Retirees, Opioids Bring More Pain," *The New York Times*, February 2, 2019, https://www.nytimes.com/2019/02/02/sports/nfl-opioids-.html.

16. Donesha Aldridge, "Unpaid Super Bowl Workers Finally Receive Paychecks from Staffing Company," 11 Alive, March 5, 2019, https://www.11alive.com/article/sports/nfl

/superbowl/unpaid-super-bowl-workers-finally-receive-paychecks-from-staffing-company/85-4d2edecb-e7f0-4bf8-9bc2-03cb76768859.

17. Donesha Aldridge, "Atlanta City Council President Sends Letter to NFL Commissioner About Unpaid Super Bowl Workers," 11alive.com, February 28, 2019, https://www.11alive.com/article/sports/nfl/superbowl/atlanta-city-council-president-sends-letter-to-nfl-commissioner-about-unpaid-super-bowl-workers/85-818cb32a-7edc-42da-8fc7-e1e49dfc7ae2.

18. Alan Peppard, "From Actors to Presidents, Everyone Wants to Watch a Cowboys Game from Jerry Jones' Suite," *The Dallas Morning News*, July 21, 2017, https://www.dallasnews.com/sports/cowboys/2017/07/22/from-actors-to-presidents-everyone-wants-to-watch-a-cowboys-game-from-jerry-jones-suite/.

19. Karen Crouse, "Snubbed Fans Given Tickets to Next Super Bowl," *The New York Times*, February 7, 2011, https://www.nytimes.com/2011/02/08/sports/football/08tickets.html.

20. Carl Nelson, "Robert Kraft Defends Patriots Amid Uproar Over Deflated Footballs," *The New York Times*, January 26, 2015, https://www.nytimes.com/2015/01/27/sports/football/robert-kraft-defends-patriots-amid-uproar-over-deflated-footballs.html.

21. Mark Leibovich, "Where Does the N.F.L. Go After a Season of Division?" *The New York Times*, February 1, 2018, https://www.nytimes.com/2018/02/01/magazine/where-does-the-nfl-go-after-a-season-of-division.html.

22. Maya A. Jones, "RISE and the Undefeated Bring Activism to Super Bowl LIII," Andscape, January 31, 2019, https://andscape.com/features/rise-and-the-undefeated-bring-activism-to-super-bowl-liii/.

23. "To Serve: Dr. Martin Luther King, Jr.," Grateful Living, https://grateful.org/resource/dr-martin-luther-king-jr-to-serve/.

15. "If it ain't broke, fix it anyway."

1. IBISWorld, "Number of Cable TV Subscriptions," August 22, 2024, https://ibisworld.com/us/bed/number-of-cable-tv-subscriptions/4625/.

2. Michael Nathanson, "NFL: Is Cheating a Good Strategy?" MoffettNathanson Research, September 7, 2023.

3. Ben Fischer, "NFL's Rolapp on 'MNF' Simulcasts: We Welcome All Ideas to Expand Reach," *Sports Business Journal*, November 20, 2024, https://www.sportsbusinessjournal.com/Articles/2024/11/20/nfl-brian-rolapp-sbj-media-innovators.

4. "NFL Network Lays Off What It Calls a 'Limited Number' of Employees," Pro Football Talk, NBC Sports, May 5, 2023, https://www.nbcsports.com/nfl/profootballtalk/rumor-mill/news/nfl-network-lays-off-what-it-calls-a-limited-number-of-employees.

5. Benjamin Mullin, Ken Belson, and Nico Grant, "YouTube Reaches Deal for N.F.L. Sunday Ticket," *The New York Times*, December 22, 2022, https://www.nytimes.com/2022/12/22/business/youtube-nfl-sunday-ticket.html.

6. Colin Salao, "Amazon Is Paying $100 Million for the Rights to One Specific NFL Matchup This Year," The Street, May 10, 2023, https://www.thestreet.com/sports/amazon-is-paying-100-million-for-the-rights-to-one-specific-nfl-matchup-this-year.

7. Alex Weprin, "Netflix Spikes the Football: Behind Its NFL Megadeal," *The Hollywood Reporter*, May 22, 2024, https://www.hollywoodreporter.com/business/business-news/netflix-nfl-megadeal-1235905666/.

8. "NFL Announces Two Exclusive Streaming Games for 2024 Season, Including One Postseason Game," Around the NFL, NFL (website), March 26, 2024, https://www.nfl.com/news/nfl-announces-two-exclusive-streaming-games-for-2024-season-including-one-postseason-game.

9. Andrew Beaton and Rosie Ettenheim, "The NFL Is Back—and It's Never Cost More to Watch," *The Wall Street Journal*, September 6, 2024, https://www.wsj.com/sports/football/eagles-packers-brazil-peacock-streaming-netflix-b55de642.

10. Michael McCarthy, "Sources: NFL Eyes Multibillion-Dollar International Rights Package," Front Office Sports, October 16, 2024, https://frontofficesports.com/sources-nfl-eyes-multi-billion-dollar-international-rights-package/.

11. Global Markets Program, NFL (website), https://www.nfl.com/international/global-markets-program.

12. Arash Markazi (@ArashMarkazi), "The scene at the Wynn Field Club for Saturday night's Cowboys-Raiders preseason game at Allegiant Stadium. The night club takes up the entire north end zone and is 11,000 square feet with 29 VIP tables, 18 dining tables, 4 bars and 2 DJ booths. There's nothing like it in the NFL," X (Twitter), August 18, 2024, video, https://x.com/arashmarkazi/status/1825040339029442898?s=43&t=pijou4aAILuwk7_rnFNzEg.

13. "NFL Game Costs Surge: A Decade of Rising Prices," Freebets.com, November 21, 2024, https://www.freebets.com/news/nfl-attendance-cost-analysis/.

14. Ken Belson, "What Makes Someone a Fan?" *The New York Times*, September 19, 2019, https://www.nytimes.com/2019/09/19/sports/rich-luker-fan-psychology.html.

15. Jenny Vrentas, "N.F.L.'s Rapid Embrace of Gambling Creates Mixed Signals," *The New York Times*, February 4, 2024, https://www.nytimes.com/2024/02/04/business/nfl-gambling-super-bowl.html.

INDEX

ABOUT THE AUTHOR

KEN BELSON has covered the business of the NFL for more than a dozen years as a writer for *The New York Times*. He has interviewed hundreds of owners, team executives, union officials, players, sponsors, network executives, and fans in the NFL ecosystem. His focus has been on how the league became a $23 billion-a-year enterprise with little sign of stopping. He has broken national stories on the inner workings of the league, including the treatment of players and efforts by teams and the league to suppress and shape unflattering news. Before covering the NFL, he wrote about the business of sports more broadly, spent three years in the *Times*' Metro Section and six years in the *Times*' Business Section, including in Tokyo, where he lived for a dozen years. He was part of two groups that were finalists for the Pulitzer Prize, and he has won numerous other journalism awards.

RAISING READERS

Books Build Bright Futures

Thank you for reading this book and for being a reader of books in general. author, I am so grateful to share being part of a community of readers with and I hope you will join me in passing our love of books on to the next gener of readers.

Did you know that reading for enjoyment is the single biggest predictor child's future happiness and success?

More than family circumstances, parents' educational background, or inc reading impacts a child's future academic performance, emotional well-b communication skills, economic security, ambition, and happiness.

Studies show that kids reading for enjoyment in the US is in rapid decline:

- In 2012, 53% of 9-year-olds read almost every day. Just 10 years later, in 2022, the number had fallen to 39%.
- In 2012, 27% of 13-year-olds read for fun daily. By 2023, that number was just 14%.

Together, we can commit to **Raising Readers** and change this trend. How?

- Read to children in your life daily.
- Model reading as a fun activity.
- Reduce screen time.
- Start a family, school, or community book club.
- Visit bookstores and libraries regularly.
- Listen to audiobooks.
- Read the book before you see the movie.
- Encourage your child to read aloud to a pet or stuffed animal.
- Give books as gifts.
- Donate books to families and communities in need.

Books build bright futures, and **Raising Readers** is our shared responsibilit

For more information, visit **JoinRaisingReaders.com**

Sources: National Endowment for the Arts, National Assessment of Educational Progress, WorldBookDay.org, Nielsen BookData's 2023 "Understanding the Children's Book Consumer"